SACRED CHARITY

Sacred Charity

Confraternities and Social Welfare in Spain, 1400–1700

Maureen Flynn

Cornell University Press
Ithaca, New York

First published 1989 by Cornell University Press

Printed in Hong Kong

Library of Congress Cataloging-in-Publication Data
Flynn, Maureen.
Sacred charity.
Bibliography: p.
Includes index.
1. Confraternities—Spain—Zamora—History.
2. Catholic Church—Spain—Zamora—Charities—History.
3. Zamora (Spain)—Church history. I. Title.
BX808.5.S7F57 1989   248′.06   88–47727
ISBN 0–8014–2227–2

To my parents

Contents

List of Figures

Acknowledgements

Many mentors walked with me through the heap of broken images that traditional Spanish culture has left behind. And if we all puzzled at times over the unusual signs of life that the archives delivered, no-one was more baffled than me. I turn with gratitude now to those who helped me find meaning. My dissertation adviser, Stanley G. Payne, provided essential guidance in the interpretation of Spanish history. His demands that I constantly subject archival facts to critical analysis and synthesize them into issues of broad intellectual appeal ring in my ears like the urgent ad all-too-distant call of a foghorn to the lost voyager. I am indebted as well to other teachers at the University of Wisconsin who have broadened the vista of this local study by suggesting issues for consideration that extend beyond Spain to include the entire European continent. Professor William Courtenay lent invaluable assistance in medieval source material to locate the roots of many sixteenth-century religious ideas. Professor Robert Kingdon's knowledge of social conditions across sixteenth-century Europe served as a mirror to catch the reflection of Spanish events in other places. With kind yet insistent patience, Professor Domenico Sella cautioned me more than once from overzealously presenting popular religious beliefs as if they were doctrine, an enchanting illusion for social historians. Professors Jerzy Kloczowski, Henry Kamen and William Christian, Jr. made useful recommendations on aspects of the social context of poverty and charity.

For opening the doors to Spain and its archives, I thank the Fulbright Commission as well as the archivists in Zamora, Valladolid and Madrid. They graciously facilitated research and have inspired in me a perpetual desire to return to the archives. Special thanks belong to José Luis Rodríguez for assistance with paleography. Many other Spaniards, some untrained in the discipline of history but eager to reveal the secrets of their past, aided in the recovery of insights and information. Guadalupe Ramos de Castro and Chano Lorenzo Sevillano assisted with their knowlege of local Zamoran history in the reconstruction of pilgrimage routes to medieval Leonese churches and shrines, and Antonio Reina Romero tracked down numerous sources on confraternities that could not have been found in archives.

For sharing all the early struggles while I set the course of dissertation chapters, Oliver Hayward, thank you. And finally Willy,

I owe you a lifetime of ritual gestures of gratitude for the innumerable acts of mercy that you offered while I wrote, not least of which was your patience in enduring periods of obsession with confraternities in conversation. But conversations, like alms-gifts, are mutually and unboundedly indebting, aren't they? My greatest joy has been in this debt of ours.

Introduction

Among the illiterate folk of medieval Europe, history shows us few individual personalities. The paucity of written records expressing their personal views makes it virtually impossible to capture the multiple dimensions of their private lives. The communal lives of the common people, however, are much more accessible to investigation. Collected into groups, the faceless individuals merge to form corporate personalities whose features are clear enough to appear in historical documents. Confraternities, guilds and youth associations of various sorts provided their undistinguished members not only the monetary means but also the self-confidence to commission scribes to document their thoughts.

Using records drawn up by confraternities in the city of Zamora, situated in the old Spanish kingdom of Leon-Castile, I have attempted to reconstruct the religious experiences of Spanish Catholics between the fourteenth and the seventeenth centuries. By tracing the activities of Zamoran confraternities across generations of membership, I was able to note long-term patterns in the devotional habits of the populace. The purpose in joining confraternities was to exercise Christian piety, particularly charity, long heralded by medieval theologians as the most desirable of the cardinal virtues. This study analyzes how members' preoccupations with charity pertained to their beliefs in the afterlife and how their almsgiving practices affected the material conditions of society's poor. It is therefore essentially an examination of the way in which religious values shaped the moral community and controlled poor relief before the creation of the modern welfare state.

The perspective presented in this local study has been deeply influenced by a group of ethnographers and sociologists whose research into spiritual customs of both western and non-western civilizations moved them away from viewing the evolution of religions as the work of founding fathers and turned their attention instead to the role of the community in the growth and development of religious systems. The sociologist Emile Durkheim argued that all religions were the product of social forces.[1] Collective portrayals of the sacred led to organized religious creeds. Durkheim specifically rejected the approach of western church historians who sought the origins of beliefs in great intellectual figures of the past. According to Durkheim, religion was created neither by nor for individuals. It is a collective pursuit that holds meaning only among many believers. Religious systems, he declared, reflect the parameters and essence of collective mentalities and are more than the designs of individual minds, divine or human. Individuals are made conscious of the sacred world through the moral force of the community and they sustain personal spiritual sentiment through social interaction. In explaining the roots of organized faith, Durkheim asserted that 'collective representations are the result of an immense co-operation, which stretches out not only into space but into time as well. To make them, a multitude of minds have associated, united and combined their ideas and sentiments; for them long generations have accumulated their experience and their knowledge.'[2]

Durkheim's sociological approach necessitated a new methodology for the study of religious life in the past. Traditionally historians had relied exclusively on written documents for their information and these essentially private records had encouraged them to interpret religion through the lives and perspectives of a small and select group of personalities. The approach paralleled the prevailing 'great man theory' of history. In western historiography, for instance, scholars often considered gospel texts or the works of Augustine or Aquinas as sufficient source material for their investigations into the origins and meaning of credo, doctrine and liturgy. For Durkheim, on the other hand, such commentaries of individuals merely reflected the beliefs and practices of the societies in which they lived, and he did not assume that their views determined the phenomena to which they referred. The origin of religious rites had to be sought elsewhere, among the people, and the meaning of those rites must be found in communal admissions rather than within personal memoirs. Durkheim challenged historians to give account of religious cults by their symbolic and functional significance in society.

At the same time that Durkheim was speculating about the nature of world religions in order to facilitate understanding of different cultures, a group of German scholars were applying sociological theory to the study of Christianity. Ernst Troeltsch sought to relate Christian ideology to the cultural environment of western Europe in *The Social Teachings of the Christian Churches* (1911). To Troeltsch, the Christian religion was not a changeless message instituted by God but a product of social forces whose doctrines, laws, and institutions changed over time in response to human needs and desires. His colleague Max Weber emphasized the manner in which western religion responded to social change in *The Protestant Ethic and the*

Spirit of Capitalism (1904/05). Weber portrayed the Reformation as a bourgeois movement which recast Christian ideals to suit the more practical needs of a society that pursued rationality in spiritual as well as economic affairs. He argued that the high value placed on reason and practicality among Protestant communities created the psychological conditions necessary for the growth of capitalism. The Englishman R. H. Tawney perceived Christianity evolving along similar lines, and attempted to show how the adoption and adaptation of Christian ethics changed the economic organization of early modern Europe.[3]

Durkheim and Troeltsch both believed that the major transformations in religion were brought about by the common people, and since the publication of their work historians who have applied their sociological method to the study of religion similarly concentrate on popular rather than elite culture. This approach assumes that Christianity was not exclusively an ideology enforced on the masses by an official ecclesiastical elite, but a living and growing system of beliefs richly influenced by lower-class culture. In Germany in the 1920s, folklorists with historical interests in the field of *religiöse Volkskunde* brought to light a myriad of popular practices that had been incorporated into the Christian religion.[4] Gabriel Le Bras encouraged historians in France to examine this evidence more systematically by applying sophisticated quantitative methodologies to the study of religion.[5]

Within the last twenty years, historians of medieval and early modern Europe have adopted some of the programmatic goals and techniques of the early twentieth-century sociologists to evoke new appreciation for popular religious practices once dismissed as 'unsophisticated' and 'superstitious'. Sharpening their interpretation of communal ritual with analytical tools offered by ethnographers, they have turned the study of religion into a multi-disciplinary endeavor. Keith Thomas, Natalie Davis, Carlo Ginzburg, Richard Trexler, William Christian, Jr., and Thomas A. Brady, Jr. are but a few who have studied religion at a local level where the efforts of the common people in creating pious practices and formulating beliefs can be most fully and easily perceived.[6]

Durkheim's appeal to historians to view religious life through the perspective of the laity has borne fruit in the innovative approach adopted by Aron Ja. Gurevich in his examination of purgatory through the use of popular visionary literature, an approach which differs significantly from that of Jacques Le Goff, who studies the origins of the same phenomenon in theological treatises of church fathers.[7] A similarly distinct methodology is manifest in Lionel Rothkrug's quest for the ancestry of the Reformation in patterns of saint veneration among German peasants, which stands in strong contrast to Roland Bainton's traditional search for the Reformation in the life of Luther.[8]

Some of the most suggestive work has been undertaken by medievalists. Regional studies of piety in the Middle Ages demonstrate that lay religious beliefs did not conform strictly to official Catholicism.[9] Popular piety was expressed in numerous local variations. Its complex system of beliefs and rituals, inherited from local custom as well as from church teachings, extended far beyond the circle of formal doctrine and liturgy established by the church. For instance, Norwich townspeople and pilgrims offered almost as much devotion to the cult of St William, a crucified child martyr, as they did to Christ.[10] In Austria and Bavarian South Germany, a number of shrines to the 'Bleeding Host' demonstrated a peculiar desire among pilgrims to observe and worship Christ's body as it became flesh outside the mass.[11]

The great diversity of Christian forms of worship described by medievalists has inspired one of the most intrepid historians of popular religion, Jean Delumeau, to suggest that we reconsider the traditional view of the Middle Ages as a period when Europe constituted a Christendom unified in belief.[12] Just as Voltaire had challenged historical terminology by asserting that the Holy Roman Empire was neither holy nor Roman nor even an empire, Delumeau and historians of local religion have suggested through their work that the medieval 'Christian commonwealth' was neither 'common' in its range of beliefs and rites, nor necessarily 'Christian' in terms of the orthodox character of those beliefs.

Applying this new perspective to the sixteenth century, Delumeau prefers not to envision the Protestant Reformation as a radical 'split' in Christendom but rather to conceive of it as the definitive recognition of regional divisions in belief that existed for centuries. The subsequent attempt by both the Protestant and Catholic churches to define precisely their doctrinal positions and to disseminate their views among the populace with improved education programs standardized Christian devotions for the first time along two distinct theological lines.

My study of popular piety in the region of Leon-Castile modifies this new interpretation with respect to the Middle Ages. I affirm the traditional view that medieval Europe did indeed constitute a religious commonwealth in a few significant areas of belief, most notably in the concepts of Christian charity and brotherly love. Without denying the existence of local variations in religious practices, I found that the medieval approach to charity was remarkably uniform across Europe. Communities shared similar ideals of charity based on biblical injunctions and observed identical religious rituals that expressed these ideals. Charitable activities were stereotyped in the Middle Ages; everyone performed the same gestures in the same circumstances. As Emile Durkheim would say, 'this conformity of conduct only translates the conformity of thought'.[13]

Charitable rituals were practiced by the ecclesiastical estate through convents, chapter houses and parish churches. They were exercised by laypeople through confraternities, and it is upon these institutions that my examination of popular piety is based. Confraternities were voluntary organizations dedicated to the practice of piety and the promotion of the spiritual welfare of the community. They existed in all parts of Europe by the late Middle Ages and included all sectors of society in their membership.[14] The confraternities institutionalized popular religious beliefs and brought diverse local strains of piety into contact with official Catholicism. They standardized popular religion by creating a network of common devotional exercises among their members.

This study concentrates on confraternal piety in the city of Zamora, but it also draws analogies to other population centers in the kingdom of Leon-Castile in order to show the similarity of religious habits across a broad region. It is offered as a basis of comparison for other geographic areas, particularly those outside Spain, to determine the extent to which the common religious experiences described here were shared by the rest of Europe in the late Middle Ages.

With regard to the Reformation period, my work accords with recent portrayals of the Catholic Reformation as a movement that sought to impose upon medieval lay piety a higher degree of uniformity.[15] The efforts toward greater standardization were not directed at completely isolated and dissimilar religious communities, however, but at a Christendom that already held in common certain fundamental spiritual principles and observances. The Catholic Reformation merely enforced a more strict devotional and doctrinal program to conform with the church's new and more narrow definition of orthodoxy. I shall show that a wide variety of confraternal devotions in Spain were replaced after the Council of Trent by a smaller selection of officially prescribed devotions designed to propagate certain themes in Catholic doctrine threatened by Protestant theology.

As part of the reconstruction of Zamora's religious sociology, I am interested in distinguishing differences in expression and application of the Christian concept of charity among people of varying degrees of wealth and social status. The manner in which the privileged orders carried out Christian charitable ethics to explain and encourage almsgiving, as well as to justify their own advantageous economic position in society, has been portrayed frequently in the historiography of poor relief[16] and my work supports the conclusions of these studies. Less well known is the manner in which the common people – artisans, tradesmen, laborers and peasants – utilized Christian ideals of brotherhood and love toward neighbors to strengthen communal ties for their own material and spiritual security. In contrast to the concentration in earlier works on aristocratic views, this study of confraternities focuses on workers' perspectives.

Unfortunately, owing to lack of information, I have been unable to deal with the manner in which the indigent and powerless may have used Christianity for their own benefit. It is characteristic of the pre-modern era that the voices of the lowest orders of society are transmitted indirectly and are difficult to hear through the perspectives and prejudices of the literate who record their words. As recipients of charity, we see only their open hands while their faces and feelings are left undefined in the records. In the sixteenth century, critical changes affecting the ways of life and status of the poor in Zamora and other parts of Spain took place, but the tales are told from the point of view of wealthy donors and the church, who, although sometimes attentive to the wishes and responses of paupers, basically express their own concerns. Is it possible to discern the real feelings of the underprivileged? Did paupers whose wardrobes came from attending funerals, or whose dinners came from extending their hands in gestures reminding benefactors of the value of their prayers, contribute at all to the ideology of charity? I suspect that they were manipulated by the system rather than vice versa, but since they have left no records of their own activities and intentions, we can only speculate.

My study of confraternities and charity in the city of Zamora has relied exclusively on archival sources, but it is heavily indebted to a number of comprehensive studies on Spanish confraternities and poor relief for comparative purposes. The most influential of these studies for my work has been Antonio Rumeu de Armas' fundamental synthesis, *Historia de la Previsión Social en España* (Madrid, 1944), which first introduced me to the subject of Spanish corporations and impressed upon me the close relationship between private religious confraternities and social welfare in Spain. Work by Teófanes Egido on Valladolid, by Pedro Carasa Soto on Burgos and by Marie-Claude Gerbet on Caceres revealed important ways in which confraternities fit into the social life of local communities.[17]

The subject of poor relief has received a great deal of attention in Spanish historiography, particularly in the last decade or two. Church historians have explored the extensive literature relating to charity penned by theologians since the central Middle Ages, while secular scholars have examined the social and material context of poverty and welfare in Spain. The classic works on Spanish poor relief are by Fermín Hernández Iglesias, *La beneficencia en España* (Madrid, 1876) and María Jiménez Salas, *Historia de la Asistencia Social en España en la edad moderna* (Madrid, 1958), both of which outline the historical development of hospitals and government welfare policies. Recently, in *Poverty and Welfare in Hapsburg Spain. The example of Toledo* (Cambridge, 1983), Linda Martz has examined Spanish welfare reform in the critical period of the sixteenth century. She has written a detailed and lucid account of the operation of Toledo's welfare institutions within the context of the city's economic and political environment. Her carefully drawn connections between Toledan reforms and central government welfare measures make her local study a fundamental work for understanding state poor relief policies. William J. Callahan and María Rosa Pérez Estévez carry the study of national reforms into the eighteenth century.[18]

My analysis of confraternities and charity builds upon these foundations with archival material from Zamora, Valladolid, Salamanca, and the national archives of Madrid and Simancas. The principal sources for information on confraternities were the parish archives of Zamora. The city's thirty sixteenth-century parishes were administrative centers where confraternal records were deposited and financial accounts were made by parish priests. Confraternal statutes, bequests, wills and parish registers were all of use in the reconstruction of Zamoran social history. In addition to these parish archives, the Archivo de la Mitra and the Archivo de la Catedral de Zamora provided documentation pertaining to confraternities and poor relief in the form of episcopal visitation reports, property transactions, wills and synodal statutes. The Archivo Histórico Provincial de Zamora stores the city's protocols, a rich source for private correspondence.

The *Libros de Actas*, or proceedings of the city council, provide a fairly regular weekly sequence of reports on city life in the sixteenth century. Records of hospitals and other beneficent institutions are stored within sections pertaining to the Diputación Provincial. Most of the documentation on Zamora's monasteries and convents which include references to confraternities is housed within the Archivo Histórico Nacional in Madrid, and demographic information is available in the Archivo General de Simancas.

To examine confraternities outside the city of Zamora, I explored parish records in small towns surrounding the capital and visited the municipal archives of Valladolid and Salamanca. The *Libros de Actas* in the Archivo Municipal de Valladolid are particularly rich sources with respect to urban affairs, and the archives of the Universidad de Valladolid contain accounts and property holdings of the regions' confraternities. In Salamanca, the protocols offer a potentially valuable source of information on confraternities among the university population, but the material is scattered among several hundred volumes and I had the opportunity to tap only a small percentage of the records. Salamanca's cathedral and university archives also contain information relating to the region's welfare activities.

Jean Delumeau and Gabriel Le Bras have offered critical assessments of the research value of such archival material for the study of western European religion.[19] A few additional comments, however, are appropriate. The ordinances of confraternities have been particularly fruitful sources of information in recovering popular religious practices. All confraternities were required by the church to draw up a set of rules to inform episcopal authorities of their intentions and activities. The official statements tell us about the conventions that confraternities observed, from mundane matters such as protocol for celebration of feast days and fees and fines incurred by members in particular circumstances, to such formal concerns as membership obligations and internal governing policies. The statutes were frequently revised and supplemented, offering historians an opportunity to observe changes in religious practices over time. Since they were considered among the most precious objects in the confraternities' possession, in part because they conserved communal traditions, they were carefully protected in locked cases. Of all the surviving documents relating to confraternities, statutes are certainly the most numerous.

It has been suggested that confraternal ordinances exerted a more profound effect on the religious conscience of the populace than sermons, and that they should be considered the 'classics' of lay piety.[20]

In terms of the frequency with which ordinances were read, they undoubtedly formed one of the most influential devotional texts of the medieval and early modern period. Officials of confraternities constantly referred to them for guidance in the management of corporate activities and regularly read them aloud to members. While holding membership, each person heard the confraternity's statutes repeated a score of times. It is not an exaggeration to say, therefore, that these corporate messages constituted for the laity as important a spiritual guideline as the monastic rules for the cloistered communities. Paul Oscar Kristeller has urged historians to make greater use of them in the recovery of popular literature, pointing out that their eulogies to Christ and the saints were one of the few forms of lay poetry of the pre-modern period. Their exhortations to the moral and spiritual perfection of members make up some of the most carefully conceived prose written by the laity.[21]

Confraternal ordinances nevertheless should be dealt with cautiously as sources of popular culture. Two important mediating factors create problems when regarding them as direct expressions of the thoughts of the common people. First, the ordinances were written by professional scribes familiar with the rules of a number of confraternities, including those of clerics and aristocrats. It is impossible to calculate how much the scribes contributed to the formulation of the goals and activities written into these statutes. Standard words and phrases frequently appear in different sets of ordinances, suggesting cross-fertilization of confraternal programs through the interaction of scribes. Secondly, it should be kept in mind that the ordinances of confraternities were written as much for the benefit of ecclesiastical supervisors as for their members, and therefore they were carefully designed to meet the approval of the church and may not necessarily reflect the true, or at least the full, intentions and objectives of members.

The use of confraternal ordinances for the examination of popular culture involves all the problems of interpretation that historians confront with other written sources of the pre-modern era. Since the data on lower-class culture is conveyed through scribes or through literate churchmen, historians must take special care to distinguish the views of the authors from those of the people whose views they are presenting.

Of primary concern in this regard is the astonishing convergence of ideas articulated in confraternal ordinances drawn up separately by clerics, nobles, and commoners. To what degree do common expressions written into their codes reflect the imposition of the language of the dominant orders over the lower order of society? Or to what degree do they manifest a free and spontaneous conformity of attitudes among all three orders? Is it safe to assume that the illiterate and subordinate population accepted the standards of their social superiors, or should we consider identical descriptions of religious ideas to be evidence of a collaborative religious culture shared by all classes?

The questions are not easy to answer. In the case of one ritual enscribed in statutes, several different interpretations are possible. All Zamoran confraternities referred to the annual feast-day distributions of money and bread to members as 'charity'. The term is especially curious when employed by the noble estate, whose members would normally balk at the thought of receiving these items in the manner of alms. One has the impression that these communal distributions were conceived as signs of spiritual charity for the nourishment of souls. But it cannot be disregarded that for members of the lower class, these distributions of 'charity' fulfilled important material as well as spiritual needs and therefore the term might be understood in a literal sense. Do we see here the dominant orders appropriating a secular practice from the common people to turn it into a ritual that would have meaning for them by serving a supernatural purpose? Or did commoners learn to express their relief activities in a language that the church would construe in a spiritual sense? The problem then is how to interpret confraternal rules established by members of the lower classes, but written by a professional group of notaries for the scrutiny of episcopal authorities. In most cases I have tried to consider implicit meanings behind the formal statements in statutes, and wherever other records, such as council proceedings and financial accounts were available, I have utilized them to supplement ordinances.

The material provided by confraternal ordinances, if evaluated critically, can reveal a great deal about popular culture. Confraternities were one of the few institutions created by the populace to meet their own needs. Unlike craft guilds, they encompassed, at least in the Hispanic peninsula, women and occasionally even children in their membership.[22] They were much more numerous than guilds in Spain. Almost everyone belonged to at least one confraternity, including the unemployed, service workers and widows, who were normally excluded from guilds. The confraternity was involved, moreover, in almost all major events in the lives of constituents. Members joined celebrations of births and marriages; they consoled families at funerals; they attended common festivities and accompanied those journeying on pilgrimages to city limits. A study of these religious corporations, therefore, offers a singularly promising opportunity to reconstruct the experiences of the entire community.

In one of the most inclusive of all definitions of confraternities, Gabriel Le Bras called them 'artificial families in which all members were united by voluntary fellowship; confraternities had as their objective to satisfy within a narrow group the most poignant needs of body and soul'.[23] This study will examine the efforts made by Spanish confraternities to meet these 'poignant needs of body and soul' through religious welfare. We will see that their corporate rituals of charity were developed over the centuries by thousands of participating members to confront problems encountered in daily life and to ease anxieties about the great unknown challenges of death and the afterlife. We are reminded of Emile Durkheim's counsel that religious rituals are made over 'long generations' with the ideas, sentiments and experiences of 'a multitude of minds'. The hallowing of confraternal rituals out of popular desires to commune with God reveal to us some of the most important and intriguing of western Christianity's 'collective representations' of the sacred.

1 The Confraternal Structure of Zamora

The traditional Catholic vision of the gates of Heaven was crowded with familiar faces. Just as Dante caught the comforting glance of Beatrice among other acquaintances during his journey to Paradise in the *Divine Comedy*, so did people count on the support of the righteous both in heaven and on earth to assuage their fears. In the early sixteenth century a townswoman in Zamora, Francisca de la Peña, prepared for her own death in her will through

> faith, hope and charity in God and in his holy mercy that compassion will greet me; and in supplication of the always glorious Virgin Holy Mary, his mother, our intercessor, to whom I humbly pray, and to all the saints who are before the eternal throne of God, [I pray] that they be my lawyers and persuade my Savior that he receive my soul. ...[1]

At the Last Judgment, Francisca, like most of her contemporaries, did not imagine herself confronting God directly and alone; rather, she was escorted by the good wishes of loved ones on earth and by the good will of the blessed, to whom friendly recognition had been offered during her life.

In popular images of the Day of Reckoning, it was not the church as an institution, nor writs of pardon, nor quantifiable lists of indulgences, nor even clerics that were invoked to facilitate entry among the saved. The primary view in testaments was that human companions would stand in defense of one's case.

The position of church leaders, by no means completely reconciled to this communal approach to salvation, nevertheless affirmed the ability of men and women to assist each other toward salvation. Medieval theologians beginning with Augustine acknowledged that at death, friends and relatives could provide spiritual assistance to sinners.[2] Augustine asserted that 'it must not be denied that the souls of the dead are relieved by the piety of their living, when the sacrifice of their mediator is offered or alms are given in church'.[3] His references to 'friends' and 'saintly friends' who could obtain through their merits God's mercy on behalf of those for whom they prayed endorsed the sense of community and mutual support in early medieval piety.

12

Church doctrine on the treasury of merits of the saints also sustained the collective pursuit of salvation among the populace. The church held that holy persons who lived throughout the Christian era had accumulated through their good works an abundance of grace that could be applied to fellow Christians. Saints of the past offered to the living a treasury of merits for their spiritual needs.

In theory all the meritorious deeds ever performed were at the disposal of the living, and all the good works and prayers accomplished by the living could be extended backward in time to the dead and forward to future generations. Perpetual reciprocity of merits and prayers between departed and living souls engendered a sense of communal immortality that transcended individual deaths. The community's ancestors depended on the supplications, penitences and indulgences of those on earth and thus the living shared responsibility in the fate of departed souls. In the judicial process of salvation private responsibility did not stand alone; the community helped redeem the faults of the dead.[4]

The idea that both the sanctified dead and the pious living could make reparations for the sins of others was a powerful incentive to the formation of confraternities for mutual spiritual assistance. To the townspeople of late medieval and early modern Zamora, confraternities offered a circle of companions who promised to provide spiritual aid upon their deaths. By joining a confraternity, individuals gained communal protection and fortified their spiritual well-being with ties of fellowship. The confraternities designed requiem masses, prayer services, vigils over tombs and almsgiving programs to assist the delivery of members' souls to heaven. They also created bonds of friendship with saints for assistance in salvation. By setting themselves up under the protection of special saints and honoring their feast days with masses, public processions and dancing, they established patronage relationships with heavenly beings capable of bestowing grace.

Seen in this perspective, the confraternities, ensurers of brotherly aid and cultivators of saintly good will, were carefully constructed death societies. They assumed collective responsibility for the guilt of individuals and established programs that made reparations for sins. Through common oaths of fidelity to corporate obligations that served the dead, cofrades sought to ensure the salvation of everyone. The breaking of a confraternal oath threatened the welfare of one's own soul as well as those of past generations and risked eternal damnation because one lost the continuing spiritual support of brothers and sisters. Outside the corporation, justification was a person's own responsibility and the way to salvation was solitary.

That lay people as well as clerics preferred the communal approach to salvation, sheltering themselves within the salvific programs, is demonstrated by the almost wholesale incorporation of Zamoran society into confraternities. The city of Zamora and its environs offer a particularly interesting and vivid example of the efforts of medieval Christians to obtain spiritual security within corporate structures. A rich and virtually untapped series of confraternal documents exists in its ecclesiastical archives that shed light on the operation of the alliances for salvation. Zamora appears to have possessed more confraternities per capita than any other city in Europe by the beginning of the sixteenth century, and the influence of these organizations on the community's spiritual life was exceptionally strong. Neither an administrative center like Valladolid or Toro, nor a commercial nexus like Medina del Campo, Zamora subsisted on its own domestic economy. Its citizens earned their livelihood in modest handicrafts like spinning, weaving, masonry and metallurgy, and their social experiences revolved around internal neighborhood activities. Zamora represented, then, a city not atypical of the majority of Spanish population centers that relied on internal resources for survival. How its confraternities fit into this domestic life is illustrative of many other Spanish townships as well.

Affiliation occurred among inhabitants who had originally immigrated from a variety of different areas in the peninsula as well as beyond the Pyrenees after the Arab conquest of the early eighth century. Situated high in the northwest of Spain's central plateau, Zamora had gathered its early inhabitants from Christian crusaders and settlers who entered the region during the Reconquest. In 748, Zamora had been razed by conquering Christian armies under Alfonso I and was periodically assaulted by both Moors and Christians throughout the ninth and tenth centuries. As a result of Zamora's strategic position on the Duero river which divided northern Christian Spain from the Muslim south, it was used as a base for colonization efforts into the center of the peninsula during the eleventh century.

In the course of the Reconquest, Zamora's population was frequently replenished by people from the northern provinces of Leon, Asturias and Galicia, and by Mozarabs from Toledo, Coria and Mérida.[5] From the late eleventh century until the first third of the thirteenth century, French immigrants also appeared and in the mid-thirteenth and fourteenth centuries Jewish immigration added to its ethnic diversity.[6]

Other geographical factors exposed Zamora to settlers and travellers from distant territories as well. The city was a natural crossroads among several regions, linking Portugal with the center of Old Castile and connecting Extremadura and Andalucia with Galicia. Most importantly, it formed a part of the primary north–south axis of the pilgrimage route to Santiago de Compostela. A glance at a sixteenth-century travel guide by Juan de Villuga shows Zamora to have been placed within the most dense network of roads in the peninsula.[7] The population density of the polygon Burgos–Zamora–Salamanca–Avila–Toledo–Madrid–Valladolid was then four times that of the rest of the peninsula.[8] Zamora's place within this mobile area shaped its social composition and destined it to deal with a continuously shifting regional mix of inhabitants. Foreign travellers, pilgrims, displaced workers and vagrants moved freely to the city, seeking lodging, employment or alms.[9] It was the fate of its people to try to incorporate these diverse elements into society, and it was primarily through the religious confraternities that they succeeded. Confraternal programs dissolved regional differences enough to create a common cultural outlook among inhabitants by the later Middle Ages.

The construction of confraternities in Zamora proceeded slowly in the thirteenth and fourteenth centuries. The earliest recorded confraternities date from 1230, and by 1400 the city possessed ten.[10] We know of their existence principally from testaments and legacies left in their name by wealthier members of society. Since wills of the third estate rarely appear before the sixteenth century, the confraternities cited in testamentary documents of the late Middle Ages reveal exclusively the involvement of clergy and nobility. Thirteenth- and early fourteenth-century confraternities were established in the old part of the city, centered around the cathedral and castle, where the upper classes and a sizeable French population resided. Some of the late medieval confraternities patronized hospitals of lodging houses below the city walls along the southern road leading from the bridge of the Duero river to Galicia – an ideal location to welcome poor farmers, travellers, and pilgrims passing through to Santiago de Compostela. The high social status and relative wealth of the thirteenth-century donors suggest that the confraternities were essentially charitable institutions dedicated to the support of poor residents and wayfarers rather than mutual aid groups for the material assistance of their own members.

Confraternities of the third estate began to appear in the mid-fourteenth century in new neighborhoods that stretched outside the city walls of the Reconquest period. They accompanied settlement of the eastern suburbs by artisans, merchants and day laborers. They multiplied as a new market expanded and allowed for the financial support of parish churches.[11] Along the Duero river at the site of an old lodging house called the 'Hospital of Shepherds', a group of merchants erected a church in 1167 under the advocacy of San Julián, the patron of pilgrims.[12] In subsequent years, several new churches were built to accommodate the growing merchant and artisan classes. The parishes of San Leonardo, Santa Lucía, and Santa María de la Horta soon joined that of San Julián. By the fourteenth century, fifteen parish churches and three monasteries for women – Santa Clara of the Clarissas, the Franciscan convent of Santa Marina and the Dominican convent of San Pable – served the new city. A second layer of walls was built to enclose the new residential area, forming an outer crescent around the original urban nucleus.

Confraternities of artisans and merchants began to cluster around the parish churches, particularly along the main street of Valborraz which served as a new artery for traders and pilgrims. By the end of the fourteenth century, four of the ten confraternities of the city were located in the new neighborhoods, and in the fifteenth century, a total of fifteen confraternities were founded in the area, compared with eleven in the old section and five in outlying rural areas.

It has been suggested by Luis G. de Valdeavellano that medieval craft confraternities in Spain originated among Mozarab or French handicraft workers, who subsequently spread them among Spanish artisans.[13] The hypothesis might be accurate for the Zamoran craft confraternities, since they appeared after both Mozarabs and Frenchmen had set up shops in the city. It is highly likely, however, that the craft confraternities developed in imitation of those established earlier by elites, for they were almost identical in function and organization. The Franciscan and Dominican orders may have introduced confraternities among all Zamoran residents since they were responsible for extending confraternities throughout many parts of Italy and France by the fourteenth century.[14]

Confraternities began to proliferate in the city during the last two decades of the fifteenth century. By the second half of the sixteenth century, 150 confraternities operated among a population which at its peak reached only 8600 residents.[15] This proportion was decidedly higher than that calculated for larger cities in Spain. In Valladolid at least 100 confraternities have been estimated for a population of 30 000, and in Toledo, 143 confraternities have been identified among a population of 60 000.[16] The ratio of confraternities to population was much higher in Zamora, where one organization existed for every fourteen households, compared to one for every 48 households in the villages of the province of Cuenca, and one for every 100 households in New Castile.[17]

Beyond the Pyrenees, confraternities appear to have been less numerous than in any of the Spanish provinces. In sixteenth-century Florence, 75 confraternities have been cited among a population of 59 000,[18] and 68 are noted in Lyon, where the population varied between 45 000 and 65 000 in the sixteenth century.[19] The northern European city of Lübeck, with 25 000 residents in 1400, had at least 67 confraternities, while 99 existed at the beginning of the Reformation among Hamburg's population of 16 000 to 18 000.[20]

The unparalleled vigor of Zamora's confraternal life may have been related to its comparatively underdeveloped economy, which failed to sustain a comprehensive guild structure. The religious organizations supplied all the mutual aid and fraternal benefits that in other cities were partially provided by guilds. It should be noted in this regard, however, that while Zamora possessed an unusually high number of confraternities, membership sizes in each tended to be smaller than average sizes of organizations in other cities. Zamoranos preferred to form intimate brotherhoods of 30 to 40 members under the advocacy of favored saints and then join several different groups to benefit from multiple intercessions.

With respect to geography, sixteenth-century confraternities were distributed fairly evenly throughout the neighborhoods of the urban center of Zamora, ranging from a low of one to every 22 households in the neighborhood of San Andres to a high of one to every nine households in San Antolín. The highest densities were to be found among neighborhoods with large numbers of lower-class handicraft workers. In San Antolín, as much as 83 per cent of the households were considered poor in a census compiled by the *corregidor* and city council in 1618.[21] Most of these poor residents were textile workers such as weavers and combers of wool, and silk-mercers. Skilled craftsmen in the allied trades of tailoring and headdress-making were also counted among their ranks, as well as a few construction workers, masons, cutlers, and shoemakers. These artisans formed small confraternities of 20 to 30 people that served as modest mutual aid groups for members whose meager incomes left them frequently in need of financial assistance.

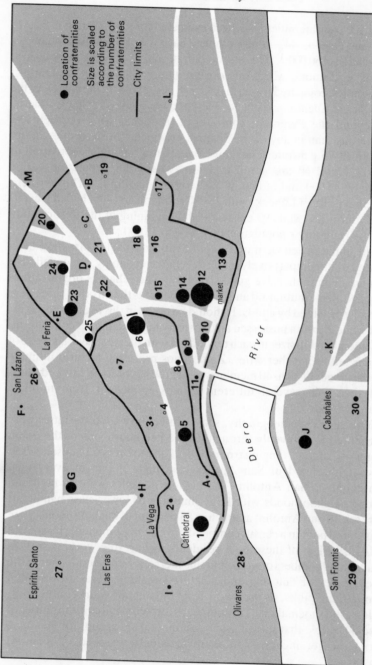

1.1 Confraternities in the city of Zamora in the mid-sixteenth century

1.2   Zamora's Parishes and their Confraternities

PARISHES	CONVENTS AND SANCTUARIES

PARISHES	CONVENTS AND SANCTUARIES
1. Cathedral: 9	A. Sanctuary of Santa Marta: 1
2. San Isidro: 2	B. Convent of Santa Clara: 1
3. San Martín: 1	C. Sanctuary of Santa Marina
4. La Magdalena	D. Chapel in the Hospital of
5. San Pedro y San Ildefonso: 7	Sotelo: 1
6. San Juan de la Puerta	E. Sanctuary of San Sebastián: 1
Nueva: 13	F. Sanctuary of Santa Susana: 1
7. Santa María la Nueva: 2	G. Monastery of Santo Domingo: 6
8. San Cipriano: 3	H. Sanctuary of Santa María de
9. Santa Lucía: 5	la Vega: 2
10. San Julián: 5	I. Church of Santiago de los
11. San Simón: 2	Caballeros: 2
12. Santa María de la Horta: 15	J. Monastery of San Francisco: 8
13. Santo Tomé: 5	K. Convent of Santo María de
14. San Leonardo: 7	las Dueñas
15. Santa Eulalia: 4	L. Monastery of Nuestra Señora
16. San Andres: 2	de la Consolación
17. San Pablo	M. Sanctuary of Santa María del
18. San Salvador de la Vid: 5	Camino: 1
19. San Miguel	
20. San Torcuato: 5	
21. Santiago del Burgo: 1	
22. San Vincente: 3	
23. San Antolín: 7	
24. San Esteban: 6	
25. San Bartolomé: 5	
26. San Lázaro: 2	
27. Espíritu Santo	
28. San Claudio: 1	
29. San Frontis: 5	
30. San Sepulcro: 3	

The numbers following each name show the number of confraternities in each parish or attached to each convent or sanctuary.

The churches of San Juan de la Puerta Nueva and Santa María de la Horta, situated in the two main market centers of Zamora, contained as well a high number of confraternities that enrolled traders and consumers frequenting the squares outside their doors. As in the neighborhood of San Antolín, most members of these confraternities were workers in the secondary sector of the economy, especially textile and leather makers, embroiderers, shoemakers, tailors and silversmiths.

There was also a high concentration of confraternities in the area of the cathedral, where a different type of poverty prevailed. Indigent families who lived principally on charity settled among the wealthy residences of canons, nobles, government officials and widows, where charitable doles were plentiful and hospitals large and adequately furnished.[22] The largest and wealthiest charitable confraternities were located in this section of the city, including the renowned Cofradía de Nuestra Señora de la Misericordia that housed pilgrims and the homeless from the province. Unlike the mutual aid groups of San Antolín and the market areas of San Juan de la Puerta Nueva and Santa María de la Horta, the charity of the confraternities surrounding the cathedral was directed entirely outward to non-members.

Neighborhoods with the fewest confraternities per capita in the urban center of Zamora were those whose residents were involved in work associated with the tertiary sector of the economy. Parishioners of San Andres were administrators, merchants and grocerers. Those of the parishes of San Cipriano and Santa María la Nueva included many government officials, military men and merchants. In addition the service workers living within wealthy districts adjoining the cathedral, such as San Isidoro and La Magdalena, erected relatively few confraternities in their local churches.

This sociological sketch illustrates that confraternities were concentrated heavily in parishes whose residents belonged to the nobility and to the artisan class. Bourgeois residential areas produced fewer confraternities than did either of these two other kinds of neighborhoods. It was indeed for patricians and for plebeians that these spiritual alliances existed – they received alms from one hand to give to the other. Charitable confraternities were a phenomenon adapted to old regime society with its wide gap between rich and poor. Corporate life was less vigorous among the self-sufficient bureaucrats, merchants and military men in the city who did not share the financial worries that induced less prosperous members of the third estate to join for their material well-being. These bourgeois residents also lacked as part of their social identity the spirit of largesse that encouraged aristocrats to participate in confraternal charitable programs.

Also illustrative of the old regime character of confraternal life was the arrangement of membership into one of the three estates of clergy, aristocracy and commoners. In Zamora five clerical societies, which were among the oldest in the city, served the first estate. Their strict entrance requirements only admitted residents born in wedlock to Christian parents, specifically barring persons with Jewish or Moorish ancestry. The most exclusive of the clerical associations was San Pedro and San Lorenzo, commonly called the 'Cofradía de los Racioneros' because its members were required to be ordained priests holding prebendary positions with the cathedral chapter. Royal privileges conceded by King Sancho IV in 1284 and confirmed by King Alfonso XI in 1338 enabled it to grow into one of the wealthiest confraternities in the city.[23] It was exempted from payments of all royal taxes and permitted to buy and sell property freely, except for land belonging to monasteries or churches which required royal permission. In return for these favors, the Racioneros were obliged to say an anniversary mass every Saturday in the church of San Pedro for the souls of deceased members of the royal family and to pray daily for the health and salvation of the regents and their children. The confraternity enjoyed such prestige that by the mid-fourteenth century over 70 high-ranking individuals had joined, including members of the royal family, bishops throughout the Spanish kingdoms, and fellows of the major military orders. Its popularity declined in subsequent years, until by the late sixteenth century revised ordinances reveal that the Racioneros had been reduced to ten clerics, all residents of the city of Zamora serving within the jurisdiction of the cathedral. The confraternity always selected members from elite ranks and closely examined the moral standing of candidates for admission. Aspirants were required to prove that they were legitimate sons of Old Christians and that they had never been condemned by the Inquisition. To ensure that they would be obedient and peaceful brothers of the society, candidates served it for a probationary period of three years, during which time cofrades assessed their characters and observed their ability to fit in amiably with the group.[24]

The largest land-owning confraternity in the city of Zamora was formed by clerics from the church of San Ildefonso, called the 'Cofradía de los Ciento' for its one hundred members. The priests of the Ciento were members of the order of San Pedro, subject to the cathedral of Zamora, and all were either born in Zamora or in charge of benefices within the city. Ten lay persons, also residents of Zamora, were permitted within the group. Due to the high entry fees required, they usually derived from the nobility. Wealthy widows were encouraged to join because of the sizeable inheritances that they had at their disposal, while workers in mechanical trades were automatically disqualified. All cofrades were required to prove through the testimony of neighbors that they were Old Christians, 'untainted' by

Jewish or Moorish blood. By the late sixteenth century, they were also required to demonstrate that they were not descendants of Lutherans, nor holders of heretical beliefs.[25]

Among the ten aristocratic Zamoran confraternities which existed in the sixteenth century, not only the religious background but also the noble rank of ancestors was carefully considered. Statutes required that cofrades not be 'of the race of New Christians, Moors, Jews, nor penitents of the Holy Inquisition, nor ever punished by it, nor infamous in any respect'.[26] Before admittance, relatives on both the matrilineal and patrilineal sides were scrutinized for loyalty to the Catholic faith in a rigorous process that made membership a symbol of honor and prestige among the upper classes. The strictest confraternities, like that of San Ildefonso, excluded all tax-payers and government officials from membership, for these persons violated the status of a true *caballero* by earning a living through work rather than rents and inheritances. Women who wished to enter noble as well as clerical confraternities were expected to prove good moral standing within the community. Blemished reputations could disqualify them from consideration.

Sufficient confraternal positions were available in Zamora for all clerics and nobles to participate if they so desired.[27] Indeed, testaments confirm that men from the first and second estate enjoyed multiple membership.[28] A single example in 1597 suffices to illustrate a common phenomenon. Antonio de la Peña, a parish priest of San Esteban, claimed active membership in the confraternities of the Ciento, the Transfixión y Angel de la Guardia, the Santa Vera Cruz, Nuestra Señora del Rosario of the monastery of Santo Domingo, the Trinidad, Santo Sepulcro y Nuestra Señora, and the Santíssimo Sacramento of the parish of San Esteban.[29]

The third estate had well over 100 confraternities in sixteenth-century Zamora from which to choose allegiance. Entry fees of the popular confraternities were generally small enough to permit the most humble artisans to join, and persons too poor to meet any financial demand could be exempted from all financial burdens in the name of charity. Fees averaged 200 *maravedís*[30] in the first half of the sixteenth century, about six days' wages for a journeyman and three and a half days' income for a master artisan. They increased to an average of 425 *maravedís* in the second half of the century, rising slightly less than wages to equal about four and a half days' worth of compensation for a journeyman and a little more than three days' income for a master.[31]

Commoners shared with clerics and nobles an interest in joining several different spiritual alliances. A gardener residing in the parish of San Juan in 1556 claimed affiliation with seven confraternities, and in 1564 the wife of another gardener claimed six.[32] The weaver Juan Mogollo belonged in 1578 to a special confraternity composed solely of workers of his own trade as well as five other devotional groups.[33] In 1598 the tailor Antonio López belonged to six and the widowed María Alvarez claimed membership in seven.[34]

Unlike the exclusive confraternities of the clerics and nobles, these salvific alliances of the commonfolk made no demands regarding family background. Their only concern was that associates hold reputations of good morality within the community. Only two of the popular confraternities, both of which charged such high entry rates that only well-paid bureaucrats and residents of the upper middle class joined, enforced purity of blood requirements.[35] The rest permitted entry to *conversos*, or converted Jews, who were denied admission into the brotherhoods of clerics and nobles, and who, in various regions of Spain, were periodically forbidden to hold public office or enter religious convents and universities. The open admission of the third estate's confraternities leads one to question the oft-cited assertion in the historiography of race relations in Spain that preoccupations with purity of blood were of plebeian origin, promoted by undistinguished men and women desperately seeking status in religious orthodoxy.[36] Confraternal practices reveal to us that, quite the contrary, the common people were exceptional in upholding in their admissions' procedures their professed aspiration to promote harmony among all Christians.

More remarkable is the fact that, unlike so many confraternities in sixteenth-century Florence and Lyon which restricted membership solely to men,[37] only a handful in Zamora excluded women. Indeed, any gender segregation that existed among Castilian organizations was just as likely to have been initiated by women as by men, for occasionally women designed their own confraternal programs to meet special needs such as assistance in childbirth. To deny women the right of participation in confraternal life would have meant the exclusion of one of the neediest and most deserving groups in society, for women, particularly the widowed, suffered under severe conditions of poverty. Widows in Castilian society were among the most dependent of the minorities, deprived of the income of their husbands and frequently forbidden to carry on family trades. Their disadvantageous position is reflected in the fact that of all the indigent households identified in Zamora in 1561, 66.4 per cent were headed by single women, and 80 per cent of these single women were widows.[38] In such circumstances, women were especially eager to secure the aid and companionship of cofrades, who acted as surrogate family members by caring for them in sickness and ensuring funeral services and prayers after death. For this reason confraternities frequently offered widows admission for half the fees of other members. Wealthy widows shared the desire of other single women to enter into these collegial alliances, and their willingness to donate generously to corporate property won them the approval of other members.[39] As a result, the vast majority of popular confraternities opened their doors to women as well as to New Christians. At times they also made efforts to encourage the participation of the poor by lowering entry fees or by abolishing financial requirements altogether. Such provisions testify that these corporate groups were willing to admit diverse elements of the population into their ranks. Both in theory and in practice, their confraternities served not to sow dissension but to encourage a sense of camaraderie among the commonfolk.

With this in mind, we need to look carefully at critiques levelled by opponents of the Old Order, starting with social reformers of the eighteenth century and continuing with many historians of the twentieth century, that the corporate structure of traditional society was inherently divisive.[40] According to these critics, both confraternities and guilds of the old regime prevented the development of broad class and national identities by training popular attention on the pursuit of narrow corporate goals. In fact, one of the principal demands of the French Revolutionary governments of 1789 to 1791 was for the abolition of all types of corporations in the hope of uniting workers' sentiment around the banner of the French nation. Was such hostility to corporate life warranted? Did confraternities and guilds isolate the laboring class into mutually-exclusive interest groups?

Confraternities in Zamora played a role in society that was by no means as corrosive of popular unity as reformers and revolutionaries supposed. Certainly confraternities were responsible for reinforcing the medieval legal segregation of society into estates of commoners, clerics, and nobles by drawing their membership almost entirely from one of the three groups. Aristocratic confraternities explicitly prohibited entry to citizens from the 'mechanical trades', and both priestly and popular corporations severely limited the number of members that they would admit from an order other than their own. But it is not evident that confraternities of the old regime were responsible for creating occupational divisions among commoners, divisions that might have prevented them from gaining a consciousness of themselves as a unique social and economic class. In fact, alliances among confraternal members in Zamora generally cut across occupational lines. Among all the artisans and professionals in the city, only a few designed their own exclusive religious groups. They included furriers and scribes, and contingents of merchants, tailors, public criers, weavers of linen, shoemakers, gardeners and students. All the other workers joined alliances that catered for a variety of trades. To describe what one of these groups might look like: the confraternity of Santa Catalina in 1400 embraced a surgeon, a blanket-maker, a blacksmith, a sculptor, a tanner, a wool-comber, a barber, a carpenter, a messenger, a censor, a weaver and a servant.[41] Another, Nuestra Señora del Yermo in the poverty-stricken extramural parish of San Lázaro, admitted 78 members in 1595. Enrolled among them were two priests, three coppersmiths, five weavers, five wool-carders, several silk-mercers, two fullers, two millers, two blind men, three teachers, a carpenter, a shoemaker, a servant, a fruiterer, a locksmith, and a washer-woman.[42] The confraternity of San Juan Bautista, founded in 1572 by a woolen-cloth weaver, included among its 29 affiliates several silk-mercers, a sword cutler, a butcher, a baker, a shearer of cloth, a servant, a blacksmith, a stone-cutter, a gardener, a shoemaker, a coachman and a messenger.[43] Such heterogenous fields of employment were found over and over again in membership lists of other confraternities.

While more than one hundred religious corporations enrolled members from different occupations, very few professional guilds, or *gremios*, brought together workers from the same trade in Zamora. Only two dozen of the city's crafts organized into corporations to pursue purely economic goals by the end of the sixteenth century, and they never attained the high degree of popular allegiance enjoyed by the confraternities.[44] Given the supremacy of confraternities over guilds, it is apparent that the overriding impact of the Zamoran 'corporate system' was to combine various occupations rather than to isolate them into separate interest groups. The majority of plebeian corporations in the city weakened distinctions of profession. Indeed, if we consider that most urban residents belonged to not one, but several, religious groups, it becomes even clearer that these associations did not divide the community along sectarian lines. No single confraternity could elicit the undivided allegiance of its constituents. Joint membership interlocked the confraternal structure throughout the community. If confraternities failed to engender workers with 'class consciousness', therefore, it was not because they divided crafts against each other.

Recent scholarship on nineteenth-century labor movements increases doubt about the supposedly divisive nature of the corporate regime, moreover, by undermining the notion that guilds discouraged unification of workers around class issues. Labor historians such as Bernard H. Moss and E. P. Thompson have pointed out that when European workers finally adopted class goals in the nineteenth and twentieth centuries, they tended to come from areas where traditional occupational corporatism in guilds had been quite strong, as in Paris, Lyon, Manchester, and Barcelona.[45] Contrary to the opinion still widely held by historians of a generation and more earlier, it was not the unorganized proletariat of the factories at all, but artisans accustomed to corporate collaboration in workshops who participated in the first workers' movements. Developing these new insights into the social background of urban revolts, William Sewell Jr. has argued that the spirit of corporatism not only survived, but indeed fuelled, the revolutionary labor movements that brought on the collapse of the old regime in France.[46] In the proper circumstances, guild co-operation readily broadened into class spirit. The conclusions of these social historians, sympathetic with the cause of the working class but by no means driven for this reason to condemn the traditional order of society out of hand, demand a clearer understanding of the nature of corporate organization in the medieval and early modern period.

If guilds cannot be blamed for the disunity of the working class, how can confraternities, which drew together craftsmen from diverse trades, be evaluated? Did confraternities have a positive role to play in the movement of labor solidarity in the modern period? Curiously, the evidence here indicates that just the opposite was true. In the nineteenth and twentieth centuries, areas with a tradition of intense religious corporatism such as Castile never developed significant workers' movements. In assessing the impact of the corporate structure on social relations, therefore, the roles of guilds and confraternities must be carefully distinguished. Only confraternities occupied a position that seemed to have deterred the expression of class goals. How was this done? Certainly not, we have seen, by instigating factionalism among trades. But it is possible that in tying communal bonds along religious rather than economic lines, the confraternities discouraged identification among workers with trade-related issues. Or to state this more accurately, the reasons why the common people never developed a strong working-class ethic during the old regime probably had less to do with the corporate structure of society itself and more with the absence of a coherent and moving political ideology of class that could compete with the vitality of religious solidarity.

In traditional European society, it was not political action after all that the underprivileged trusted to further its own welfare. In both material and spiritual affairs the common people turned for help to religious ritual. Their confraternities were instruments for soliciting divine assistance; they were intended neither to facilitate nor to obstruct political activities. Security lay not in their own hands but in the hands of divine beings to whom they offered allegiance. It was for this reason that confraternities, and even most guilds in the old regime, dedicated themselves in name to saints who would favor their causes. Let us look more deeply into the mentality that underlies the old corporate order of Zamoran society in order to sight its emotional distance from the pragmatic political orientation of the modern world.

Patron saints were selected carefully according to status or perceived sympathy for particular needs of members. Thirteenth-century Zamoran confraternities picked universally-known saints as their protectors, apparently because those with greater fame were thought to possess more influence with God. Primary among them was the Virgin Mary, who guided the first known Zamoran confraternity and became the most popular and enduring of all patron saints. Four fourteenth-century confraternities and ten fifteenth-century groups in Zamora chose Mary as their advocate, designing special honorific titles to distinguish her patronage among them. Santa María de la Vega, Santa María del Val de Mora, Santa María del Caño, and Santa María de la Cabaña associated Mary with favorite natural settings around Zamora and domesticated her powers within private shrines. Other epithets attached to her name singled out special events in her life such as the Annunciation, the Purification, and the Visitation, or identified prized attributes – la Santa Caridad, la Misericordia, la Piedad. Across Spain, hundreds of confraternities became Mary's children by adopting her various matronymics into their titles. Through language, they fulfilled their wishes to develop intimate relationships with the mother of God.

The populace fashioned the image of the Virgin into a patroness whose solicitude extended over the entire range of human needs. Unlike the other saints, she was never identified as a special guardian against particular bodily ailments or natural calamities. She remained a universal symbol and could be called upon in many circumstances. R. W. Southern explains that since the twelfth century, the Virgin's reputation was based on her willingness to extend aid to anyone who called upon her in need. 'Like the rain,' he comments, 'this protective power of the Virgin falls on the just and unjust alike – provided only that they have entered the circle of her allegiance.'[47] The notion that Mary, the epitome of human goodness, never exercized her compassion in a judgmental manner by making it contingent upon either the moral character of the supplicant or the seriousness of the cause was of utmost importance to theologians at Salamanca in the development of scholastic thought on the nature of mercy[48] and more generally to the common people in conceptualizing ideal charitable behavior. The Virgin Mary succoring the needy personified the spirit of beneficence and Christian love. Cofrades did not hesitate to perform their charitable acts in an emotional manner, emulating her display of pity and pleasure. Their beneficence was personal in the way that she bestowed her own divine favors, and indiscriminate in the way that she gave to all who asked.

Mary was considered a more dependable ally to salvation than Christ for her mercy softened the justice of her son. Despite attempts beginning in the twelfth century to render the figure of Christ in a more human and compassionate form, he frequently displayed the traditional appearance of a stern judge almost as unapproachable as God the Father. Mary stood closer to human frailty and weakness and received the first requests for assistance among the mediators with God. Expressing such confidence in the mother during a period of pestilence and civic strife in 1466, the entire village of Villalpando bargained by promising to honor her Immaculate Conception if she would

> undertake to plead with her glorious Son Our Lord Jesus Christ; that He, by mercy and pity, and by the holy passion which He suffered for our sins, should listen to her, and grant her request ... and order His Angel to desist from wounding and killing us.[49]

This was one of the earliest communal demonstrations in Europe in favor of the notion that Mary had been conceived without sin, initiating a movement of popular support for her cause that finally forced the papacy to admit the Immaculate Conception into dogma in 1854. It was not merely coincidental that pressure from below to glorify Mary came in times of desperation, when earthly measures

failed to heal the troubles of society. In vowing to believe in the
miraculous, the village surrendered confidence in man-made remedies
– and in man himself – and placed its trust in divine auspices. Its
guardian would henceforth be raised above other humans in the
unnaturalness of her birth, freed from all traces of original sin that
subjected the rest to the material world. The people's female paragon
embodied to perfection all those qualities traditionally associated with
the maternal in western thought – soft and yielding, kind and tolerant –
which made her desired even before Christ in times of stress. Her
sacred womb represented new life, perhaps the only hope from the
all-consuming death around them.

> As Christians, we have no other medicine, nor any other support or
> remedy or helpmate to assist us in our griefs and miseries and
> tribulations, except the glorious Virgin Mary, she who without sin
> was conceived in the womb of St. Ann ... because as a result of our
> sins, we are not able nor dignified enough to seek the help of God.[50]

Fortunately for those in search of her favors, she was also subject to
flattery – an indispensable weakness in an effective intercessor.
Complimenting Mary on her superior standing among celestial court
lawyers, cofrades of Nuestra Señora de la Anunciación dedicated
their pious work

> to the honor and veneration of the Virgin Holy Mary, His mother,
> our Lady, who as the flower of all virtues, mother of orphans,
> consolation of the disconsolate, glory of widows, and crown of
> virgins, deserves to be honored more than all the saints and raised
> above all the choirs of angels, and by whose merits the whole
> Christian commonwealth is aided forever.[51]

To those in need, no other divine figure equalled the status of the
mother and no other sacred symbol so calmed their anxieties and
indulged their fantasies. She was *parthenos* or Virgin, the guarantee of
man's soul for having refused to admit his body.

Other holy patrons favored by the confraternities were men and
women who, like Mary, had rejected the flesh for a life of ascetic piety.
There was Catherine of Alexandria and Catherine of Siena who
followed in Mary's footsteps by devoting their lives to their 'bride-
groom' Christ. St Susanna too had rejected man's overtures for sexual
contact.[52] Among the male patrons of Zamora's confraternities was

St Ildefonso, the seventh-century archbishop of Toledo who wrote a book to prove the holy mother's perpetual virginity. St Lorenzo, one of the earliest patrons, was a Venetian nobleman who rejected marriage to devote his life to prayer in the cloister. St Lawrence had suffered a martyr's death, roasted on a grid-iron at the hands of a Roman prefect for spending the church's treasure on the poor. What all these holy patrons had in common was to have conquered the flesh in their lifetimes. It was this that gave them special graces for assisting those feeble mortals who wept and wearied under the pressures of earthly existence.

To ensure adequate protection, cofrades occasionally enlisted two, or sometimes more, despisers of the flesh, one of whom was almost always the Virgin Mary. The Cofradía de Nuestra Señora de San Antolín y del Señor Santiago invoked the Virgin and the 'blessed Apóstol Señor Santiago, Light [and] patron of the Spanish lands, whom we take as lawyers in all our deeds so that they be guards and defenders of our souls, bodies, and property, that we not perish by our errors, but that they guide us and place us on the right road of salvation ... '[53]

In the suburbs and rural areas outside the city, the Holy Spirit was a conspicuous patron. The third person of the Trinity had been called upon in many parts of Europe since at least the early thirteenth century,[54] and was possibly even more popular an advocate than Mary in the small villages where the mendicant orders had not been quite as successful as in the cities in extending the cult of the Mother of God. The Holy Spirit typically reigned over confraternities with hospitals, for even earlier than Mary it was seen as a symbol of charity. In the original Greek definition, Paraclete was 'comforter' or 'advocate'.[55]

With the multiplication of confraternities in the second half of the fifteenth century, less celebrated saints, many of them recognized only among the local communities, were invoked as patrons. They included such holy souls as Tortijo, Boal, Amaro, and Mamed. The presence of saints' relics inspired the creation of confraternities for the utilization of their powers. San Cucufate's relics had travelled all the way to Zamora from the Catalan coast, and the remains of San Ildefonso came from Toledo. The latter's cult required special armed defense because the Toledans contested the right to possess his bones and frequently sent delegations of church authorities to have them returned, officially or surreptitiously. The potential threat to Ildefonso's intimate presence among the community gave Zamoran aristocrats, privileged in the right to bear arms, special incentive to claim him as their patron.

There was a paradox connected with the cult of the saints, a paradox evident at least to the modern mind. The saints had received their powers by overcoming the trials and temptations of the material world, and yet they manifested their holiness most conspicuously in material objects. It was in their bodily remains or in their waxen images that their spiritual graces resided for the community to tap. After nominating for sainthood those men and women who had denied the world of fleshly pleasure and pain, the people proceeded to endow them with special influence over earthly affairs. Saints were called upon to assist the community in problems encountered on earth as well as on the way to heaven. They were asked to appease God for offenses made by the people and to bring peace, health and good weather. For these purposes, the church recognized two types of rogational processions, those instituted by ecclesiastics, and those acclaimed by public vote.[56] During processions, confraternities brought out their most cherished relics to solicit spiritual assistance. Promenaded under the skies in public streets and squares, these physical remains communicated with the supernatural, exerting a force on the heavens set off by believers' passions. To draw down divine grace upon a scorched earth, cofrades marched with their relics through the fields which thirsted for water. To bring supernatural control over a swelling river, they submerged their relics and holy images in the flood waters. The Cofradía de Nuestra Señora de los Remedios extended special confidence to its icon of the Virgin. During a drought in the spring of 1589, the city council discussed and approved the request of the confraternity 'to take out into procession its image so that, by means of Our Lady, God Our Lord would be induced to send water from the heavens for the bread and fruits of the land'.[57] Nuestra Señora del Socorro was another statue especially favored to invoke supernatural aid in the belief that God would be 'attentive to the devotion and affection that this confraternity and its cofrades have accumulated in her service'. The confraternity customarily petitioned for good weather and rain; and in 1651, during severe devastations of crops by insects, it set out to beseech 'our Lord Jesus Christ so that He would be so served as to placate His anger and liberate the fruits from locusts'.[58] The vows made by cofrades in personal service to God or the saints could extend indefinitely in time, binding future generations to observe corporate pledges.

The divine favors that the confraternities cultivated over the years in religious services to patron saints prompted civil authorities to seek their aid in endeavors affecting the commonwealth. From time to time

the crown called upon them to assist in national crises. In 1588 King
Philip II ordered all Spanish prelates to organize processions for the
successful completion of the mission of the Armada against England.
Zamora's bishop proposed taking out into the streets the most
influential of the city's relics, those of San Ildefonso and San Atilano,
patron saints of the municipality and bishopric. In deliberating upon
the matter, the city council, the cathedral chapter, and the confraternity of San Ildefonso which held the keys to their remains decided to
parade only San Atilano for fear that the people from Toledo might try
to steal Ildefonso's relics if they were taken from safekeeping.[59] The
city took its chances on exposing San Ildefonso to the skies in a more
immediate crisis in the closing years of the sixteenth century when the
bubonic plague broke out in neighboring villages. After enforcing all
the customary sanitary restrictions to preserve the health of the city,
magistrates decided that it would be 'more advantageous and useful to
employ spiritual measures by entreating Our Lord to protect the city.
This should be done through the intercession of the blessed patron
saints San Ildefonso and San Atilano, by making processions and
orations ... and by extracting all available charity from residents'.[60]
Charitable giving discharged spiritual graces among the population at
the same time that it filled depleted municipal coffers for the
enforcement of relief programs.

Confraternities were also called upon to commemorate national
triumphs. Their processions served not only to foster national pride
and convey joy in communal solidarity but also to circulate the news
among the population. In 1563 Zamoran religious corporations
welcomed the closing of the Council of Trent with a general parade,
and in November 1571 they celebrated the victory of Lepanto in
procession with city officials and church prelates.[61] Cofrades had
special reason to cheer, for Pope Pius V confirmed that their role in the
actual victory over the Turks had been decisive, and instituted a yearly
feast of Our Lady of Victory in gratitude to all the confraternities of
Europe that had prayed rosaries for the triumph of the Holy League.

These efforts on behalf of environmental control and national
political causes extended the area of confraternal social concerns. Like
all private organizations, their first commitment was to their own
constituents, but this did not necessarily mean that they acted to
impede the growth of broad regional or national identities. Indeed,
confraternities were one of the few agencies that central governments
and national churches could rely on to gain the attention of the
population in the absense of an adequate communication network.

When called upon, confraternities were prepared to move beyond concern for their own affiliates to serve the large community.

Such concerted activity for the benefit of others was, after all, the professed goal of these spiritual alliances, and it is not surprising that they should respond occasionally to governments' calls for assistance. As conceived in the minds of members, confraternities were microcosms of the ideal Christian world of love and equality among believers. They were intended to instill in individuals a spirit of co-operation and mutual support. Like all higher ideals, however, this world of brotherly love was easier to conceptualize than to practice. The tactics adopted by confraternities to transform their ideals into reality were not without flaws and inconsistencies. Consider, for instance, the internal governance of a confraternity. Here we can see both the achievements and the failures of corporate policies.

The political structure was designed to uphold Christian belief in the equality of all souls before God.[62] Members rotated official positions in order to prevent concentration of power, and they arrived at important decisions through consensus by vote. The *mayordomo* took charge of co-odinating group activities. His duties included managing property transactions and other financial matters, presiding at meetings, enforcing statutes to ensure the performance of spiritual obligations, and organizing banquets, processions and feast day celebrations. Little status was attached to the position, and in fact the work was considered so onerous that harsh penalties had to be imposed for refusing to serve once elected. The mayordomo held office for one year and received a salary from communal funds. Assisting him were other officials whose positions similarly held little prestige. The *cotanero* assumed the duties of calling members to attendance for meetings and services, and, if the society supported a hospital, regulated entry of patients. Accountants handled budgetary matters. Members shared the remaining responsibilities, working either together or in turn depending on the character of the job at hand. In this manner, no single cofrade assumed a disproportionate amount of labor or prestige.

So far so good. But 'Christian democracy' had its limitations, important limitations of which members may or may not have been aware. The denotation of the male gender in the terms *brother*hood (*herman*dad) and con*fraternity* (co*fradía*) makes an important mark in internal politics. For although both men and women were admitted into membership, only men were allowed to hold governing positions and not infrequently women did not hold voting privileges. Indeed the only time that women enjoyed all the rights of members and fully exercized democratic principles was when they formed their own organizations. The way in which male colleagues dealt with them as incomplete creatures of God compelled the Cofradía de Nuestra Señora in the suburb of San Frontis to demand firm independence from the control of men. Its female clientele formally mandated in statutes that 'no man, not even the abbot or curate, may interfere by inspecting our confraternity'.[63] The inconsistencies that they experienced in Christian attitudes about human equality were not unlike the experiences of women in the late-eighteenth- and nineteenth-century 'republican' states of the west that restricted suffrage and office holding to men.

Among male cofrades, the notion that brotherhoods should be run democratically was conceived not so much with respect to equality of men and women as to equality of laymen and clerics. All precautions were taken to prevent a hierarchical distribution of power and prestige in favor of the priestly order. In old regime society the potential for clerical domination over lay brothers was an important concern. Most lay organizations limited the number of clerical members to two or three, or else requested that priests and friars enter as 'laymen'. The ecclesiastics were called upon to perform scheduled masses and attend at funerals, for which they received monetary reimbursement from confraternal funds that supplemented their parish salaries or prebendary stipends. Since the annual income of many clerics was notoriously low, service in confraternities could be a highly-prized position among them. Until Trent, cofrades maintained exclusive control over choosing their own clerical brothers, a privilege that helped create a system of lay piety relatively free from ecclesiastical manipulation.

CORPORATE FINANCES

Not by sentiment alone were these representations of the mystical body of Christ to survive on earth. An enormous amount of wealth went into fashioning corporate entities out of Zamora's heterogenous population. Canon law provided the necessary guidelines for the acquisition and management of material goods. It designated that organizations dedicated to pious or charitable purposes were 'moral persons', a juridical status that enabled their members to possess and administer property as a unit under the authority of the bishop.[64] This status was obtained through formal decrees of the bishop or his delegate, and allowed confraternities to receive and distribute donations for pious causes. Groups that sought formal episcopal authorization were placed under the jurisdiction and protection of the cathedral chapter and given the same privileges granted churches and other sacred places, including exemptions from royal tributes and excise taxes. With such favors, confraternities built up their estates and became major property owners.

Corporate land was donated principally by testators requesting that rental income be applied to charitable causes or liturgical services for the welfare of their souls. Since last wills and testaments had the force of civil law and the protection of the church, they furnished a stable source of financial support to the religious groups.[65] Unless the specific requirements accompanying bequests were not being fulfilled, the church had no power to confiscate property holdings. Donors left their bequests in confraternal hands with the binding agreement that certain services be fulfilled, pious services that were incumbent on all cofrades, present as well as future. Members took solemn oaths of fidelity to these confraternal agreements with the dead, the breaking of which constituted a mortal sin. No greater commitment could have been given to those who wished to buy spiritual insurance. Cofrades incurred upon themselves the penalty of eternal damnation for failure to complete their vows on behalf of donors' souls.[66]

Another important incentive guiding individuals when they invested their wealth was that confraternities were obligated to protect possessions with communal funds. They assumed any legal costs that might be incurred in the process. The Cofradía de los Ciento annually sent eight members to inspect the conditions of its estates and to report back to the council in order to keep up with necessary repairs.[67] As a group, members decided to rent property or convert rents into long-term leases. Such policies ensured donors that their property would be managed wisely, for cofrades were generally concerned about maximizing corporate income. Only in the event that a fellow member required financial assistance might decisions be made differently. Brothers and sisters could be given priority over outsiders in renting corporate property even if the price that they were able to pay fell below other offers. For poor widows especially, this practice was a valuable form of welfare assistance and an important benefit of membership.

In no circumstances, however, were confraternities free to dispose of donations as they pleased, for they acted strictly as bearers and executors of individual bequests, bound by law to respect the purposes and qualifications under which they were granted. When, for instance, the Cofradía de la Caridad attempted to sell a donated *censo* of 14 000 *maravedís* in order to obtain funds to repair its fulling mills on the Duero river which had deteriorated to such an extent that fishing from them was impossible, the cathedral chapter filed a civil suit against the misapplication of corporate funds. 'The confraternity has all [these] goods deputed to saying daily masses, by the authority of the Ordinary of this bishopric, and by a written public contract made with the oaths of its cofrades.' The chapter argued that 'since it is legally prohibited to alienate these goods without license, and since the *censo* is not ecclesiastical property, nor were the people who donated it ecclesiatics', the Caridad could not transform the capital to ends other than those intended by the donors. 'There never has been, nor is there now, a confraternity erected with the necessary authority and license, not even those sanctioned by the pope', to manipulate testamentary bequests.[68]

How much property was invested for the salvation of souls in Zamora can only be guessed. What is certain is that the amount was sizeable. If we look at the larger pattern of land ownership in the kingdom first, we see that property as a whole expanded greatly between the eighth and the thirteenth centuries, obtained in large part from small private estates turned over by individuals for just such purposes. During the Reconquest, southern Asturias, Leon, and Castile, particularly around the valley of the Duero river, had been repopulated by peasants and humble adventurers. Over a period of three or four centuries, a seigneurial regime such as that found in northern Europe replaced this early medieval freeholding system. It was a massive transformation in land ownership that the eminent medievalist Luis G. de Valdeavellano attributes to the channeling into church hands of donations on behalf of souls, or *donationes pro anima*.[69] Of course not all this wealth went into estates of the confraternities, for in the tenth and eleventh centuries cathedral churches and monasteries received the vast majority of bequests, but in subsequent centuries lay-dominated organizations accumulated more and more of the donations.[70] After immediate families, they were the most preferred group to which testators bequeathed property in the late medieval period.[71]

Confraternal estates together in Zamora undoubtedly formed one of the largest patrimonies in the province, surpassed only by the cathedral chapter and monastic orders.[72] Although many of the poorer organizations possessed no land or rents, accounts of the confraternities of clerics, nobility and prosperous artisans reveal extensive land holdings both within the city and in outlying territories of the province. Their wealth was a matter of great concern to the city government, particularly because they did not pay tributes on the value of goods and property nor excise taxes to the king. One of these groups, the most well endowed in Zamora, was in a particularly advantageous position. The members of the Cofradía de los Ciento accumulated property at such a rapid rate in the sixteenth century that in 1588 an alarmed city council moved to contain further appropriations. According to city magistrates, it was said throughout town that the growth of the Cofradía de los Ciento caused

> great danger and harm to the lay residents of this city and its environs, because it already holds *fueros* and *censos* over the majority of houses and properties in this city, and every day there are many complaints about this confraternity over repairs on these estates.

How its members got such vast holdings becomes clearer:

> since they are pastors of the parishes of this city, it is a well-known fact that for their private interests, they seduce those who come to them for confession to leave their estates to the confraternity.[73]

The price paid for spiritual security was high indeed. And people did not donate to these collective insurance agencies only on their deathbeds. Throughout their lives they contributed to corporate revenue with entry fees, yearly dues, and fines for non-compliance with statutes. Members also regularly dropped small coins in confraternal almsboxes placed at convenient public sites to finance the illumination of chapel images. Confraternities of the Souls in Purgatory reserved special places for their boxes along the stone bridge leading into the city from the south, converting the roadway into a sacred passage reminding travellers of the transportation of souls through charity from one world to the next. When these proceeds fell short, mayordomos appointed delegates to ask for contributions among members or to solicit donations from homes throughout the city.

How was all this income used? Masses had to be financed, liturgical supplies needed replenishing, property required repairs, and festivities required large quantities of food and drink. These were the quotidian expenses incurred by the holy alliances. By design, however, the money was to go into charitable services either for members or for worthy poor of the neighborhoods. Among the charitable items, funerals were high on the list of corporate expenses, for all groups guaranteed burial services to their clientele. Entry fees were usually assessed at values that would cover costs of funeral ceremonies, which explains why married couples and families were required to pay more than single cofrades. Like modern insurance companies, some confraternities measured the risk value of members, soliciting higher entry fees from candidates who joined after reaching the age of 60. The noble Cofradía de San Nicolás required that members make additional donations through testamentary bequests in its name. If members passed away without leaving gifts, the confraternity claimed the right to recover 100 *maravedís* from their estates unless they were poor.[74] Non-members who commended themselves to confraternities for burial were also expected to leave something for services, unless once again they were too poor to 'donate'.

In their concern for personal sanctification, the Zamoran people elected to invest substantial portions of their wealth in corporate projects for the salvation of souls. As soon as private donations entered confraternal coffers they became a part of collective property and entered the exchange of charitable services that continuously reactivated graces among the community. Members distributed corporate revenue among themselves on special occasions, hoping to invigorate communal morale. Some groups made a practice of dividing half the entry fees of new members among the rest of cofrades to encourage attendance at initiation ceremonies. The confraternity of Valdés distributed part of its yearly gains to cofrades on election day to induce members to come and vote for their officials.[75] Others distributed money at celebrations of patron saint days and anniversary services, withholding it from those who did not attend without valid excuses.[76] Corporate funds could also be used to regulate behavior and prevent tardiness, a technique employed by the Cofradía de Nuestra Señora de la Visitación in refusing to give individual allocations to those who had not arrived for mass 'before the raising of the chalice', or not 'standing in their places with hats off for the sermon ...'.[77] The wealthy confraternity of the Racioneros, whose members were all beneficed clerics, offered a special policy to those who had served the organization for ten years by inviting them to give up their benefices and receive the rents and fruits of communal property. Non-veterans received bonus gifts of wheat and barley from confraternal lands after August's harvests, and chickens in the Christmas season.[78]

Collective distributions of money were also common at burials, offered in the name of charity either by the confraternity or by the dead. The regular policy of the Cofradía de San Nicolás was to distribute 300 *maravedís* among members for attending funerals, provided that they were present from the time that the body was taken from its house until they returned back to the door for prayer.[79] Testators offered charity to confraternities for distribution among participants at their own funerals. A donor to Nuestra Señora del Rosario allocated three *reales* to the confraternity's priest for saying mass and ringing the bell four times at his funeral, one *real* to the poor who were present, and six *reales* to attending cofrades.[80]

Distributions of communal funds and offerings of gifts by testators to cofrades served several different purposes. Practically (and unofficially) the doles compensated individuals for time lost on the job while attending confraternal services. At funerals, the money covered ceremonial expenses of candles or torches and the mourning robes in which cofrades were dressed. The purpose explicitly stated for the doles, however, was more holy-minded than all this. They were expected to elicit memories of the dead and touch off prayers among members for the benefit of the departed's soul. How many times, we will see later, would exchanges of material goods be sublimated by religious sentiment!

RITUALS OF SOLIDARITY

The corporate personality of the Zamoran social structure exerted tremendous influence over the character of urban life. In the medieval and early modern period, confraternities assumed many of the functions that are relegated today to civil administration and judicial bodies for the preservation of social order. More than any other institution, the confraternities were responsible then for maintaining public peace. They acted as police forces by disciplining the social conduct of their members and as lawyers and judges by arbitrating their own disputes. Like modern legal and ethical codes, their religious contracts attempted to shape people's character. While social harmony today depends upon the regulation of individual behavior, during the Middle Ages urban peace rested upon corporate rules.

Cofrades entered into voluntary agreements, sealed by oaths, to preserve the well-being of the community. Inside each confraternity, there was no distinction between separate rights of constituent members. The corporate personality took over, and all members became their brother's keepers for the good of the whole. Each cofrade understood that he or she shared responsibility in the welfare of the organic community.

And yet it must not be assumed that members succeeded in creating fraternal bonds out of the goodness of their hearts. Elaborate and even stringent mechanisms had to be devised to maintain a sense of fellowship within the community. The smooth functioning of these voluntary groups depended on the existence of good relations among cofrades, a goal that was carefully, and at times precariously, preserved. In all the confraternities of Zamora, friendship was formally cultivated, tested and ritualized. Interaction among members was prescribed rigorously, to the point of being subject to written decree and enforced by officials. Extreme care was taken to ensure that incoming members would not disrupt this harmony. When a person wished to join a confraternity, three council sessions were held to discuss the aspirant's character and explore reactions of cofrades to the admission of the new member. Anyone who wanted to enter, according to the Cofradía de Santo Cristo de la Agonia, 'must be a gentle and pacific person, and of good conduct, in order to avoid occasion for scandal and tumult, or the altering of the peace and blessed union that all of us, as Catholic Christians, are obliged to maintain'.[81] If any member objected to a candidate, admission proceedings were terminated or acceptance was delayed until the objection was withdrawn. The Cofradía de Nuestra Señora de San Antolín specified in 1503 that if any cofrade complained that a candidate 'is his enemy, that he [the candidate] not be received until they become friends, because it is not right that among brothers who are to live in concord there be hostility and discord'.[82]

Aristocratic confraternities that required strict purity of blood and noble status for membership appointed special committees sworn to secrecy to review testimonies on the qualifications of candidates. Once this step was successfully completed, admittance of candidates passed into the hands of members for majority, or, in some cases, unanimous approval.

General meetings were dangerous opportunities for disagreements and harsh words between cofrades and everything possible was done to ensure that discussions proceeded smoothly. To prevent persons from talking simultaneously and to ensure that each would have the opportunity to voice his opinion, a *vara* or rod symbolizing authority and justice passed from hand to hand of those who spoke. Cofrades of San Antonio Abad in the church of San Antolín recommended that in their meetings they be

> quiet, peaceful and calm, and that no-one carry on noisily nor cause a disturbance; and if the mayordomo should see anyone in anger, or beginning to fret or raise a commotion, he is to take the precaution of allowing him to speak. He who speaks must do so with the *vara* in hand and without passion, and if he be ordered to be quiet, he must be quiet; and if he remains pertinacious and rebellious and obstinate after being reprimanded, he should be punished by the Council ... [83]

Fines and penalties confronted the audacious cofrade who unsheathed the sword or shouted obscenities in anger.[84] Aristocratic brotherhoods forbade the carrying of arms to council meetings, masses, and burials to prevent violence.[85] Methods of correcting slander or injury perpetrated by one cofrade on another had to be devised because members did not always meet standards of sociability which, as one organization put it, compels 'all we cofradas to be very sisterly and honest, and not rambunctious'.[86] Harsh words, squabbles and name-calling between members were brought before mayordomos and offenders were 'fraternally castigated'.[87]

Morality was controlled, and to a large extent perceived, within the context of collective devotion. Artisans who organized the confraternity of San Cucufate enforced fines of a pound of wax for insulting each other at council meetings; they insisted upon two pounds for second incidents and finally threw offenders out of the meeting for further transgressions while demanding that apologies be made to injured parties.[88] Cofrades of San Nicolás reacted in indignation if one of their group criticized the confraternity or the proceedings of its council whether in the heat of anger or in a completely sober temper. If cofrades went about saying that they no longer wanted to be part of the group, they were charged 25 pounds of wax each time that the sentiment was uttered and to top matters off they were not permitted to leave without the consent of all the members.[89]

The confraternities served as private guarantors of law and justice within their own communities, taking the opportunity for vengeance out of the hands of individuals. According to the rules of the Cofradía de Nuestra Señora de la Antigua in 1566, if one cofrade injured another 'the aggressor is to ask pardon from the entire council and the injured one, and to be friends. Furthermore, if the offense were grave and the aggrieved does not want to forgive, our cofradía will raise the hand for punishment ... and if the misdeed merits, and the aggrieved persists in holding back pardon, the council can freely expell [the agressor from the organization] and receive another in his place'.[90] A cofrade of Santa María Tercia y Santa Catalina would bring up complaints of mistreatment or disrespectful dealings by another member before his general council, which named four members to examine the case. If found culpable, the offender was ejected from the group for four years.[91]

In their preoccupation with social harmony, confraternities performed religious rituals designed to appease tensions. At group activities such as pilgrimages and feasts, members were required to be on good terms. The Cofradía de Nuestra Señora de San Antolín fined those who were not in a state of friendship before leaving on its yearly pilgrimage, while cofrades of the Santa Cruz in the village of Villalpando made it a practice before sitting down to their annual Palm Sunday meal to offer a communal pardon for all injuries and ill intentions that had been committed.[92]

Concern to maintain peace also carried over into their private lives. Some confraternities required that members not take in domestic servants or hired hands of another cofrade without consent. No legal suits could be filed against another member of one's confraternity, for disputes were handled by the society. Nor could one cofrade buy a bond weighing over another.

Such artificial measures may have seemed doomed to generate a mere facade of fellowship, but a more hearty congeniality was fostered among cofrades by common festivities, banquets, and processions. These shared activities contributed to the formation of a collective mentality. Cofrades prayed for each other at masses and identified their fortunes with a common patron saint. They revered the same statue and guarded the same relics. In the penitential confraternities, members even wore the same dress for processions, donning long hooded robes that covered the face and made each of them an anonymous participant of one mystical body recognizable to the public only by corporate banners.

Their central communal event was the annual banquet that celebrated the spirit of brotherhood among members. According to the church, 'this fellowship or covenant meal ... externalized the supernatural faith of the participants'.[93] It was a ritual act that emulated the Last Supper when 'our Redeemer, in an attempt to show his disciples a sign of his love, wished to dine with them'.[94] Confraternities recognized that their meals served the purpose of nurturing bonds of charity and love among communicants. The confraternity of San Ildefonso asserted that 'in accordance with our humanity, love always increases at social gatherings and banquets'. Every year members feasted on the day of its patron saint 'so that love and charity grow among us'.[95]

Municipal police might view such disingenuous claims more cynically, for confraternal festivities were frequently the occasion for rowdy dancing and brawling in the streets. Mutual love and joy created in an atmosphere of food and drink did not always coincide with law and order and the city council from time to time was forced to ban communal feasting in the interest of public peace. Christian ideals here as elsewhere did not translate into reality. Corporate disciplinary mechanisms failed to contain conflict in all circumstances, as quarrels over precedence in processions also attest. But it is not surprising that cofrades occasionally failed to obey the spirit of their laws; and indeed the remarkable fact is that they did demonstrate a more constant commitment to keep it. As we shall see in the next chapter, the deepest bonds of fellowship, ones that were rarely violated, appeared in welfare programs for the relief of sickness and poverty and the salvation of souls. The sick and dying called to their sides, around their beds or caskets, the brothers and sisters of their confraternities. To be 'accompanied' was one of the most frequent and heartfelt concerns of testators, and one of the main reasons why they joined confraternities and donated generously to them at the end of their lives.

For it is certainly true that however short of their goals these alliances may have fallen, their corporate ritual, like their politics and finances, made a concerted effort to realize within the microcosm of membership the spiritual ideals of brotherhood and social equality. Their constitutions and oaths on matters of policy denote not the vertical paternal contracts characterizing medieval kingship and feudalism but horizontal fraternal agreements among equals. They were the first self-consciously democratic organizations in Zamora, founded upon the religious concept of *universa fraternitas*. The confraternities constituted one of the clearest institutional expressions of religious ideals in society, matched only perhaps by the monasteries.

2 The Charitable Activities of Confraternities

Drawing upon the notion of the *vita activa* and rejecting the contemplative tradition of the cloister, confraternities organized the pursuit of salvation through the practise of good works. Pre-eminent among the good works were those of mercy, and it is my contention in this chapter that in observing merciful works as devotional exercises, confraternities created one of the first 'institutions' of social welfare in western history. To understand how private gestures of charity, today only a minor and ephemeral part of the welfare process, could have formed the core of traditional poor relief requires that we enter the spiritual consciousness of the past. We must in the first analysis recognize the powerful stimulus provided by the Christian faith to charitable giving.

In the attainment of salvation, the medieval church accorded varying degrees of credit to both grace and works, but it was the notion of works which chiefly manifested itself in Christian social ethics and which particularly interested commonfolk in confraternities. Their corporate statutes were concerned not so much with setting private inner standards of belief over members as with regulating collective behavior for the purpose of stimulating communal piety and earning spiritual merits. As Pierre Chaunu has remarked, medieval Christianity was expressed not as much through beliefs as through deeds.[1]

For theologians concerned with guiding the faithful in their achievement of merits, the crucial Scriptural text was Matthew, chapter 25, on the Last Judgment. Conditions necessary for salvation were delineated in the key verses 34–6:

Come blessed of my Father, take possession of the kingdom prepared for you from the foundation of the world; for I was hungry and you gave me to eat; I was thirsty and you gave me to drink; I was a stranger and you took me in; naked and you covered me; sick and you visited me; I was in prison and you came to me.

The Biblical image in Matthew of God as a hungry, thirsty, naked and homeless pauper, ushering the blessed to his right side on the basis of their generosity to him, and damning misers and inhospital folk to his left, was invoked before the public in sermons to stress the value of

44

charity. Theologians considered almsgiving the most worthy expression of love for God and for neighbors. It was, they believed, the most
effective manner of obtaining spiritual purification. Medieval and
early modern Catholic theologians discussed charity in terms of its
redemptive value.[2] According to Friar Tomás de Trujillo, 'he who
gives charity, extinguishes hunger, and covers nakedness, extinguishes
his own faults and covers his own sin'.[3] Paraphrasing Ecclesiasticus
3:30, the confraternity of San Ildefonso announced its charitable
activities with the declaration that 'charity kills sin as water puts out
fire'.[4]

From the early centuries of Christianity, charitable deeds worthy of
divine recognition were incorporated into literature and sermons on
the proper Christian life. Augustine was among the first of the church
fathers to cite specific acts of mercy for the instruction of Christians. In
his discussion of faith and works in the *Enchiridion*, Augustine
presented almsgiving as a way to atone for sin. To make up for the
commitment of serious sins, he argued that charity must be performed
during one's lifetime, for these transgressions cannot be redeemed by
purgatorial fire after death.[5] Augustine offered a long list of spiritual
acts to be practiced in obtaining forgiveness of sin. This list included
feeding the hungry, giving drink to the thirsty, clothing the naked,
offering hospitality to the stranger, sheltering the fugitive, visiting the
sick and incarcerated, ransoming the captive, bearing the burdens of
the weak, leading the blind, comforting the sorrowful, healing the
sick, guiding the lost, counseling the perplexed, providing for the
poor, correcting the unrighteous and pardoning the offender.[6] To
these imperatives he later added the burial of the dead.[7]

Augustine's list was refined in the Middle Ages and eventually
assembled into a moral code. One of the earliest expressions of this
was contained within the Benedictine rule which commissioned
several acts of charity for observance by the monastic community.[8] In
AD 802 a Carolingian capitulary entitled 'Admonitio generalis' which
dealt with the basic precepts of Christianity enjoined the practice of
charitable acts with the injunction that 'faith without works is dead'.
To follow the ideal of treating others as oneself, the capitulary
prescribed feeding the poor, taking pilgrims into one's home, and
visiting the sick and incarcerated. As works which would clean away
sins, it mentioned redeeming captives, assisting those unjustly
persecuted, defending widows and orphans, ensuring justice, prevent-
ing iniquity, curbing prolonged anger, and avoiding excessive drinking
and banqueting.[9]

By the late eleventh and twelfth centuries, the acts of mercy were established as formulae for lay spiritual behavior. Pedagogical texts such as the 1093 cartulary of Mas-d'Azil advised Christians to 'keep charity always in your heart', by calling into fraternal peace those who complain, supporting the poor, visiting the sick and also burying the dead.[10]

In the *Siete Partidas*, Alfonso X's law code compiled in the second half of the thirteenth century, a section concerned with managing beneficence in society divided the acts of mercy into spiritual and corporal types. It considered the spiritual acts of pardoning the injurer, punishing the wicked, and instructing the ignorant superior to the material forms of mercy, likening them to the souls' superiority over the body. The corporal acts consisted of feeding the hungry, giving drink to the thirsty, clothing the naked, and visiting the sick and imprisoned.[11]

The earliest thirteenth-century Latin catechisms reduced the acts of mercy to seven for easier memorization. Once cast into seven, a number that held special ritual significance in Christian thought,[12] the merciful acts remained spellbound to the present day. In Juan Ruiz's fourteenth-century account of the acts of mercy in the *Libro de buen amor*, they had become something of a talisman for the faithful. Ruiz argued that these charitable acts could conquer the evil forces of the world, the devil and the flesh.[13] Regularly to feed the hungry, house the wayfarer, dress the naked, give drink to the thirsty, visit the sick, dower orphans and bury the dead might fend off impurity and preserve the soul, sanctified by baptism, for entry into heaven.

In the catechetical treatise of Pedro de Veragüe, the merciful acts were introduced with the warning that

> Esperança perderás
> E la feé quando serás
> Delante Dios, berás
> Con gran liberalidad
> Fas obras de caridad
> Que la linpia boluntad
> La caridad es tan alta
> Que todos bienes alcança
> De quien non resçibio falta[14]

In the catechism, seven spiritual acts had been added to the corporal, and in time this dual moral code became the standard format of the merciful works presented in Catholic educational texts. The spiritual acts, invoked less frequently, included teaching the ignorant, counseling the doubtful, admonishing sinners, bearing wrongs and adversity patiently, forgiving offenses willingly, comforting the afflicted and praying for the living and the dead. Among the corporal acts, dowering orphans was permanently replaced with burying the dead, and cited along with feeding the hungry, giving drink to the thirsty, clothing the naked, lodging the homeless, visiting the sick, and ransoming the captive. These seven acts were versified in Latin as 'pasco, poto, coligno, tego, visito, librero and condo'.[15]

The merciful acts were propagated along with the Creed and the Ten Commandments as part of the attempt to turn late medieval and early modern Europe into a Christian society. One finds them in confessional manuals and mystical literature, among preachers' sermons and lay devotional guides. They were painted and sculpted in church interiors and posted on church doors.

As the charitable works were standardized in written religious treatises and catechisms, they became formalized in practice. The seven corporal works took on stereotypical dimensions in the charitable work arranged by benefactors. Every testator aspired to perform an act of mercy upon his or her death. Wills of the late medieval and early modern period are filled with carefully formulated bequests in demonstration of the donors' charitable virtues in order to ensure the safety of their souls. Even testators from small villages, where one might have expected poor understanding of catechetical precepts, revealed a striking familiarity with the seven acts of mercy. In 1545, Juan Gregorio ordered the sale of all his clothes in order to buy simple woven garments to distribute to the poor.[16] A townswoman of Zamora, Catarina Alvarez, chose to feed the hungry by giving two pounds of bread to four needy people every Sunday.[17] Francisco de Verástigui, resident of the village of Calabazanos, named most of the acts of mercy in his testament in 1554, making donations to the confraternity and hospital of the royal court and to a confraternity in charge of caring for poor orphans in the place where he would die. He left 50 ducats for the redemption of captives, 50 ducats to free a pauper from jail, and provided for dressing and giving money to 13 paupers who accompanied his body to the grave.[18] Any one of the merciful works – freeing a prisoner, or clothing the poor – carried with it the explicit message that the service was holy, offered to the needy in the image of Christ.

Enshrined as religious ritual, the acts of mercy possessed a significance transcending the utilitarian functions that they served. It was the religious meaning attributed to the merciful works that accounts for their influence in social custom and that ensured their continuous observance by the populace. The performance of an act of mercy was a means of acquiring grace, a wholly efficacious rite that communicated with God even as it relieved the physical discomfort of one's fellow Christian. But the practical role of charity should not be obfuscated by the formality with which it was exercised. As the anthropologist Victor Turner has said of many communal rituals, 'a creative deed becomes an ethical or ritual paradigm'.[19] Almsgiving was commuted in Zamora into a religious paradigm and in this routine became all the more effective as a program of daily welfare. Beggars required feeding every day, three times a day if they could get it. Whenever they sat at a resident's doorstep at dinnertime they represented an opportunity to exercise one of these charitable virtues.

The acts of mercy became institutionalized as soon as they attained the status of ritual. Zamoran confraternities, in their concern for the sanctification of members' souls, adopted the merciful acts among their earliest activities. The first documentary references to confraternities in the city in the thirteenth century are, in fact, private deathbed donations of blankets to them for distribution to the needy.[20] In later centuries, confraternal statutes explicitly declare that their objective was to pursue charity. A standard introduction to the individual programs of charitable confraternities proclaims that they were 'founded primarily to accomplish the "obras de misericordia", that is, true charity, which is the principle upon which all similar confraternities ought to be founded'. The reason given for such work – 'so that the living grow in devotion and that the dead never lack divine offices' – equated almsgiving with soul-saving.[21] Mercy propagated graces among the community for the collective sanctification of souls.

In pursuing acts of mercy, confraternities worked in conjunction with private individuals, canons, priests, friars, nuns and *beatas* to create a comprehensive welfare program for society. At a time when the government was unable or unwilling to allocate aid to the indigent, who constituted a significant proportion of the total population (almost 30 per cent of Zamora's residents, a figure that most Castilian towns matched[22]), these individuals and private religious organizations shared responsibilities for relief. Their actions were conditioned not merely by the needs of society and the means of assistance at their disposal. They meticulously observed the merciful works when turning to care for paupers. It was the imitative quality of their charitable gestures that gave direction to almsgiving in Catholic society. Religion ritualized relief to the poor, creating a welfare system with its own distinct organization and rhythms. Alms were by no means given in the spontaneous and haphazard manner in which traditional scholarship has portrayed pre-industrial attempts to administer to the poor. The methods adopted to provide poor relief in the past were standardized by the acts of mercy. Let us see how this operated.

2.1 The Acts of Mercy: The Distribution of Bread and Wine to the Needy
[Source: *Entrada de Carlos V y del Papa Clemente VII en Bolonia*]

'To feed the hungry, give drink to the thirsty, visit the sick and clothe the naked ... '

The management of hospitals was one of the most ambitious ways that confraternities chose to observe the merciful works. At least thirteen confraternities in the city of Zamora ran their own hospitals. Others assisted monastic infirmaries and privately endowed hospitals where their devotional concerns were applied to the permanent care of the sick and homeless. Although it has been recognized in the literature on poor relief that medieval health care facilities owed their existence to religious organizations and pious individuals in the service of God,[23] what remains to be clarified is the manner in which religious preoccupations conducted actual nursing services.

One of the oldest hospitals in Zamora was called the Hospital of Shepherds. Established in the twelfth century by a group of merchants, the hospital was taken over by furriers of the Cofradía de Santa María y San Julián from the mid-fourteenth to the mid-fifteenth centuries.[24] It was located in the church of San Julián at the entry to the city from the bridge over the Duero, where it welcomed pilgrims passing through from the south. Pilgrims were considered particularly worthy recipients of charity due to their homeless status, and the confraternity sought to provide them with food and shelter along their journey. The hospital also cared for the sick, housing patients until they were fully cured and able to earn a living. An attendant living on the premises supervised patients and ensured that they received communion and made confession. By late medieval standards the hospital was relatively well supplied with fourteen beds and twenty-five wool blankets.[25] In addition, twenty-five sets of used clothing were reserved as burial garbs for those who might die within the hospital. The clothing was donated by furriers from their personal wardrobes at their deaths, a ritual of charity pledged by all members upon entering the Cofradía de Santa María y San Julián. This contribution of clothing to the needy, referred to as a 'falifo', was shared by other confraternities in the province of Zamora for the maintenance of their hospitals and earned them the name 'cofradías de los falifos'.[26]

Collective almsgiving supplemented these private donations of clothing and food to provision patients. Once a year, in ritual profession of clothing the naked, the furriers of the confraternity gave to each of their patients a cape of coarse goat's hair, a fur robe, and shoes. In compliance with their commitment to feed the hungry, on major feast days they distributed to patients portions of rabbit and pork with bread and wine. Together, food produced by the furriers' own hands and clothes offered from their own backs entirely supported the health care facilities of the hospital.

Not all confraternities concocted such imaginative rituals to furnish hospitals but they all offered equally intimate gifts and services. Aristocrats of the two most extensive welfare facilities in sixteenth-century Zamora, Nuestra Señora de la Candelaria and Nuestra Señora de la Misericordia, went out into the streets to find homeless paupers to lodge in their hospitals. They then visited patients, bringing along food and firewood for their needs. On a more modest scale, cofrades of the Ciento extended hospital care to sick clerics, and commoners in other confraternities worked in their own small institutions, furnished with only a couple of beds, when needy members required special nursing attention. These private hospitals brought cofrades into direct contact with the poor and infirm, offering them opportunities to perform religious services through countless daily ministrations.

People gave what they had to supply the institutions. Antonia Martín donated two small pillows 'for paupers who are well behaved'.[27] In 1566, a cleric, Francisco Aguilera, gave to one of his confraternities two ducats to buy its patients bread and to another confraternity he donated two ducats for clothes.[28] It was particularly common for members to offer their bedding to hospitals at the time of their deaths. Leonor de Cormega gave a mattress, a blanket, two sheets and two pillows to the poor of the Hospital of the Candelaria, and a mattress and a blanket to the Hospital of the Misericordia in 1546.[29] Such careful allocation of the goods of one's estate, each gesture crafted to imitate an act of mercy, constituted the sole source for provisioning some of the tiny confraternal hospitals.

Due to the personal nature of endowments, administration of health care in these hospitals was extremely cumbersome. Beds, clothing and food rations provided by individual bequests were saddled with special stipulations and could not always be allocated efficiently. Confraternities were bound by law to preserve the intention behind each donation and to protect the integrity of the pious endowment with corporate funds. Imposing a degree of order over these multiple sources of funding was the most serious challenge faced by hospital management.

Some confraternities handled the situation exceedingly well. An outstanding example was set by aristocrats of the hospital of San Ildefonso who moved beyond literal implementation of the merciful acts in designing an elaborate therapeutic program. Hospitals in this period were not known for their doctors (indeed, few employed trained physicians at all, and offered only nursing care), but cofrades of San Ildefonso sought out and elected the most qualified physicians within several hundred leagues of the city and placed them on salaries.

They also appointed apothecaries, barber-surgeons and hospitallers to treat their patients. Every month, cofrades nominated among themselves two people to make weekly inspections of sanitary conditions and ensure that patients were adequately fed and properly treated. To assist in maintaining order, they posted tablets on the wall near the hospital entryway that informed new-comers of residence requirements.[30]

The hospital of San Ildefonso accepted as many patients as facilities permitted, giving preference to resident paupers over those from the province and foreigners. In aiming to restore the sick to complete health, it accepted only those with curable illnesses, whether of the non-contagious or contagious type (including in this category cases of the bubonic plague). It rejected terminal cases such as leprosy. Since the hospital owned only a few feather mattresses and sleeping mats, most patients slept on the floor or on wooden benches in blankets and sheets.[31] The confraternity provided paupers with daily rations of meat, wine, bread and other food and invited them to semi-annual banquets on the two feast days of San Ildefonso to enjoy members' ritual gifts of 'feeding the hungry'.

In addition to these services, the hospital offered two 'general cures' in May and September for paupers who wished to be purged, fed and housed for a month. Cofrades advertized services throughout the city by a public crier and examined those who gathered at the hospital door to ensure that they were poor and in need of medical aid. The confraternity hired as many physicians and surgeons for the cures as was necessary, paying them 12 to 16 bushels of wheat for their work.

Under the scrutiny of one or two members of the corporation, paupers were bled and administered medicinal purges by physicians and apothecaries. The hospital personnel induced sweating with 'purges, sweet juices and other unctions', including cathartic teas from the wood of the guayaco tree, imported from the New World.[32] To prepare this latter purgative, they chipped and pulverized guayaco tree bark and then boiled it for a long period over low fire. After cooling, the liquid was strained and poured into small sealed bottles. Patients drank nine cups in the morning and another nine in the afternoon, repeating the process an extra day if they required more extract to complete the sweating process. The entire cure lasted 30 days, with paupers heavily clothed and blanketed and under strict dietary regimens.

Fortunately for the health of the poor, purgations were performed only if adequate resources of food and bedding were available to carry patients through the period of convalescence. These cures were paid for by sales of wheat and barley produced on confraternal land, a stable source of income that generally assured the hospital the means to extend treatment to 25 to 40 persons. In famine years, however, the confraternity was forced to divert cash reserved for annual banquets in order to maintain the semi-annual cures. In 1601, following several very difficult years in which peasants on its land could not meet rental payments, the confraternity barely managed to treat 20 paupers by selling 160 bushels of barley at the crown's established price.[33]

Cofrades supplemented property income with membership fees and gifts to support the hospital. In the sixteenth century, each paid between 500 and 1000 *maravedís*, four pounds of wax, and a blanket or mattress upon joining the organization. Private endowments varied yearly. The most common arrangement was for individuals to endow beds and pay for patients' residence in the hospital. In 1586 for instance, a resident of Zamora, Luis Docampo Ordóñez, willed two beds with sheets for convalescent paupers after the May cure, providing 60 *reales* in perpetuity for their maintenance. Several years later, his wife donated in her own testament 60 *reales* for two more convalescents after the September cure, along with extra money for clothes, new mattresses and soap.[34] Endowed with permanent rental property, the beds could be occupied as long as income continued to cover costs. By directing pious aspirations such as these to its therapy services, the confraternity of San Ildefonso extended a relatively high degree of corporate management over private charitable offerings.

Other confraternities played a less important role in the medical process; many acted merely as auxiliaries to hospitals under separate management. The largest in Zamora in the sixteenth century, the hospital of Sotelo, was managed by a combined committee of city council members and the cathedral chapter. Confraternities attached to it were limited to saying masses in its chapel and providing funeral services for patients who died.

In the nearby village of Toro, cofrades assisted in nursing duties at the privately financed and administered hospital of Nuestra Señora de la Asunción. Its founder, Juan Rodríguez de Fonseca, bishop of Burgos, limited appointment of administrators to the clerical order but explained that 'since charitable causes ought to be communicated and used for the good of all', he would invite lay cofrades of the village to perform charitable services in his institution. The founder ordered that his hospital receive 50 cofrades to attend to the sick and bury those who died 'since we know that other hospitals are aided by the visits and attendance of cofrades, who are provided the opportunity to perform the acts of piety for which they are created'. The 50 cofrades took turns visiting the hospital once a week throughout the year to inspect nursing care and ensure observance of doctors' orders. In the process they fulfilled their own personal duties of charity for the sanctification of their souls. For this work in visiting the sick, they enjoyed plenary indulgences from the pope.[35]

Additional opportunities for pious lay people to perform good works existed at the large pilgrims' hospital of the Catholic Monarchs in Santiago de Compostela. Construction of the hospital in Santiago began in 1503 by Queen Isabella, who had been informed of the pressing need for a large hospital to accommodate paupers and pilgrims who gathered from all over Christendom to visit Santiago's shrine. The Queen promised that anyone who joined a confraternity dedicated to Santiago and its hospital, or donated one twentieth of a ducat to the institution, would enjoy remissions of their sins through future masses said by the confraternity in a chapel of the hospital. Men and women from all estates throughout Spain and France joined the Cofradía de Santiago and with the authorization of the Emperor Maximilian and Archduke Carlos in 1508, its membership expanded to include Germans.[36]

A major responsibility of the confraternity was to hear masses regularly for the souls of cofrades, the monarchs and the poor, which yielded indulgences and graces for all who contributed to the hospital. It was also responsible for publishing notices of collective indulgences and encouraging donations. Initially, rental income provided by the Catholic Monarchs supported hospital services, but by 1511 the regent Juana was compelled to seek additional donations from the public to cover increased costs. She distributed among cofrades licenses to preach and solicit charity in parishes on Sundays and holy days.[37] In the following years, cofrades throughout Spain organized a comprehensive campaign to collect funds by sending out letters soliciting donations to major cities and increasing their own private membership fees.

Except for volunteer services offered by cofrades, nursing and medical care was performed by hired personnel and clergymen. They too carefully followed the prescriptions of the acts of mercy, for despite monetary reimbursement they considered their work holy. In addition to treating the sick, they fed beggars who came to the door for alms, cared for abandoned children and offered hospitality to pilgrims in need of lodging.[38] The hospital had three separate infirmaries in the mid-sixteenth century, each with six of its beds reserved for pilgrims. It was expected that only one person would occupy each bed, although over-crowding periodically forced patients to share facilities. In 1568, two additional infirmaries opened to admit more patients and the hospital sent out German and French chaplains to search the streets and churches of Santiago de Compostela for foreigners in need of nursing care.

It is apparent in Santiago's hospital that the act of mercy of sheltering the homeless was closely allied in practice with caring for the sick. Many pilgrims to shrines were seeking cures for illnesses and disabilities, and required medical attention. Late medieval Zamora supported at least five confraternal hospices (the term *hospital* referred to both hospices and hospitals) along major thoroughfares and near bridges for the convenience of travellers. City residents who sought to assist travellers donated to Santa María y San Julián, Santa María de Tercia, Santa María de los Alfares, Nuestra Señora de la Misericordia, and San Juan de Acre, the groups in charge of these hospices. Again, the main burden of administrators was to co-ordinate the idiosyncratic wishes of private donors to the needs of the poor. Only the most street-wise of the city's beggars knew, for instance, that every Saturday and Sunday cofrades of Santa María de Tercia distributed bread to each pilgrim in their hospice and to travellers and paupers who gathered outside the doors for charity.[39]

More extensive than the institutional nursing care provided by cofrades was the private care that they extended to sick people in their homes. In pursuit of the act of mercy of visiting the sick, virtually all confraternities developed policies for attending to their own members when they became ill. A system of vigils was set up whereby cofrades took turns caring for sick brothers and sisters. The usual custom was to have two cofrades attend at one time. Beginning with those who resided nearest to the home of the invalid, members rotated visits day and night to maintain constant attention at the bedside. Cofrades brought candles, food, medicine, the eucharist, and, if necessary, oil for the Last Rites, seeking to comfort the sick and nurse him back to health or ensure a Christian death. Many of the confraternities of commoners, unable to afford charitable programs for paupers hardly worse off than themselves, concentrated solely on aiding each other in this manner.

While non-members were obliged in receiving charity to recompense benefactors with spiritual services, brothers and sisters received help without incurring the duty to reciprocate. In delivering charity to members as a right of fellowship without strings attached, cofrades were less concerned with literally fulfilling the acts of mercy and came up with ingenious methods to assist each other. The aristocratic confraternity of San Ildefonso paid debts of members unable to meet their obligations. Rural confraternities formed their own type of mutual assistance network, aiding impoverished members by permitting them use of the corporation's land, providing wheat, and sending hands to aid in the cultivation of farms for those unable to work. The Cofradía de la Vera Cruz in the village of Villalcampo stipulated that its cofrades would hand over a day's earnings to a sick member who called upon it for aid. It also guaranteed that if a cofrade fell ill outside the village without means to support himself or people to nurse him, the confraternity would retrieve him, journeying up to a day at the cost of the organization.[40] One of the most useful functions of the rural confraternities was to act as agencies supplying seed to needy farmers.[41]

By breaking away from ritual, the assistance programs to members met circumstances in a manner creative and flexible enough to prevent as well as to alleviate poverty. During the sixteenth and seventeenth centuries, craft confraternities in more industrially advanced areas such as Madrid developed sophisticated insurance programs for their members. Antonio Rumeu de Armas provides fascinating information on confraternities that subsidized members through periods of sickness, joblessness, and, in the case of a few confraternities consisting solely of women, of help with pregnancy and early childcare. A confraternity of cobblers in late sixteenth-century Madrid furnished sick members the services of a doctor and a barber-surgeon as well as medicine (except for women), and seven *reales* a week in indemnity payments for time that they lost at work while ill. The Cofradía de Nuestra Señora de las Nieves y Jesús Nazareno and the Cofradía of San Antonio Abad in the same city extended extraordinary support for risks associated with motherhood. These two confraternities allocated sums of money to cofradas upon the birth of children, giving lower amounts for miscarriages. Subsidies for miscarriages were delivered only if the fetus were at least three months old, confirmation of this to be made by an experienced member. If women fell ill after giving birth, they received daily allowances for periods up to one month.[42]

'To offer hospitality to the homeless ... '

As part of the fulfillment of the prescription to aid wayfarers, some confraternities took upon themselves the duties of maintaining bridges for safe passage across the countryside. According to Marjorie Boyer, medieval churchmen had encouraged the widespread notion that bridge construction and repair were pious activities by demanding that travel across them be gratuitous and forbidding fortification on bridge premises.[43] In fact, these strategic nexus of communication were endowed more frequently with chapels and shrines than with parapets in the Middle Ages. Clerics' sermons also invoked the sanctity of bridges by employing imagery of the viaduct in drawing a connection between the material and spiritual worlds. The most famous analogy was, of course, Bernard of Clairvaux's depiction of the Virgin as an aqueduct of grace from the heavens to individual souls.[44] A sixteenth-century Spanish treatise propounding the spiritual rewards of charity commented that 'the bridge to the glory of paradise is mercy',[45] a figurative statement that the Zamoran confraternity of the Animas of San Simón manifested quite literally by painting images of souls on bridge walls near its almsbox to stimulate donations for souls in purgatory.[46] It was a culture and a period that took symbolism seriously.

Brotherhoods of bridge-keepers lined the roads of major pilgrimage routes in the Spanish peninsula as well as in parts of England and France.[47] The oldest appeared in the late eleventh and early twelfth centuries in the valleys of the Rhône and the Loire rivers, performing the functions of bridge construction and repair, charity collection, and accommodation for travellers.[48]

The most active bridge-keeping confraternity in the province of Zamora was located in the northern village of Rionegros. Dedicated to Nuestra Señora de la Carballeda, it was commonly known as the 'Cofradía de los Falifos'. According to the confraternity's papal bulls, the earliest of which dates from 1342 and attests to the existence of the organization during previous pontificates, the confraternity participated in extensive poor relief programs for pilgrims throughout the province of Leon. The bull of Pope Eugene IV of 1446 recognized its pious activities, claiming that since its establishment, the confraternity had erected 35 bridges over 'several different and dangerous rivers for the greater security of pilgrims who travel to visit the temple of the Apostle Santiago and other pious places, and founded 30 hospitals for the lodging and sustenance of the frail, of abandoned children, and of sick people and orphans'.[49] In 1538, Paul III conceded to its members numerous indulgences and complete pardons of ecclesiastical penalties to encourage support of its estimated 20 hospitals, its many bridges and roadways, and its dowry programs for young girls and education of abandoned children.

The pious activities of Nuestra Señora de la Carballeda were financed completely by voluntary donations of members from villages in the north of the Zamoran province. According to the organization's statutes, revised at the end of the eighteenth century, cofrades sustained the work for many centuries 'without further resources than charity and the contribution of the Falifa, that is, a piece of the best clothing that they had, like a cape, a coat, a jacket, a petticoat, a doublet or whatever was the style in the territory'. The clothing was used by the poor or sold on the market for money to finance bridges and facilitate the travels of pilgrims in inhospitable regions of the province.[50]

'Offering hospitality to the homeless' was not a rigid prescription. It was pursued in many forms. Besides hospices and bridges, orphanages were also constructed to heed the call of this particular holy deed. Care of foundlings and orphans became an important concern of Spanish confraternities in the sixteenth century, when several organizations under the advocacy of Mary or Joseph were established specifically for rearing homeless children. In addition, many medieval confraternities that once had been dedicated to aiding travellers and sick people began to focus on the young as pilgrimages to Santiago declined in popularity. In the early modern period, Nuestra Señora de la Carballeda transferred funds which had been directed towards the maintenance of bridges and hospices to care for foundlings and poor children in the village of Rionegro and its countryside. Hospitality to infants abandoned at its chapel doors involved hiring wetnurses to raise the minors until they reached the age of seven, when they were placed in schools and trades.[51]

Foundling confraternities were established in Salamanca and Valladolid in the sixteenth century to care for unwanted children in the southern realms of Leon-Castile. The Cofradía de San José y Nuestra Señora de la Piedad in Salamanca offered protection to foundlings deposited at the Door of Pardon of the cathedral, sometimes left by parents who travelled several dozen miles. The confraternity hired wetnurses, primarily Portuguese peasants, at approximately 5000 *maravedís* a year for the care of each child.[52] It also provided the women regular provisions of baby clothes and shoes and covered baptismal costs. Between September 1590 and July 1596, the confraternity recorded expenses on 500 children, the vast majority of whom died within the first year of their care by the hospital.[53]

Funding for these services depended heavily on public support, and the confraternity called upon the assistance of the citizenry of Salamanca in yearly demonstrations. Parades have always served as means to rally popular support, and the confraternity excelled in utilizing them to further their charitable cause. Once a year the children of the orphanage circulated through the city streets brandishing candles and incense and holding in their hands a few *reales* of charity as tokens of the care accorded them by the confraternity. At the head of the procession, cofrades of San José mounted their icon of Nuestra Señora de la Piedad on a scaffold over their shoulders and several dozen priests carrying crosses surrounded the patron saint. Steadily pounding kettle-drums, cofrades called the attention of the public to their holy work.

In Valladolid the Cofradía del Niño Jesús y San Jośe that raised infants set out at doors of churches and wealthy homes found a no less grandiloquent way to attract public attention. It sponsored local theatrical productions and utilized the proceeds to support annually an average of 100 children with wetnurses, dowries and religious and educational services. In 1638, the crown conceded to the foundling program additional revenue from taxes on oil consumed in Valladolid.[54]

In the city of Zamora, canons of the cathedral assumed responsibility for raising foundlings,[55] assisted by several confraternities dedicated to dowering poor orphans once they reached marriageable ages. Dowering orphans had long been recognized as a charitable deed in Spain, although in the formal listings of the acts of mercy, it had been replaced by ransoming captives or burying the dead. Dowries remained nevertheless one of the most popular forms of charity because donors visualized their gifts protecting the virture of poor girls from prostitution. The 1389 testament of Gomez Martínez, for example, attests to the sentiment of piety surrounding this particular act. He ordered his cousin 'to look for four poor virgins in Zamora for God and for the souls of my father and mother and brothers', and to help find them husbands with money donated to their dowries from his estate.[56]

Of all charitable offerings, dowries permitted donors the greatest opportunities to exercise their personal preferences in the choice of recipients. Donors dictated the moral character of the women who were to receive the gifts, and frequently specified the family lineage or neighborhood from which they were to be chosen. It is with the dowries that we see the patronage system of old regime society most grievously manipulating with private prejudices the fate of the poor.

Eighty members of the aristocracy formed the confraternity of San Nicolás to dower young women and reap the spiritual rewards of this act of charity. The process of selecting candidates was long and rigorous, characterized by a great deal of publicity and ostentatious display. In one of their programs, members of San Nicolás chose four cofrades to examine young women for the dowry provided by a Franciscan friar, Rodrigo de Villacorta, who left 200 gold ducats, 12 bushels of wheat and one bushel of barley for marrying a woman every year. The four deputies distributed application forms among the preachers in the city and posted notices in public places to inform all who might know of poor orphans wishing to marry to bring their names and places of residence to the attention of the confraternity.[57]

The four deputies carefully reviewed qualifications of the nominees, questioning neighbors and acquaintances as to their moral standing and reputation. In making their choices, they followed criteria set up by the confraternity which established that they give priority to women with noble blood over commoners, and to residents over non-residents. These standards also obliged that deputies give preference to nominees without parents or relatives who might provide for them 'because the intention of our confraternity is to help the poorest who live in the most licit and honest state'.[58] In addition, they gave an advantage to older candidates whose time for child bearing was running out. If more than six women remained eligible after this screening process, deputies wrote the names of the candidates on slips of papers and threw them into a container for a child, whose innocence and impartiality in the matter could be assured, to draw six finalists. At a mass held near the end of May, the six names were put again into a container and placed on an altar. Cofrades commended the lottery to Christ in the hope that the final choice might be the woman in most need. After services, the presiding priest reached into the basin and pulled out the name of the woman who was to be married that year.

Immediately after the drawing, the mayordomo and deputies of the confraternity called upon parents or relatives to select a husband for the winner. On the day of San Nicolás, she and her fiancé were married during high mass at the church of Santa Olaya in the presence of all cofrades and parishioners. In this elaborate and prolonged preparation for marriage under the confraternal system, the woman's own wishes were never consulted, nor was it assumed that she would feel anything but gratitude in fulfilling the spiritual obligations asked of her by the father of the fund. Every Sunday for a year following the wedding she took on the task of offering bread, wine and candles provided by the confraternity at the sepulchre of Friar Rodrigo in the monastery of San Francisco. The following year, the duties were taken over by another newly-wed woman, ensuring continual attention over the grave of the donor. In this manner his dowry gift, designed to protect and ensure woman's virtue through marriage, capitalized on the sanctifying powers of the prayers of the pure.

The concern to regulate the sexual morality of the poor was just as obvious in the confraternity of Nuestra Señora de la Anunciación. Founded by the bishop of Zamora, Diego Meléndez de Valdés, in the early sixteenth century, it was modelled after the Anunciata established in Rome in 1460 for the purpose of dowering poor women.[59] The choice of advocacy was not an arbitrary one. The Annunciation honored the miraculous conception of Jesus by Mary, 'announcing' her favored status in the eyes of God. To Catholics the Annunciation represented the supreme achievement of marriage and motherhood, when mortal woman became vessel for the God-head. Unable ever to attain a similar position, young women nevertheless were asked to recognize the Virgin as their role model.

The 110 members who first joined the Anunciación in Zamora consisted of both clerical and lay men and women who claimed for themselves 'pure Christian lineage'. Special privileges of the confessional that were conceded by the papacy permitted members to elect their own confessor, who had the power to absolve them of all their sins and to commute almost any vow or act of penance imposed on them in the past into the performance of an act of mercy.

The pious works of the confraternity began with the will of its founder, who donated 200 000 *maravedís* to buy land and possessions for rental income applied to a permanent dowry fund. The mayordomo and ten elected deputies managed the program. They selected recipients for the dowry among nominees offered by other members of the Anunciación. The eleven cofrades granted gifts to as many 'poor, honest and well-reputed' women as could be endowed, estimating that at least 160 bushels of wheat in rent were necessary to put together a dowry for one woman.[60] To guarantee objectivity in choosing among eligible candidates, the committee was instructed not to favor daughters or servants of members, nor to admit well-to-do women before poor ones. Moreover, women living with their parents and relatives or patronesses were favored over those working for wages outside the city, and once again natives of Zamora were given priority over those born elsewhere. Requirements tightened in the seventeenth century, a tell-tale sign of a growing austerity during the Counter Reformation, when deputies began to examine rigorously the reputations of the women in question and inspect baptismal records for certification of age and place of birth. Revised ordinances of 1644 reveal a growing preoccupation with the morality of the poor. Since 'the life span of people is shorter now', the organization despaired, 'evil enters at a much earlier age'. Cofrades decided to reduce the age of eligibility from 18 to 16 in an effort to reach innocent young girls 'before they destroyed themselves' through promiscuity.[61]

Many other confraternities acted as supervisors of small dowry funds provided by their members or by parishioners of their church. A chaplain of the cathedral asked the confraternity of the Misericordia to marry one orphan girl for his soul every year with a perpetual *fuero* of 3500 *maravedís*.[62] Women were particularly active as donors of dowries. The widow Leonor Rodríguez left to the confraternity of the Santíssimo Sacramento de San Antolín 28 864 *maravedís* in annual rents to dower an orphan girl on the day of Nuestra Señora de Septiembre every year. She authorized the confraternity to buy more property for the dowry fund with additional rental money and asked it to inspect her possessions every two years to ensure that they were in good repair.[63] To the same confraternity in 1592, Francisca Valderas left 400 *reales* to be given to an orphan in quantities of 10 000 *maravedís* yearly on the anniversary of Nuestra Señora de Septiembre, asking cofrades to pray for both her own and her husband's soul.[64] Several women contributed to dowry funds handled by the confraternities of the Ciento, Las Huérfanas de San Bartolomé, and Nuestra Señora del Rosario.[65]

It is impossible to quantify the number of needy women married by confraternities in the city each year in order to assess the relative economic importance of this particular act of mercy because dowry money, like other charitable donations, varied from year to year. Every parish had at least one marriage program to offer neighborhood residents, but none of them possessed funds sufficient to cover all the city's poor women. Unlike the wealthy confraternity of the Encarnación in Seville, which alone dowered over 100 women every year,[66] the modestly funded Zamoran confraternities generally offered only one or two annual dowries. The significance of these marriage gifts was as much moral as economic. Poor young women would wait for years in expectation of a dowry, and all the while their reputations were on the line. Their dependence on dowry money to marry gave society an important tool with which to discipline and control their sexuality.

'To redeem captives ... '

From the bridal altar to the jail cell the acts of mercy followed the needy. The prescription to 'ransom prisoners' involved either assisting local folk in city jails or captives in foreign lands. For the latter, the large crusading orders of the Santísima Trinidad and the Merced had been established in Spain.[67] For prisoners at home, the confraternity of Nuestra Señora de la Piedad y Pobres de la Cárcel had been founded to free those in the public jail. This confraternity accumulated donations and rents for the purpose of assuming debts of poor people and providing them with food, clothing and firewood in jail. Its property extended into small villages of the province, having been donated by wealthy individuals concerned with helping the indebted, who always included peasants from the countryside.[68]

Contributors to the acts of mercy of freeing prisoners frequently made discriminate selections of recipients. Juan Vázquez de Zeynos and his wife María de Zarate offered the rents of houses in the village of Fuentes to the confraternity 'to redeem from Zamora's public jail those held for debts, on Christmas and Easter'. The couple insisted that the funds be used for no other purposes and asked that the confraternity delegate one of its members to keep accounts without salary. Eight days before Christmas and Easter a record of prisoners in jail was to be taken and as many prisoners as possibe to be freed, beginning with those held for the smallest amounts. The debts of farmers were to be paid before those of city people, with first priority to those from the rural area of Madridaños. Cofrades were instructed not to free prisoners accused of stealing or of crimes of infamy, and those whose debts were taken over had to have been jailed for at least 15 days. The money was deposited in the cathedral of Zamora, and if the Pobres de la Cárcel failed to fulfill its duties, the sum was to be transferred to the Misericordia for the same purpose.[69]

Most major towns in Spain had confraternities similar to the one in Zamora attached to jails for the care of prisoners. Ciudad Rodrigo possessed the Cofradía de Pobres de la Cárcel, run by scribes, and Valladolid had the Cofradía Nueva de la Redención de Presos de la Cárcel.[70] In Salamanca 24 noblemen who aspired personally to visit and redeem prisoners founded in 1500 the Cofradía de Caballeros Veinte y Quatro de las Reales Carceles. Two of them visited the jail every month to hear grievances and offer meals. After ascertaining which of the persons incarcerated for debts were truly poor and unable to pay, they freed those whom they considered worthy. At a special monthly mass the two cofrades discussed their services with the entire group, explaining who had been imprisoned, for what reasons, and whom they had released. When money was needed to pay off debts, two to four cofrades solicited charity throughout the city for their cause. In their monthly visits to jail, cofrades also identified prisoners who were condemned to death and after hearing their confessions, helped them make wills and gave them food, beds and heat if they were poor. In the early years of its foundation, the confraternity was supported solely through the charity of members and the public, and by the turn of the century it had accumulated an enormous amount of rental income in money and kind which vastly surpassed expenses in the jail. By then it had become one of the wealthiest and most prestigious charitable organizations in Salamanca. Even officials of law and order applauded its work in freeing prisoners, no doubt in part because it reduced the number of inmates lodged in crowded quarters and improved living conditions for the rest. But in language more appreciative of the religious than the practical accomplishments of the confraternity, city officials praised its 'divine services' on behalf of the souls of cofrades.[71]

'To bury the dead'

Of all the merciful acts, the burial of the dead was considered the holiest.[72] It was the last rite of corporal mercy that the community could offer its members, and thereafter only the spiritual act of prayer for the dead remained to assist souls to paradise. Virtually all confraternities offered funeral services to members, their families and the poor. The principal burial society in Zamora was the Misericordia, one of a category of large and prestigious confraternities throughout Europe dedicated to caring for paupers who could not afford the costs of Christian rites. The Misericordias earned the designation of arch-confraternities by affiliating with two brotherhoods operating in Rome, the white penitents, established in 1264, and the black penitents, founded in 1488. Both of these had gained papal approval along with special indulgences for their work. The white penitents assumed responsibilities for treating the sick and offering dowries to poor girls as well as burying the dead. The black penitents buried dead paupers found within the limits of the Roman compagnia and consoled criminals condemned to death. Their duties, according to accounts of Hippolyte Hélyot (1660–1716), a Third Order regular of St Francis, were especially lugubrious. When judges sentenced persons to death, they notified the black penitents who sent four of their number to condole with the condemned in prison and help them make general confessions. The four members remained with prisoners all day and night until their call to execution, when the rest of the brothers gathered to escort them in procession amid crosses draped in black cloth. Slowly and solemnly cofrades moved with lighted candles chanting the seven psalms of penitence until they reached the gallows, where they dressed the convicts in confraternal robes, symbolically turning them into brothers, then attended their executions and burials, and prayed for their souls.[73]

By emulating these activities, Misericordias outside the Papal See shared in the same indulgences granted to the Roman penitents. In the Spanish peninsula, the black penitents were noted for their presence at *autos de fe*. The white penitents, always more numerous, followed their Roman counterparts by engaging in a variety of charitable services. They found especially favorable conditions in Portugal where the Crown gave approval to the establishment of 114 Misericordias btween 1498 and 1599.[74] The work of Portugal's white penitents included all 14 acts of mercy, both spiritual and corporal, which they channelled through almshouses and hospitals.

Zamora's Misericordia was known by travellers throughout the province for offering lodging to the homeless and burying dead paupers. It operated a hospital in the parish of San Martín to shelter those seeking beds and warmth in the winter and administered to them the sacraments. Since its principal duty was to bury the dead, it provided funeral services for all those unable to afford rites, including the patients of the poor leprosarium of San Lázaro outside the city walls. Cofrades regularly searched the inner city and its suburbs for sick and dying paupers, prepared to carry them to the hospital or arrange proper Christian deaths for them. During years of pestilence cofrades were particularly active, coming out two by two into the streets with wooden planks and coffins to recover plague victims and bury them in cemeteries.[75]

The Misericordia also provided burial services for well-to-do persons who commended their bodies to it at death, especially non-residents who had no other confraternity to administer to their needs. During an illness which kept him hospitalized in Zamora, Juan Gáez de Segura from Vitoria commended his body to the Misericordia. 'Since I am a stranger', he expressed his wish, 'that it bury me and spend the wax, and say the masses that it is obliged to perform, and customarily performs, for other strangers...'[76] María del Valle, a poor woman from the city without money for burial services, asked the Misericordia to bury her in any manner in which its cofrades saw fit.[77] Amaro Hernández de Losada was similarly obliging. In 1577 he arranged in his testament that at his death the 'cofrades of the holy Cofradía de Nuestra Señora de la Misericordia take pity on my soul and do that which it is obligated to do... and bury my body in the church of Santa María la Nueva, and perform that which it usually does for other poor persons'.[78]

In the village of Villalpando, it was the penitents of the Vera Cruz that buried poor men and women 'as if they were members'.[79] In Argujillo, penitents buried all villagers who sought its services and paid special attention to wrongdoers condemned to death. They promised that if any criminal commended himself to their confraternity, they would seek authorization from the local judge to detach the body from its place of execution, parade with it through village streets under the brotherhood's special cross as it did with bodies of cofrades, and bury it with religious ceremony.[80]

What was done for society's wretches was done with heightened enthusiasm for a brother or sister of one's own confraternity. The dying cofrade counted on his brotherhood to attend to his burial by setting up funeral processions and offering prayers. Customarily members gathered together at the home of the deceased dressed in special funeral garbs to accompany the body to mass. Draping the coffin with a pall designed in a color distinctive of their brotherhood, cofrades carried the body to burial. The number of candles held by mourners as they bore the soul through the city streets was a matter of utmost importance. They carried only half as many for a servant or child under the age of 14 as for a full-fledged member. Similarly, the number of requiem masses and prayers that cofrades offered during the subsequent mourning period depended on the deceased's membership status.

Special procedures were followed for burials at the pilgrimage shrine of Santiago de Compostela. When a pilgrim died in Santiago's hospital, a cofrade walked through the city's main streets ringing a small bell to announce the impending funeral to anyone who wished to go to the service. If the deceased should happen to have been an affiliate of the brotherhood of Santiago, all members present in the city were obliged to attend the funeral and they were called by the ringing of a bell larger than that used on behalf of non-affiliated pilgrims. Any cofrade who died in another city could be buried in the hospital's cemetery if he wished his body carried back to Santiago. There he received all the honors and religious services promised by the confraternity to Santiago's members.[81]

Except for this international pilgrimage confraternity which extended burial services to members residing outside the seat of Santiago de Compostela, confraternities restricted their burial services to members who were residents of their own town. So important was the home base that if a member died outside the confines of the town, cofrades had the obligation to journey only to the edge of municipal limits to greet the body and carry it back inside for funeral services. And if the deceased had wished to be buried outside the town, members were obliged only to accompany the body in procession to the urban walls, leaving the burial to others.[82] In contrast to this concern that funeral ceremonies be held within the neatly circumscribed spatial setting of the city, the remains of the body itself were not always required for the execution of a funeral. If a member died in a distant place, services would be offered in town for his body *in absentia*. The soul apparently could be saved anywhere, as long as loved ones prayed on its behalf at home.

A widespread and curious custom practised at funerals in Zamora tells more about popular religious ideas concerning death and the afterlife. Offerings of food called *limosnas* and *animeras*, usually consisting of bread and wine, were placed over sepulchres or graves of the dead immediately after the burial. Later in the day, they were consumed by relatives, paupers and priests. What the rituals meant for mourners is something of a puzzle. Possibly the bread and wine represented the body and blood of Christ that brought the redemption of mankind. Such an interpretation is suggested by the arrangement of straw baskets containing bread, two liters of wine and four candles that the confraternity of the Ciento customarily offered to members who died.[83] But why did some people request that additional food stuffs be placed before their graves? Catalina Fernández furnished her Cofradía de Santa Ana with property for purchase of a bushel of wheat, 60 *maravedís* worth of bread, six decanters of wine, a pair of rabbits and some wax to offer on the day of her burial.[84] A not uncommon request was for fruit and cheese. The large quantities and peculiar choices of items intimate that the offerings may have derived from an old pagan custom of distributing food at tombs for sustenance of the dead.[85]

In fact, during the early years of the Christian church, theologians had recognized a similarity between the offerings of Christians over graves of the dead and traditional pagan burial rituals. Both Augustine and Ambrose condemned the custom called *refrigerium* of feasting over the graves of the dead. Pagans thought that the deceased were actually present and partaking in the food of the living at the meal.[86] Augustine attempted to eradicate the heathen element in the funeral banquet by bringing the offerings in line with orthodox views on the resurrection of the body with the soul after death. He also wanted to

2.2 A man and a woman in mourning in Castile

'In this manner the rich men in the kingdom of Castile mourn when a friend dies.'

'In this manner the women of Castile grieve and cry out reprehensibly because she has died, having been beautiful and gracious, wealthy and pious.'

[Source: *Das Trachtenbuch des Christoph Wieditz von seinen reisen nach Spanien (1529) und den Niederlanden (1531/32)* (Berlin: Verlag von Walter de Gruyter & Co., 1927), Laminas LII and LIII]

reduce the opportunities for excessive drinking and eating that the ceremony engendered. So he recommended that Christian mourners share only moderately-sized meals at tombs, and then insisted that a portion of the aliments be distributed to the poor.[87] In the form of alms, the funeral banquet was transfigured into a cult act consistent with Catholic belief in the power of charity to assist the souls of the dead to heaven.

But old habits return. Church synods in medieval and sixteenth-century Castile continued to regulate distribution of burial food to paupers in order to preserve its character as alms. The bishopric of Astorga agreed to honor the disposal of 'caridades perpetuas' of the dead because it was traditional in the area, but carefully apportioned amounts to their proper sources. One third of the charity was delivered to paupers, one third was given to the church's accounts of the dead and another third went to the local council.[88] The church found it repeatedly necessary to caution relatives of the dead not to impoverish themselves, for in addition to offering food over gravesites, they began to distribute doles to paupers outside the doorway of the deceased's home on interment day.

Alms were the food that nourished blessings and prayers for the dead. Testators who requested funeral meals for the welfare of their souls '*como de costumbre*' may have been taking advantage of the goodwill which, as they undoubtedly had experienced, accompanies a feast. Or perhaps they were exploiting the sense of gratitude and the desire to recompense that all guests feel toward their hosts. In any case, heirs of the dead faithfully fulfilled obligations to wish a safe and speedy delivery of souls to heaven during feasts. On All Saints' Day the populace in Aragon, Catalonia and Valencia developed elaborate memorial uses for the *rosca*, a wreath of bread made of wheat and oil topped with sugar and honey. After mass, mourners placed a large lighted candle inside the *rosca* and carried it to gravesites where they sat and prayed until the candle burned down and extinguished itself, melting the sugar on top of the *rosca*. Then celebrants consumed the loaf.[89] The name of this dish, *almitas*, is strikingly similar in meaning to the Zamoran funeral offering of *animeras*. Both referred to the soul. Identical sentiments underlie All Saint's Day ceremonies in Galicia and Asturias, where mourners prepared plates of chestnuts in amounts corresponding to the number of souls that they wanted freed from purgatory.[90] Such rituals have been interpreted by scholars in various ways, as expressions of solidarity, gratitude, renewal, even, Mikhail Bakhtin suggests, toasts to the health of the dead.[91] But running through all the rituals is the theme of alms as a means of transporting the soul to paradise. We have seen that cofrades employed the currency of charity in many imaginative forms, but nothing quite surpassed the extraordinarily graphic ritual use of it at the last stage as souls left the community of providers and recipients at funerals.

THE CONFRATERNAL WELFARE 'SYSTEM'

In late medieval and sixteenth-century Castile, religious beliefs generated welfare practices singularly different from modern secular programs to fulfill basic material needs of society. Catholic ideology and ritual provided a common framework in which individual neighborhoods arranged charitable assistance. Welfare in Zamora and surrounding population centers was delivered, to use Clifford Geertz' term, through communal ritual 'thick' with symbolism. Principal among the sacred symbols were the seven acts of mercy which dramatized Biblical history. The merciful acts simulated Matthew's exhortation to provide for the needy, and their constant repetition by lay and religious people constituted the praxis of medieval Christian poor relief. This shared meaning created a uniform pattern for charitable activities, producing what might be called a poor relief 'system'. How was Biblical metaphor translated into an active moral code that reflected Christian precepts so precisely that no-one could mistake its meaning? The representative power of the written word in traditional society was unlike anything known today, as Michel Foucault has explained so breathtakingly to us in *Les Mots et les choses*.[92] To find in the natural world resemblances of metaphysical concepts was considered the pathway to knowledge in the medieval period. The pious Christian believed that the legible words of Scripture should stamp visible marks over the surface of the body. To emulate in gesture was to 'know' Scripture.

Among illiterate folk in particular, imitation, however crude and unimaginative, was indeed an effective and powerful testimony of faith. For centuries Christian creeds had been sustained within a primarily oral civilization that expressed its spiritual ideals through deeds rather than through abstract and silent meditation. In the Middle Ages, sermons and sacred drama were the media through which religious history and morality were brought to the people, who then confirmed their understanding by acting them out in daily life. Their gestures of piety were explained in psychological terms by Thomas Aquinas. According to the Dominican scholar, abstract philosophical and theological statements slipped easily from the minds of the common people unless they were given overt expression.[93] 'The condition of man is such', Aquinas stated when explaining the value of the sacraments, 'that it has to be led by things corporeal and sensible to things spiritual and intelligible.'[94] Just as Biblical texts utilized parables to elucidate moral principles, the preaching habits of churchmen, especially of the Dominican order, involved drawing analogies to visual experiences. Clothing spiritual concepts in physical images was designed to facilitate retention as well as comprehension, a process that Frances Yates has identified as part of the 'scholastic memory'.[95] Christian didactics sought to impress indelible images or codes on the mind which could be imitated as models of virtuous conduct.[96] Aquinas explains that this was done by creating 'corporeal similitudes' of spiritual ideas in art, in the sacraments, and in physical gestures, which excited the memory through visual appearance.[97]

Like the parts of the church liturgy, the acts of mercy were not apprehended as completely meaningful in themselves; they were symbols of a spiritual order.[98] Just as the prayers, ceremonies, hymns and dramatic representations of church liturgy were external and discernible signs of spiritual phenomena,[99] so the acts of mercy signified in gesture the highest forms of Christian love. The corporal acts of mercy symbolized divine love in the same manner that water, associated with cleansing qualities, represented in baptism the spiritual cleansing of the soul, while the sustaining qualities of bread and wine, when administered in the eucharist, stood for sacred nourishment. Within a culture which understood liturgy to synthesize and mirror spiritual phenomena, the acts of mercy embodied the broadest dimensions of the virtue of charity. Reflected in the microcosm of an individual deed toward one's neighbor was the divine macrocosm of love and charity toward God.

After grasping the full meaning of these acts, it becomes clear why they were the object of solicitous ritual performance in popular religion. On account of their spiritual significance the acts were incorporated into nearly every type of social celebration. When the city council in Zamora held its annual banquet on the day of San Juan in June with justices, secretaries, and other municipal officials, it invited prisoners from the local jail to commune with them at supper and distributed fine pastries to paupers in the plaza.[100] On Maundy Thursday, church prelates, friars and city fathers ritually washed the feet of the poor in public in addition to distributing meals. In Villalpando, the feast of the Immaculate Conception was honored by seating 20 paupers at table to eat, and in Burgos, the entry of the queen was honored by freeing prisoners from jail.[101] Even in the midst of such boisterous activities as bullrunning, a common form of entertainment during confraternal festivals, the poor were not forgotten. After running bulls through streets and slaughtering them in makeshift rings in neighborhood plazas, celebrants sent carcasses to butchers and distributed the meat among paupers.[102] In Valladolid, before holidays the city council carefully selected worthy recipients of the bulls' meat among residents of hospitals, jails, and monasteries of the city.[103]

Infusions of charity periodically lit up every market place in Zamora, like flares illuminating the torn surface of ghetto accidents. Habitually and without failure the devotees of Nuestra Señora de la Antigua gave a *real* for food to six paupers on the days of San Miguel and Nuestra Señora de las Candelas, while cofrades of San Ildefonso conscientiously distributed its feast day leftovers to beggars. On the eve of the festival of Nuestra Señora de la Visitación, its confraternity allocated 170 *maravedís* for an expected 114 alms-seekers to congregate at the church door after mass the next day.[104] Such feast days came up over and over again during the course of the year, commemorated by other confraternities in other neighborhoods. Holy days would not be fully commemorated without remembering the poor, for charity was the highest celebration of the concept of Christian brotherhood and love. What cofrades had in mind by garnishing every feast day celebration with invitations to a few paupers to dine was to consecrate poor relief. With such token gestures, cofrades affirmed in solidarity and strengthened in spirit the virtue of charity that they sought to uphold in their everyday lives.

The timing of events heightened awareness of the sacred nature of charity. Alms distributions coincided with births, marriages, funerals and saint days. The most numerous of the confraternities, the Marians, commemorated with almsgiving several annual feasts to the Virgin. The majority of celebrations occurred in the late summer months (in honor of the Visitation of Mary on July 6, her Assumption on August 15, her Consolation on September 4, her Birth on September 8, her Sorrows on September 15 and her Mercy on September 24). Christmas and Easter also heralded geat outbursts of generosity, while patron saints' days earmarked charity at various intervals throughout the year. These holidays regulated the pace of public almsgiving, subjecting paupers to the seasonal cycle of the liturgical calendar.

The charity practiced in Zamora offers an excellent example of how thoroughly a society's culture affects the lifestyles, even the chances of survival, of its members. Within a regime of privilege in which the distribution of property itself was sanctioned by cultural codes, the only mechanism that ensured a flow of goods to sectors in critical need was religion. Catholicism orchestrated the rhythm of charity by ordaining certain holy occasions for the dispersal of alms. Then it further keyed the content of charity to the tune of the seven acts of mercy. Most importantly, Catholicism created the instruments, so many confraternities, through which lay charitable services were played out.

One of the most practical aspects of this traditional welfare system was that the mold cast by one confraternity could readily serve another in a different parish or town. Poor relief activities written into statutes and sent on to ecclesiastical authorities for approval frequently fathered new confraternal devotions and this propagation of techniques gave rise to what appears to have been standardized programs throughout Castilian towns. Indeed, imitation advanced to such a degree that different villages possessed confraternities of the very same advocacies specializing in related forms of charitable work. In some cases, the church hierarchy actively promoted the extension throughout Christendom of certain types of confraternities and therefore should be considered directly responsible for harmonizing poor relief facilities. We have already seen how the international arch-confraternities of the Misericordia buried paupers in various parts of Europe with identical techniques and aspirations. Monks of Rocamador at the famous Marian shrine in France sponsored the establishment throughout Europe of another order of confraternities, that of Our Lady of Rocamador, for communion in indulgences and exchange in prayers.[105] Zamora, Valladolid and Salamanca each had a confraternity of Nuestra Señora affiliated with the monastery of Rocamador which hospitalized the sick and lodged pilgrims.[106] All shared the patronage of the virgin of the healing shrine and each of their members aspired to make a pilgrimage to France at least once in a lifetime.

In other cases, however, the church does not appear to have sponsored the confederation of brotherhoods operating under the same name in pursuit of identical devotional tasks. These developed more spontaneously, mirroring each other in common allegiance to saints known to favor special causes. Quite a few villages in Castile, for example, had confraternities under the advocacy of San Juan de Letrán to care for the aged by providing them with housing and assuming responsibility for their debts. Advocacies of San Roque and San Sebastián, protectors against the plague, characteristically ran pesthouses.[107] Cofrades in all parts of Spain invoked Nuestra Señora de los Pobres de la Cárcel to guide programs for assisting prisoners in jail. Recent research reveals that her patronage over confraternities extended across the Atlantic into Spanish America as well – evidence of the eminently exportable character of Catholic poor relief.[108] Even Zamora had its own internationally famous cult. San Julián the Pauper was a Leonese penitent sentenced for murdering his parents to spend the rest of his life as a hospitaler with the additional duty of carrying pilgrims across the river Esla. Legends of his good deeds performed in a tiny village outside Zamora were related throughout Europe and remained remarkably consistent in the telling.[109] In the high and late Middle Ages he inspired creation of a number of hospices dedicated to facilitating the travels of pilgrims. Hospices under his patronage such as those in the cities of Zamora and Burgos and as far north as Paris appeared near rivers on pilgrimage routes. Local saints added variety to this renowned cast of healing patrons which confraternities called upon for assistance. Out of this cult of saints materialized an international network of poor relief.

Today it is startling to reflect on the fact that through ideology, and without the aid of a large bureaucratic apparatus, Catholicism provided a means by which communities across Castile, and indeed across Europe, developed similar expressions of welfare assistance. Symbolic mimesis became a routinized form of poor relief. Local confraternities practicing merciful works offered doles and services to the hungry and the homeless, the infirm and the dying, in ritually determined and consistent patterns. The cult of the saints, by offering common models of charitable virtues, extended its patronage over confraternities and provided a universal nomenclature to this welfare system.

The power of cultural symbols to move the population extended beyond the momentary feelings of piety at the religious ceremony. Charitable ritual defined the social role that the possessors of the world's wealth adopted in other situations. Rituals, Clifford Geertz has reminded us, induce a certain set of dispositions among participants, dispositions which remain long after the ceremony itself has ended to enter into the realm of everyday life.[110] It was indeed the continual and all-pervasive influence of ritual that made religion such a powerful force in traditional welfare. In modern times, only the compulsory and inescapable hand of the state has been able to match its effect in distributing material goods to the poor.

3 Welfare Reform: Attempts to Displace Charity

In constructing poor relief on private acts of charity, the confraternities subjected paupers to a religious code of ethics that was formulated only partially with regard to their material needs. The indigent and disabled were dependent for their livelihood upon rituals of religion fashioned across the centuries from biblical injunctions, soteriological concepts and saints' cults. For those of us living in societies in which welfare systems are centrally organized and relief is allocated strictly according to income levels of recipients, the traditional foundation of poor relief upon religious prescriptions is apt to appear unreliable. To modern eyes, there is something capricious about confraternal welfare, in the way that it carefully emulated sacred images of charity with little regard for the peculiar circumstances of individual paupers. Could symbolic charity respond to changing economic conditions? Did religious ritual adequately provide for the physical needs of paupers?

Such questions were raised as early as the sixteenth century. Throughout Europe, but especially in Spain, enquiries over poor relief provoked deep introspection and intense debate. It was a moment, unusual in western history, when society looked into itself to evaluate critically its own customs. Once rituals become an integral part of the life of a community, their functional purposes are rarely questioned. Only with great difficulty, moreover, are these practices, especially religious practices, ever rejected. Should these questions about relief to the poor have led to direct challenge of confraternal charity, they would have threatened both Catholic soteriology and the collective orientation of traditional life. It would have amounted to an 'epistemic' change in thinking,[1] a subversion of the entire symbolic order, for charitable ritual consecrated a particular moral and aesthetic perspective. Ritual was a language through which the Spanish populace expressed its views not only about the afterlife but also about the place of man in the natural world. As anthropologists who study consecrated behavior elsewhere have insisted, ritual is more than mere ceremonial or festive action; it helps manage human and natural resources.[2] The acts of mercy gave order to and made sense of the unequal and potentially divisive distribution of material goods in

75

society. In Zamora they assumed the important task of sustaining individuals who lacked remunerative employment or capital resources for their livelihood. Christian rituals of charity instigated social action on behalf of the poor. This consecrated routine was by no means inflexible. I have shown that the system of confraternal charity adapted to many varied circumstances in the kingdom of Leon-Castile. Confraternities were established wherever large numbers of poor appeared, whether in hospitals, orphanages, pesthouses or jails. They also followed the course of pilgrimage routes, conforming geographically to the contours of poverty.

The ritual enactment of charity in Zamora shaped the social order by defining relationships between certain classes. Charity brought rich and poor together in co-operation and mutual exchange of goods and services. Confraternal welfare was designed to benefit both the wealthy members of society, who donated charity for the sake of their souls, and the poor, who received alms as if they were representatives of Christ. The confraternity of San Antolín announced that it was 'established for the care of paupers and the honor of the rich, and for the salvation of all in common'.[3] Many people did indeed believe that poverty was a providential condition ordained by God to aid mankind in attaining salvation. Poverty provided opportunity to exercise the virtues of resignation and humility to those who suffered, and compassion and charity to those who responded.[4] It was considered a permanent, even a useful, aspect of the human condition. Paupers served as a medium for the wealthy to gain salvation, almost as significant as Mary and the saints in facilitating their entry into heaven. According to one Spanish friar, 'God made the poor to aid the rich, rather than the rich to aid the poor'.[5] Another commented that 'God did not institute charity so much for the poor as for those who give', a concept that the picaresque writer Mateo Alemán explained more fully when he said that 'to the rich are given temporal goods and to the poor are given spiritual goods, so that in return for distributing earthly possessions among the poor, grace is bought'.[6]

Such views endowed paupers with a moral role in society that was contingent upon their low economic status. This was especially evident at funerals, where paupers were asked to bear witness to the good deeds of the well-to-do and pray for their souls. The wealthier the individuals, the more paupers were invited for spiritual insurance. While kings and queens might have a couple of hundred paupers attending their funeral processions,[7] most who could afford them at all chose to invite 12 in honor of the apostles. Even a modest woolcarder in Zamora was able to invite 12 paupers to accompany his body to the grave by commissioning the two confraternities to which he belonged to provide them meals after services.[8]

We will never know what went through the minds of paupers as they stood over graves, ostensibly holding in their hands the fate of dead men's souls. But surely they apprehended the spiritual reasons for which they were called! For their presence was crucial in the transfer of funereal graces. How could the six poor women who donned the short white capes bequeathed them by Juana de la Peña have failed to understand their role when she requested that they accompany her body to the grave and attend a rosary novena to save her soul?[9] Every gift had its obligation – that they knew. Whether or not their prayers were sincere is another matter. Lazarillo de Tormes's comment may not have been purely fictional, although it would never have been stated aloud in real life: 'and thinking of burials, God forgive me, I was never an enemy of the human race except then, and that was because we ate well and I stuffed myself at funeral feasts. I hoped and even prayed to God that each day should kill its man ... '

The food and clothing given out at funerals were not insignificant items to one whose wretched existence was a constant search for material necessities. Thirteen paupers received shoes, shirts, frocks and pointed hoods at Alonso de Sotelo's funeral.[10] Another twelve put on hooded capes of dark cloth at Pedro de la Torre's burial.[11] Inés Delgado asked her weaver to prepare the fine linen in her possession for a few poor women 'so that they pray to God for my soul' – cloth not as sturdy as the usual dark, coarse wool left to funeral attendants, but draped, nevertheless, into formless capes of mourning.[12] Such graveclothes were prized possessions. Paupers rarely discarded their old rags except at such occasions, and they continued to wear the garments acquired at the cost of prayers until invited to another funeral.

Circulating through the streets in clothing designed in mourning styles, paupers were grim reminders of the burial of the dead. These walking symbols of the corruption of the flesh, of the ephemeral nature of material goods (goods which they were never fortunate enough to have been burdened with) may not have had a choice in the role that they played, but they played it. By participating in funeral rituals and offering prayers for the dead, the poor assumed the guilt of the wealthy for their lifetime enjoyment of wordly pleasure and co-operated in an ideal of universal Christian brotherhood. The charity delivered over mortal remains to praying paupers mitigated economic inequalities in the social order. Reconstruction of an ideal world of generosity and compassion through charitable ritual prevented the most serious afflictions of poverty in the real world from disturbing and destroying social equilibrium, for it provided opportunities to transfer wealth in an orderly and limited manner to those in need. Thus the perceived purpose of charity, a means of discourse between rich and poor, actually affirmed disparities in the economic status of men and acted as a stabilizing influence on the social establishment.[13] Obviously the high spiritual value placed on the condition of poverty did not threaten the position of the wealthy on earth, for the intercessory powers that paupers enjoyed carried no political weight which might have helped them redress the unequal distribution of wealth in society. The material conditions and social prestige of the poor remained so low, moreover, as to prevent them from ever coalescing into a viable force to challenge the economic order. In the same ironic manner in which the church's incredibly high estimation of the ideal woman, the Virgin Mary, ignored the real status of women,[14] the spiritual value attributed to paupers did not raise their position on earth. Ritual giving healed wounds in the social order, but in no way subverted that order.

Christian ethics sought to prevent the worst ills of poverty from festering by encouraging assistance to the weakest, most pitiable, members of society. Churchmen urged donors to discard personal prejudices in distributing relief, advocating instead that they give to those who were most needy regardless of moral deportment. Even from the earliest centuries of Christianity, church officials argued that charity should be given freely to all who asked for assistance. Partially in reaction to Manichean practices of withholding alms to sinners, Augustine denounced the 'horrid cruelty' of denying food to the hungry on the basis of unsatisfactory behavior or religious differences. He argued, as clergymen almost unanimously argued down to the sixteenth century, that the poor deserved charity purely as a result of their human status, and invoked natural law to assert their right to subsistence. 'Let us treat them with human decency because they are human beings.'[15] According to Ambrose, 'mercy is accustomed not to judge on merits but to assist in situations of need, not to be on the lookout for righteousness but to help the one who is poor'.[16]

In the sixteenth century the majority of Spanish theologians, still faithful to medieval tradition, adopted arguments of natural law when discussing the value of giving indiscriminately to the poor. They noted the practical dangers involved when donors claimed a right to judge the character of those to whom they gave alms. In 1563, Friar Tomás de Trujillo criticized those who 'investigate with great care and take a lively interest in identifying what type of person a pauper is' when they gave alms. Because if they 'ascertained that the pauper behaves wrongly, they do not want to remedy his misery, nor take care of his need'. Citing Augustine, he argued that charity should be given to all supplicants, good or evil, who required assistance.[17] The cleric Bernardino Sandoval tried to encourage almsgiving to prisoners by relieving donors of qualms they might have had in succoring a person guilty of crime. He assured them that 'you do not give in order to reward the sinner, nor because the misdeed pleases you, but because he is a man. Providing for and maintaining a pauper is in itself a good deed, because you love in the recipient not his guilt, but his human nature'.[18]

But the principles of universal Christian charity were not always respected by cofrades. As we have seen, they were usually violated in their dowry programs to poor orphans. Young women's reputations were regularly scrutinized to maintain whether or not they 'merited' charity. The European-wide practice of dowering women on the feast of the Annunciation, honoring the miraculous conception of Christ by Mary, placed women under the idealized standard of virginal purity by which their pasts were rigorously judged. In many other situations as well, donors were influenced by factors other than pure economic need when choosing recipients for their gifts. The confraternal system of welfare favored certain individuals over others. Those most likely to find assistance were members themselves. Confraternities gave their own constituents first priority in their limited number of hospital beds or alms distributions. The artisans, tradesmen and professionals of Zamora who belonged to confraternities were the real beneficiaries of a system of social welfare based on 'brotherly' love.

Next in the chain of confraternities' beneficiaries were paupers living within the inner walls of the city. These residents knew where and when to show up for crucial events at which alms would be distributed. According to an official survey in 1561, Zamora had 581 indigent households, which constituted 27 per cent of the entire number of family residences. 468 of these households, or approximately 21 per cent of the population, were unemployed and required continual support.[19] Since their needs were known in the community, they were apt to receive alms much more readily than outsiders. The so-called *vergonzantes*, or 'shamefaced poor' were targeted especially for charity and sympathy. They were formerly self-sufficient residents struck down by misfortune who were ashamed to beg. It was acknowledged within the community that benefactors 'should take extra care to seek them out, without forcing them to come to doors to ask for help, because to some we should give charity on demand, while to others we should place it quietly in their hands'.[20] In Salamanca, a confraternity of notables dedicated itself specifically to helping these *vergonzantes*. Elected officials distributed weekly rations and special holiday gifts to the poor, particularly to mothers and widowed sisters of ecclesiastics as well as widows and daughters of the lay cofrades. They divided the city of Salamanca into six sections and regularly sent a cleric and a layman to visit each area to account for all who required assistance. Members included two physicians, two surgeons and two apothecaries who practiced their crafts without reimbursement for the paupers whom the confraternity took under its care. At least once a month, cofrades begged for charity at homes and churches as well as other public sites for the local 'shamefaced'.[21] According to Juan Luis Vives, these people merited special compassion because they were reminders of what could happen to any one after misfortune, and because their misery, in contrast to the happiness that they had once known, appeared all the more stark and cruel than the poverty of the lower classes.[22]

Among the lowly folk who had never tasted wealth, those who evoked pity had better chances of receiving support than those who hid their pains and afflictions. To take advantage of the charitable system, the indigent begged conspicuously in city streets; they kept close to church entryways and hung about confraternal festivals. They regularly approached the homes of the wealthy, especially during mealtimes, and nestled down to sleep at their doorsteps. It was notorious that beggars openly displayed their wounds and disabilities, and it was not uncommon to find them feigning blindness or actually maiming themselves or their children to attract sympathy.[23] Competition within a system that could not guarantee care for everyone resulted in great injustices. Crafty beggars often ate before the truly weak and hungry. Those who conformed most closely to the categories described in the seven merciful acts: the homeless, including both pilgrims and orphans, the imprisoned, and the infirm had an advantage. Foreigners pretending to be pilgrims frequented the city all too often to enjoy the hospitality of lodging houses specifically instituted to aid wayfarers in their journeys to Santiago and other shrines. There was an art to begging, to making use of the acts of mercy, and the ingenious forms that this art took caught the attention of writers of the picaresque genre.

The people who were least likely to be aided by confraternities were the wandering, dispossessed poor. Unfamiliar with the city's charitable geography and calendar, and nameless to cofrades, they formed a troublesome crowd in the streets. City officials frequently complained that there was not enough charity to take care of these people. They arrived from the poor regions of Portugal, Galicia and Asturias, especially during times of famine, to beg alms from city residents and to seek lodging in the Misericordia and other hospices. By the sixteenth century, the major relief institutions in Zamora had settled within city walls to care for residents. Migrants could be shut out of the gates during the night. Without trades, kindly masters or permanent homes, these paupers could not afford the luxury of being modest, of having *vergüenza*, and were not likely to find regular support. Their lives were characterized by uncertainty; many became vagabonds, constantly travelling in search of the next meal and a place to lie for the night. Encountering a generous almsgiver, they gorged themselves to nausea after suffering weeks of hunger.

It was this mass of non-resident, mobile poor outside the effective care of confraternities that disturbed the local and national governments and that provoked them to question the traditional confraternal relief system. Complaints about an increasing number of vagrants in the cities of Leon-Castile were first expressed in 1523 at the Cortes of Valladolid. Representatives of the 18 Spanish cities with a voice in national government, including Zamora, Salamanca and Valladolid, petitioned the crown for enforcement of a law which restricted the movement of paupers through the kingdom and allowed them to beg only within their own townships. This request, repeated at Toledo in 1525 and at Madrid in 1528, was intended to eradicate vagabondage and encourage the poor to seek jobs.[24]

Ordinarily poverty in the countryside was only slightly higher than in urban areas. Approximately 30 per cent of village residents claimed the status of indigency compared to 27 per cent of residents in the city of Zamora.[25] But the number of poor peasants increased frightfully in the third decade of the sixteenth century after a particularly bad harvest in 1522 raised wheat prices over affordable rates. Zamoran officials complained that residents could not assist all the beggars coming in search of alms. The municipal government had its hands full already dealing with the starvation and sickness that it claimed was beginning to depopulate the city. Charity dropped to such a low level that the monastery of San Francisco, traditionally one of the most popular recipients of alms, was heavily indebted and about to sell its silver and reduce the number of its friars to continue in operation.[26]

Another meager harvest in the fall of 1530 brought more poverty-stricken rural workers into the city and renewed concern to curb vagrancy.[27] During the following summer, the amount of charity required to feed the displaced exceeded residents' resources. On 3 July 1531, the city council ordered that within five days all peasants leave the area and return to their land under penalty of 100 lashes.[28] A week later the council decided to issue begging licenses to poor folks who lived in the city in order to identify resident from non-resident mendicants. But this alone could not deter the hungry. By September 1531, public criers at each of the major monasteries, entryways and thoroughfares where paupers congregated again announced that all non-resident beggars, both those from outside the municipality's jurisdiction as well as those from the immediate hinterlands, must leave the city. They were threatened with the customary 100 lashes.[29] Throughout the following winter months, Zamora tried desperately to limit public begging to licensed residents and force all paupers sleeping outside hospices to leave.[30]

Poverty was clearly more extensive than private charity could handle. In the following years, more and more relief was shouldered by the government. The city council became involved increasingly in the plight of beggars, taking into its hands responsibilities formerly held by the church and confraternities. It stepped up police action against vagrancy, intent on keeping homeless paupers off the streets at night by lodging them in poor houses and hospitals. In 1535 the council organized permanent surveillance of these institutions by one of its members along with the Crown's representative, the *corregidor*. Together they carried provisions to patients. This experience provoked discussion among magistrates about reducing the number of hospitals in the city to five for greater efficiency in the distribution of resources.[31]

But serious reform was long in coming. It took another crisis, the famine of 1539–40, to finally propel the city into action. At this time the Crown enforced the *tasa*, fixed maximum grain prices, that strangled peasant income and forced many off their lands to urban centers for charity. Once again Zamora was inundated with mendicants. Taxed with the burden of feeding the city's own population, the council decided to expel non-residents. On 21 April 1539 it ordered that between the hours of seven and ten the next morning, all foreign beggars should gather at the bridge of San Julián to receive a loaf of bread and two *maravedís* and be on their way. Six hundred loaves of bread, each weighing a pound, were made from the public granary for the purpose.[32] A guard stood at the bridge to ensure that they did not return. But the situation was hopeless. During the following months the city continued to attract peasants from the countryside and had to turn them away repeatedly. The municipal government elected a constable of paupers to punish begging in the streets and placed guards at the city's main gates to prevent entry to vagrants. Citizens were asked to help distribute public bread among hungry folk waiting outside the confines of the wall.[33]

The principal concern during the difficult spring of 1540 was to supply enough grain to feed residents. Wheat and barley were difficult to obtain and prices began to climb despite the royal tasa.[34] Officials travelled throughout the province in search of grain at affordable rates and they then distributed the food among needy households using poor lists drawn up by parish councils.[35] But municipal funds were limited and it quickly became clear that a wider source of support had to be tapped. On 16 April the city government took its most drastic step thus far. In an attempt to eliminate begging entirely, even by residents, it assigned responsibility for care of the poor to affluent families in the city. 'The paupers, who are to be given all that they need to eat, are not to go door to door, and every one of them must wear badges over their chest with the names of the persons who are giving them food.'[36] The cathedral chapter, the monasteries of San Francisco, San Jerónimo, San Benito and Santo Domingo, clerics of the parish churches, and of course deputies of the city neighborhoods all concentrated efforts to identify paupers living within the city and congregating at entryways.

It was a radical move. Without levying taxes, the municipality managed to make charitable giving almost obligatory by assigning charge over paupers to individual households. In addition, councilmen and elected citizens solicited alms house to house to support the institutionalized, acting as 'advocates' of the poor. They sold festival bulls, normally given to monasteries and beggars on holidays, for funds to provision paupers under the government's charge.[37] The council also supplemented the resources of confraternal hospitals with municipal funds and hired a public physician to help administer medical aid.

The Zamoran government was not alone in its search for a 'nuevo orden' of poor relief. It shared in a European-wide problem of peasant immigration into the cities. A number of municipalities, particularly in northern European countries and the German states, had already begun to explore new methods of dealing with beggars. The first cities to centralize poor relief under the control of secular authorities were Nuremberg (1522), Strasbourg (1523), and Mons and Ypres (1525). Charles V requested a copy of the municipal reform program in Ypres and a month after receiving the information issued a pragmatic prohibiting vagrancy throughout the empire.[38] In 1531, the same year that Zamora licensed its beggars, Henry VIII in England authorized Justices of the Peace to license all the poor worthy of charity and a few years later provided the additional administrative machinery that would differentiate between those paupers who were able to work and those who were incapable. The Crown prohibited begging, encouraged voluntary contributions for maintaining the genuine poor, and attempted to put vagrants to work. Also in 1531, Francis I ordered each parish in France to maintain a list of its poor to facilitate equitable distribution of relief from charitable gifts, insisting that able-bodied beggars find useful employment.[39]

It is unclear why poor relief reform and stringent controls over begging swept through a number of European cities simultaneously. Imperial legislation discouraged begging but provided no practical program for the poor, leaving the initiative to the cities. Some scholars have assumed that reform was a logical result of the Protestant Reformation. Ernest Troeltsch and other nineteenth- and early twentieth-century historians argued that the new Protestant theology, denying that works contributed to salvation, encouraged the transfer of welfare from private individuals to civil authorities who handled it as a matter of secular government.[40]

It is a controversial thesis that has been challenged seriously in recent years. Research on poor relief in Catholic countries has demonstrated that centralization of welfare was by no means a Protestant prerogative. Natalie Davis and Brian Pullan have thrown doubt upon the assumption implicit in this argument that Catholic believers opposed welfare reform in order to preserve the poor in conditions of indigency and ensure the means to earn salvation through private good works.[41] Lyon's municipal relief agency, the Aumône-Générale, serves as an excellent litmus paper measuring the effects of religious belief on charitable practice because the institution was directed by both Protestants and Catholics. Davis shows that when Huguenot replaced Catholic administration in 1562, basic policy changes were negligible. Members of both religions approved of the services that the municipal program offered. For

Catholics, the Aumône-Générale was a genuine expression of charity, fulfilling all the psychological needs produced by a doctrine of salvation by good works.[42] Brian Pullan has shown that Catholic confraternities in Venice were no less interested in tackling the sources of poverty than Protestant relief agencies. Venetian philanthropists, although certainly concerned with the spiritual merits they might accrue by giving charity, did not offer doles indiscriminately to all who asked. Members of the Scuole Grandi, the principal Venetian charitable fraternities, scrupulously refused alms to the sturdy rogue and paid particular attention to beggar children in order to make them responsible and self-sufficient adult citizens.[43]

If reformation theology was not a necessary factor in the acceptance of reform, it was nevertheless an important stimulus to change in local welfare. When city governments officially turned Protestant, they generally dissolved confraternities and convents that handled almsgiving, which forced them to find a new administrative approach. Nuremberg's city council brought most of the medieval charitable institutions under its direction during the Reformation. A bank for the poor was set up on the model of the Italian Monti de Pietà, supervised by a council member and begging was forbidden except for people with physical disabilities.[44] The *Ratsherren* in Strasbourg assumed control of charity and relief in that city, and demanded that all gifts to the poor be channeled through civil authorities. Legislation of 1523–24 abolished begging and established a special committee called the *Almosenherren* to distribute relief to the needy in their homes.[45] Both Wittenberg and Leisnig set up common chests in the early 1520s into which all public donations, church funds, and properties were deposited to care for the indigent who were forbidden subsequently to beg.[46]

It is possible that the plans for reform enacted in the Low Countries and northern France in subsequent years imitated those first instituted in the cities of the Holy Roman Empire, as the German historian Otto Winckelmann has assumed. It may also be, as Paul Bonenfant more reservedly has suggested, that the plans amounted to 'an unconscious introduction of Lutheran principles into the legislation of Catholic countries.'[47] But we must heed the words of Robert Kingdon who acknowledges the similarities of the German and Flemish programs but cautions that no direct influence has been found.[48] His sobering position exposes the inadequacy of current explanations for the remarkable resemblance of welfare reforms in early sixteenth-century cities.

P. A. Slack has offered some potential clues in suggesting that social and economic problems shared by early modern urban areas were responsible for directing reform schemes along similar lines. He advises that scholars look for several conditions to explain this phenomenon: first, the presence of sophisticated and centralized administrative structures and facilities for hospitals; secondly, an increase in the number of beggars on the streets; thirdly, the cycles of temporary crises, economic depressions, inflations, famine and plague; and finally, rapid immigration. He holds out the hope that a comparative study of these features in European cities will enhance our understanding of why changes in poor relief took the form of centralized administration and institutionalization of the needy.[49]

We also need to understand how attitudes toward poverty itself could have undergone such extraordinary changes in the sixteenth century. Why was it that after centuries of toleration, begging was suddenly looked upon as an undesirable activity? What cultural changes sanctioned the appropriation of poor relief responsibilities by the government from private hands?

Undoubtedly, economic considerations played a role in this transformation of values. In the legislation of European states, already a century before the reforms of the early sixteenth century, there appears a more positive attitude toward work and its value in the material development of nations.[50] Legal codes recognized that the conservation and increase of wealth was intimately dependent on reducing the number of idle citizens. Such ideas challenged old views that limited paupers to a spiritual role in society. Men from a wide range of religious and cultural backgrounds agreed that healthy paupers should be put to work. Their high estimation of the value of manual labor was the basis for efforts to discriminate between 'deserving' and 'undeserving' paupers. The deserving ones, also called genuine poor, impotent poor, and the poor in Christ, were all those who lacked sufficient means to support themselves because of physical or mental disability, illness, old-age or a social status that enforced dependency, which included the very young, orphans, foundlings and widows. Undeserving paupers, variously called lusty, able-bodied or illegitimate poor, were those individuals who were capable of working but who preferred to live on charity. Most municipal welfare reforms attempted to separate the two types of needy by licensing only those found worthy of charity in the hope that the others would then look for employment.

Demands that the government intervene in assisting and disciplining the underprivileged members of society for the good of the common-wealth were expressed particularly during outbreaks of the plague. National and municipal legislation attempting to control mendicity, ration food supplies, and employ sturdy vagabonds accompanied nearly every epidemic in the late Middle Ages. Plague exacerbated poverty and increased begging to such a degree that strict social control became desirable. To contain disease, governments thought it efficacious to cut off trade between infected and healthy areas. Within epidemic areas, they shut down industries and quarantined businesses and homes. Just as production and trade declined, public expenses increased to compensate constables, physicians, surgeons and sanitation workers. Private needs increased as well when people began burning their clothes, bedding and household articles to prevent further spread of disease. Beggars were accused of carrying the malignancy on their bodies and they were pressured to stop walking the streets. And then the plague took its inevitable toll on population sizes. The wake of epidemics resulted in smaller labor forces which pressured governments to put able-bodied paupers to work. The first measures to abolish begging came in the mid-fourteenth century after the Black Death. In 1349 Edward II of England prohibited alms distributions to able-bodied beggars and compelled them to accept work when offered. In 1350 the French King John II also forbade alms to able-bodied beggars. Prohibitions were similar in Spain. First in the Cortes at Toro in 1369, then at Burgos in 1379 and Briviesca in 1387, John I ordered that all sturdy vagabonds be severely punished if they did not accept work.[51]

These growing fears about health hazards and economic dangers of unrelieved poverty were accompanied by humanist concerns to improve the conditions of men. In 1526 the great Valencian humanist, Juan Luis Vives, published in Bruges his masterpiece *De subventione pauperum* which provided European cities with a clear model for reform. Quickly translated from the Latin into French, Italian, German and English, the treatise was the most widely read statement invoking governmental responsibility in alleviating poverty.[52] Vives's main thesis was that the state should be involved directly in working against poverty by offering employment opportunities for the jobless, constructing centers for the physical support of the needy, and aiding poor families in their homes. 'Just as it is disgraceful for the father of a family to allow any member to suffer hunger, nakedness, or the embarrassment of wearing rags,' Vives wrote, 'so it follows that in a wealthy city, it is unjust that magistrates

permit any of its citizens to be pressed down by hunger and misery.'
The humanist suggested the possibility that poverty was an accident
resulting from bad government and not an inescapable and divinely
ordained condition of man. He pointed out practical advantages that
would accrue to government with the elimination of begging. Fewer
poverty-stricken residents would bring honor to a city, lessen crime,
foster great peace and concord, enliven urban aesthetics and animate
the spirit of society.[53] Vives then gave his support to programs
undertaken in Nuremberg, Strasbourg, Mons, and Ypres, and
encouraged reforms in Lille, Brussels, Oudendarde and
Valenciennes.

Back in Castile, reform was tardy. Charles V had been an advocate
of reform in the Holy Roman Empire, authorizing more laws
prohibiting begging and centralising relief than had any ruler during
the entire medieval period.[54] The scarcity in the years 1539–40 brought
pressure on him to improve care of the poor in his Spanish dominions.
Cardinal Tavera of Toledo wrote to Charles early in spring 1540 urging
him to take notice of the many letters lamenting miserable conditions
in the kingdom, especially in Castile, and warned him of serious
depletions in the stock of grain. Burgos faced enormous pressures as
hundreds of peasants and shepherds unable to survive in the
mountains invaded the city.[55] In June the Cardinal asked the king to
consider giving his support to poor relief reforms initiated by the
alderman of Madrid when vagrants from the surrounding countryside
appeared in search of alms.[56] The Cardinal wished to see paupers
taken into hospitals or poor houses and offered complete care, and he
also advocated that vagabonds and persons able to work be prohibited
from begging in the streets.

On 25 August 1540, the king responded to the calls for reform. He
issued throughout the Spanish kingdom a set of instructions demanding a new approach to local poor relief.[57] Charles V limited begging to
the 'truly poor' within specified areas around their homes. In all cities
and villages of the kingdom, the poor could beg only where they
claimed residency or within the hinterlands and areas under the
communities' jurisdictions. If a community did not have enough
territory to provide for their needs, paupers could obtain authorization to beg within six leagues of their homes.[58]

In order to identify the 'truly poor' and locate their residences, the
instructions required paupers to register with their parish priests and
obtain licenses approved by local justices. They cautioned priests not
to authorize begging permits to those who could work for a living, nor

to those who had not confessed their sins or received communion. The licenses recorded paupers' names, places of residency and 'any characteristic features by which they can be recognized'. Given out at Easter, these licenses remained valid for the entire year. If famine or pestilence should strike an area, a bishop or civil justice could, informed of just causes, give licenses to whomever needed them so that they might beg alms for a limited period of time. In such circumstances, the licenses would record reasons for granting permission. Parents were forbidden to bring children over the age of five to beg with them, 'to avoid turning them into vagabonds'. The laws instructed prelates, ecclesiastical judges, justices and councilmen to take special care that children receive sustenance so that they might have no reason to take up begging. At early ages, the children should be placed with masters or taught trades.

The instructions made special provision for certain types of poorfolk. Pilgrims to Santiago could beg within four leagues of routes to the sanctuary. 'Genuine' blind men could beg without licenses within six leagues of their residences. Travellers who fell ill could be given temporary begging licenses to cover the periods of their illness and convalescences. Students were also allowed to beg with the permission of rectors, both in the locale of their studies and in their home territories. Mendicant friars were required to obtain permission of prelates or provisors of the bishoprics wherever they intended to beg. And those 'commonly called *envergonzantes*' received especially generous terms in the royal decree. Charles V requested clergy and local magistrates to succor those who 'out of timidity or some personal indisposition are unwilling or unable to beg for charity' by appointing someone to beg as their substitute.

The Crown's instructions were flexible and moderate in permitting begging in a regulated fashion. They took into account the special needs of persons for whom begging was considered indispensable. The king tried to restrict beggars to their own localities where better control could be exercised in licensing only those unable to work for a living. He did not demand that cities and villages go so far as Zamora had already done by finding alternatives to begging, but he did express approval of such steps. In the final article, Charles hinted that it would be of great service to God if cities could relieve the poor of the burden of begging in the streets. To this end, he asked civil and religious authorities as well as hospital administrators to supply local governments with information relating to rental income and charitable donations. By applying these resources more efficiently in centralized institutions, the poor might not need to resort to begging. It is important to note here that Charles did not perceive reform as a means of appropriating poor relief duties from the Catholic church. Both civil and ecclesiastical officials participated in the new program. In the 1540s, as in later periods of reform, the point of contention was not between state or church control over charity; but between public or private, centralized or decentralized relief.

The royal decree of 1540 compelled each town in Spain to turn attention to its own poor, for within 60 days of its publication all beggars were to have returned to their homes. The challenge to reform presented by the decree was by no means easy for local governments to take up, for little information was provided on financing and enforcing the new welfare scheme. Without energetic co-operation on the part of municipal authorities in drawing up local policies, the call for reform fell impotent.

A few Castilian cities, however, made every effort to meet the king's challenge. In Madrid, the laws received backing by village physicians who had been warning that paupers' bodies left dead in the streets threatened the population with disease. Late in 1540 the alderman doubled his efforts to institutionalize both resident and non-resident beggars in hospitals and poor-houses where they received food and medical treatment.[59] The Royal Council gave its full support to Madrid's reforms, acknowledging that they had cured many illnesses and prevented able-bodied paupers from earning a living by begging.[60] Charles V remarked that the measures 'seem to me very good, and ought to be extended throughout the kingdom'. He expressed satisfaction that the Royal Council no longer placed stumbling blocks before reform proposals.[61]

In Zamora, the royal law also encouraged further reform. At the initiative of Bishop Pedro Manuel, cathedral prelates, the prior of San Juan and mendicant friars met with the city council to discuss reorganization of the traditional charitable system. Together, these religious and secular leaders designed the first comprehensive relief program in Spain. Radically conceived, it elicited diverse reactions within the population and stimulated the most thoughtful and critical analysis of any poor relief reform in Europe.

The Zamoran reformers sought advice and approval for their new order of welfare from doctors at the University of Salamanca. Among the theologians was the noted Dominican friar from San Esteban, Domingo de Soto, who was intensely involved in the plight of the poor in Salamanca at the time.[62] Soto observed that he and other university theologians took issue with some of the plans of the Zamoran reformers, but agreed to consider authorizing a set of ordinances for the regulation of welfare in the city.[63] Sometime in late 1540 or in 1541, at a special session held by the Zamoran city council, the civil authorities formally approved new prohibitions on begging.[64] They sent a copy of the reforms on to the University of Salamanca for the promised signatures. Almost unanimously the theologians, including Domingo de Soto to his later regret, confirmed the ordinances.[65]

Unfortunately a complete set of these regulations has not survived. Our only information on their existence comes from a summary sent to the Crown in 1545 by Juan de Medina, also known as Juan de Robles, abbot of the Benedictine monastery of San Vicente in Salamanca, who was an advocate of the reforms. According to Medina, the reforms in Zamora comprised seven essential points.

Chapter I. Great care will be taken that true paupers not be compelled to beg publicly, and to ensure this, they must be given all that they need during the period of time which they reside [in this city]. They are to be given doles one day for the duration of the entire week, in portions of twelve *maravedís* a day for a man, ten *maravedís* for a woman, and six for a child, in the event that they cannot earn their livelihood by work.

Chapter II. No paupers, not even foreigners, will be excluded from this charity. If they arrive in ill health they will receive medical assistance. And foreigners who wish to live in this town and abide by the system here prescribed will be treated as residents. And he who passes through in need of refreshment before going on his journey will be provided for without being forced to prove his poverty. His word alone if it be given honestly will be trusted. And he may stay as long as the Administrator who is in charge of wayfarers allows.

Chapter III. This charity will not be given except in cases of extreme need to those who do not demonstrate that they have gone to confession or received the Eucharist when the Church requires, nor to those who notoriously lead bad lives.

Chapter IV. This charity will not be given to the idle nor to vagabonds who are capable of working. These people will be compelled to work and earn what they eat by the Chief Magistrate and *corregidor*.

Chapter V. Extra charity which remains after true beggars and travellers have been provided for will be given to the shamefaced, to the extent that the charity can help them. Special care will be taken of the sick who are not hospitalized and who lack sufficient means in their homes to cure themselves. These provisions and alms will be given discreetly, in order that the true paupers not experience affront in receiving them. And young orphans and foundlings will be sheltered and indoctrinated in religion until they are ready to be placed in crafts to which they are inclined. And those who die without means of decent burial will be conveniently interred, according to the status of each.

Chapter VI. In order to accomplish all these pious works, there are two methods of obtaining charity: one is public, of amounts that residents wish to give or promise to give in the future. And (because some people do not want to give more than they can afford, and others do not want to be embarrassed for giving little), no-one can donate more that two *maravedís* a day, and they may give as little as they like, to a single *blanca* [the smallest coin available, amounting to half the value of a *maravedí*]. Since this charity is voluntary, people may notify the Receptor if they do not want to give in the future, and after doing this, they will no longer be asked to provide donations. The other method [of financing the program] is secret, for which there are charity boxes in some churches, located such that no-one is far from one of them.

Chapter VII. To administer this holy business, every half year conscientious people without material need will be elected by the estates of the town. The money will be held in the possession of a Receptor and distributed by him alone. And (since this is a matter of numerous tiny donations), every month the Receptor will register accounts in the presence of the Prelate and *corregidor* or their representatives. A constable or two with badges or recognizable emblems of authority on their night sticks will be appointed to guide travellers to the place where they are to receive their alms, and to place them with masters should they decide to stay and serve the town, and to prevent those who are maintained from begging.[66]

The Zamoran ordinances closely resembled both the Catholic reforms undertaken in Ypres (1525) and Bruges (1526) as described by Vives, and the Imperial Poor Ordinance issued by Charles V at Ghent in 1531. In all the programs, elected officials sought charity in the name of the poor and administered it at central stations once a week. All of them were concerned with properly rearing and educating children and protecting the shamefaced. Moreover, each program denied relief to able-bodied paupers and attempted to provide them with useful employment. Zamoran ordinances were distinctive in taking special precautions to conform with qualifications placed on reform by theologians at the Sorbonne.[67] While the city's reforms discouraged begging, they did not take punitive measures against beggars who did not receive assistance, a requirement not always observed in legislation of the Empire. Zamoran officials felt that since the city was one of the first in Spain to reform public welfare, it would be unjust to exclude non-residents from its program until the other areas provided for the needs of their own poor. This was a remarkably generous action, for the location of Zamora near the poorest provinces of the peninsula guaranteed that if would attract immigrants. And unlike imperial ordinances that limited non-resident support to one day, those of Zamora allowed pilgrims and travellers to stay in the city indefinitely at the discretion of welfare officials. They also attempted to reduce opportunities for ostentatious display of giving in order to prevent embarrassment on the part of those residents with little to donate. The new program would succeed, its designers believed, with voluntary donations.

Relief was administered through the city parishes. Priests worked along with appointed laymen to notify the Administrator of their parishioners' needs. Every Saturday, they distributed food and money sufficient for the entire week to those in need. All was done in secret of course to protect *vergonzantes*. Pilgrims travelling through the city were directed to the home of the Administrator who calculated how much support they would need for the length of time they intended to stay in the area. With his signature, the pilgrims moved on to the Receptor who provided them with food or placed them in hospices.

After their implementation in Zamora, the ordinances were adopted by the cities of Salamanca and Valladolid. In Salamanca as in Zamora, religious and civil authorities worked together in the new program and contributions remained voluntary. Canons of the cathedral and theologians of the university assembly acted as constables of beggars and administrators of charity with the aid of the city council and the Count of Monterrey.[68] Domingo de Soto too took his turn among the theologians in examining the poor for begging licenses.[69]

According to Juan de Medina, the charity received was sufficient to support the poor even though an estimated one-third to one-half of the population did not contribute. Medina believed that since the representatives of the poor who asked for charity were city authorities and priests who wielded considerable influence over the consciences of residents, most who could afford to give did so and he praised the overall efficiency of the program.[70]

In Valladolid, welfare reform proceeded more slowly. After publication of the royal decree of 1540, the city attempted unsuccessfully to prevent non-residents from begging. In accordance with royal regulations, beggars caught without licenses were imprisoned for four days for first offenses and eight days for second offenses, which only resulted in an overcrowding of hungry prisoners in the public jail.[71] It was no place to discipline young people, city authorities lamented, and they began to search for alternative means of support for orphans wandering the streets. Their first step was to work with the confraternity of the Misericordia to institutionalize orphan boys and girls, educate them in Christian doctrine and teach them trades.[72] Then they organized poor *vergonzantes* into a confraternity of their own and solicited donations from the public on their behalf.[73] Council men encouraged other confraternities to increase their aid to urban hospitals in order to institutionalize more beggars and they accompanied cofrades of the Nuestra Señora de la Piedad as they begged food and clothing for their hospital.[74]

It quickly became apparent that work within the existing system was not adequate to accommodate all the city's poor people, and in the summer of 1543 Valladolid decided to reform its welfare situation using the ordinances of Zamora as guidelines. Prodded by the Count of Monterrey who had been active in implementing the new method in Salamanca, city officials applied the rules more rigorously than in Salamanca and Zamora.[75]

But the reforms were beginning to evoke criticism from Castilian townspeople. Indeed it was said that except for the articles of faith, nothing stirred up more controversy than these new ordinances of reform from Zamora.[76] Cardinal Tavera, eager to ascertain learned opinion, questioned Domingo de Soto during his visit to Valladolid in 1544 concerning his views on the regulation of begging. Soto expressed his reservations and confessed that he had been careless in setting his signature to the initial set of ordinances sent him by Zamora, for it had included extreme measures of which he would not have approved had he read them with greater scrutiny.[77]

In November 1544, Prince Philip, regent for his father Charles V, asked Soto and Juan de Medina, known to have encouraged the reforms in Zamora, to present their views. The two theologians from Salamanca addressed the impassioned controversies over public versus private welfare in Castilian as well as in Latin because the subject 'concerned everyone'.[78] Confronting fundamental issues raised by the new restrictions on paupers, their discussions examined the role of the state in the private lives of citizens, expounded and criticized theories of progress, and held up to scrutiny centuries-old Catholic beliefs.

Domingo de Soto objected on both theological and practical grounds to the new prohibitions on mendicity. He considered begging a fundamental human right of which no government should deprive its citizens. In a society afflicted by local pestilence, famine and unemployment, he argued that to curtail paupers from begging outside their birthplace would be to endanger their lives. The state is one body with wealth concentrated in certain areas and poverty in others. Nothing should impede the transfer of material goods to those parts in need, and charity was the normal channel of exchange in this process. 'By natural law and the law of the people,' he asserted, 'everyone can go freely where he can best provide for his necessities.'[79]

Soto also took issue with the rash attempts by municipal officials to identify and punish 'illegitimate' beggars. No-one has the right or the ability to judge whether another is morally justified in receiving charity. Similarly no-one can ascertain material need by weighing all the circumstances compelling a person to solicit assistance. 'For one to be legitimately poor, it is not crucial that one be sick; it is enough to be aged, or frail or possessing some other impediment which prevents one from performing such work as is necessary to sustain oneself and family.' Some people through no fault of their own have no means of support. Persons of high lineage for instance who lose their possessions lack occupational skills to earn their living and they should not be denied the right to beg. Certainly few commoners beg out of laziness. Many of them actually have been forced into indigency by the privileged orders who fail to provide them with land or employment. Soto could be a fierce critic of the upper class, claiming that it promoted the new order to justify its own parsimony in almsgiving. To allocate charity to beggars on the basis of their moral worth, as the reforms attempted to do, is wrong, Soto admonished, for even a most degenerate sinner should not be deprived of life. When some reformers objected that among the poor there were some who had not gone to confession in ten to twenty years, Soto admitted that it might be true, but he turned the argument around in suggesting that 'the same case applies to the rich, and yet no-one takes away their life and food.'[80]

Soto proceeded to provide moral reasons why government should not forbid the poor to beg. He argued with an impeccable sense of justice that before the state could tie beggars' hands, it must secure provision of all the material needs of the people. But this condition, he submitted, was morally as well as practically impossible for government to meet. Consistent with Catholic views on mercy, men of means could not be constrained by force to give alms. Yet only by constraint, in effect only by appropriating the wealth of the propertied classes, could the state assure for itself the means of providing for the poor. And this was not even an option. No-one at the time doubted that the rich had both unquestionable proprietary right to their fortunes and complete personal liberty to either withhold or donate charity. Given the initial premise, the conclusion was inescapable: it was morally unjustifiable to take away paupers' rights to beg.[81] As long as private property remained the foundation of the economic order, the poor could not be deprived of their private right to appeal for sustenance.

In reply to Soto's defense of mendicity Juan de Medina wrote to Philip two months later justifying the city ordinances. He refuted point by point the objections raised by his opponent. While Soto's criticisms of reform were based on the natural rights of the individual, Medina's affirmation stressed the general welfare of society. He favored discrimination in poor relief, arguing that all recipients must be truly in need of material assistance to take advantage of the limited amount of natural resources available. In distributing alms, society should distinguish carefully between Christians and non-Christians. And even among Christians, he argued, care should be taken to select only the righteous. Medina recognized that Christianity encouraged people to give 'to all who beg in the name of God', but he submitted that 'for the good governing of a state, it is best that they give only to those who are deserving'.[82] It was a new type of social engineering that he advocated in transferring welfare from private to public institutions. Political authorities would decide for the first time in the Christian era who would and who would not receive the benefits of charity. Centralised control over alms-giving would have two advantages. It would guarantee that the limited amount of charity or donated money would go to those who really needed help; and it would ensure that these recipients were morally upright citizens of the community.

Medina did not consider begging a right but rather a necessity, a necessity that paupers would relinquish gratefully if other means of support were available. He cited the occasion in 1544 when paupers at the public almshouse in Zamora were asked if they were content with their maintenance, or it they would prefer to be given a license to beg as before. The paupers reportedly answered that they preferred the new method because with it they avoided the affronts that they had encountered while soliciting alms. They were also pleased to be relieved of the endless string of chores that donors had demanded of them on their begging rounds. So for the common good, Medina adduced, law rightly interferes with the individual's freedom.[83]

Medina set his goals high. If Spanish towns co-operated in reorganizing the welfare system, not only would the economy be fortified, for able-bodied beggars deprived of alms would be forced to work, but the international reputation of the country would be raised as well. With this new order, 'the poor will no longer disgrace our Christian towns as they have in the past, crying out, as paupers are wont to cry out through the streets, against cruelty and lack of good government because they are not taken care of except by shouts and importunities.'[84]

The fundamental area of disagreement between Soto and Medina was over the nature of mercy. It was a theoretical issue, the resolution of which would have serious implications for future designs concerning the role of the government in care for the poor. Soto believed that compassion was essential in any charitable program. Isolating paupers in institutions and removing them from the sight of benefactors deprived mercy of its virtue and of its strength. He placed a high value on personal contact of benefactors with the poor, believing that 'the presence of the recipient greatly tends to sway the will'. Soto felt that if welfare were placed in the hands of the state and Christians were forced to donate alms to impersonal institutions, the amount of charity would inevitably decrease and paupers would be in an even worse situation than before the reforms.[85]

Medina disagreed. For him, compassion was not a critical element in an effective welfare system. A sentiment such as compassion was merely a means to an end. Like pity, sadness or pain, this feeling exists, he contended, in order to propel us into action. We should not value the emotion itself but rather the result that it produces. Compassion really means nothing unless it bears fruit in good works. Therefore society should concentrate on the actual relief of the poor rather than on the process whereby donors experience pity for them. He had heard objections 'that whoever removes the poor from the eyes of Christians removes that which is finest in the virtue of charity, which is compassion for the wretched'. But he brushed aside the concern, arguing that there would always be other occasions for the wealthy to be moved to perform acts of mercy. And Christians well might question their own motives in giving alms, he warned. For unless their esteemed compassion derived from natural inclination and not the desire of reward, it was not virtuous. The only genuinely virtuous behavior, he asserted, was to alleviate the suffering of others. It was not only cruel but also deceitful for people to value so highly their own charitable feelings provoked at the sight of misery. His insistent demand was that people concentrate their efforts on eliminating that misery. It was difficult for him to swallow the nostalgic idea that 'during Semana Santa the voices of the poor are needed as much as gentle music is needed at good festivals'. It is far better, he cried out, to take the poor away from their miseries, wounds, lamentations and hunger than to indulge in one's own feelings of compassion.[86]

Medina's pragmatic spirit has inspired later commentators to disparage the claims of Soto as unrepresentative of Catholic opinion.[87] But if we compare the two men's views with the actual practice of relief in Spain, it is clear that Soto's position predominated. The peculiar character of Spanish philanthropy with its ceremonial display of intimately hand-crafted endowments reflected the sentimental attitude expressed by Soto. Zamora enforced the debated ordinances for only a few years and then ceased,[88] with Salamanca and Valladolid following suit. Although the requirement of 1540 that beggars be licensed remained formal law for the next 200 years, it was generally enforced only during periods of crisis. That Soto's views found favor among Spaniards is evident in the fact that his treatise was reprinted twice more in the sixteenth century while Medina's was not published again until the mid-eighteenth century. According to the historian Diego de Colmenares, writing in the early seventeenth century, the arguments in Soto's book were so compelling that they put an end to the many disputes over this issue.[89]

In contrast to the dispassionate and almost undisputed acceptance of reform for the poor in northern Europe and Italy,[90] vehement objections were raised throughout the sixteenth century in Spain. Castilians in particular expressed a fundamental aversion to the transfer of charitable functions from private to government control. They were convinced that poverty was a God-given status that had its own purposes in society, purposes that they felt would be destroyed by bureaucratic administration of poor relief and isolation of the indigent in hospitals. The flames of controversy were stoked with the belief that even the poor enjoyed certain natural rights in society. Some Spaniards protested that the new public welfare schemes were too harsh, for the needy 'are enclosed so that they do not ask for charity, and castigated if they beg; and so many superintendents and officials supervise the poor, that it all seems more like abhorrence of paupers than mercy'.[91] The theologians' criticism that the new order violated the natural rights of paupers to move freely were reiterated to protest the creation of almshouses for their permanent institutiqnalization. Licensing the indigent to beg also appeared inhuman to Castilian townspeople. 'It seems a harsh and humiliating thing to make paupers wear badges.'[92] It is impossible to know how the poor felt about these reforms. Critics of the prohibitions on begging suggested that paupers were not satisfied with their new homes. 'They flee from the back doors of hospitals as if from jails.' Beggars on the streets 'incur the envy and rage of those who must remain in hospitals'.[93]

Medina's ideas surfaced sporadically in Spain during plague epidemics when fear about contagion spread by beggars overcame such concern for the 'liberty of paupers'. During the plague years of the early 1570s, Zamora attempted to place all sick paupers in hospitals but closed its doors to healthy peasants. To protect the city, officials distributed loaves of bread from the public granary to Portuguese, Gallegan and Asturian paupers outside the gates, and sent donations on to Asturias, where they had heard that the population was dying of hunger.[94] During these same years, wandering beggars also found it difficult to obtain lodging in Valladolid, though the city council provided hospitals with additional money for food and medicine.[95]

At this time another reformer, Miguel Giginta, canon of Elna in the arch-diocese of Tarragona, began proposing a new poor relief scheme that attempted to resolve the problem of the traditional liberties of the poor. His ideas were based on a program devised by the Camara of Lisbon for the local confraternity of the Misericordia in the Portuguese capital. Forty cofrades, mostly notables, joined in a compact to purchase housing in one of Lisbon's neighborhoods for the city's poor.[96] They offered the 'Casas de Misericordia', as the institutions were called, to beggars as a place where they could eat and sleep and still retain their freedom of mobility in society. Unlike other reformed poor houses in which patrons solicited charity to support inmates, the Lisbon homes allowed the poor to beg publicly for their own support at carefully prescribed times. Cofrades assumed duties within the Casas. An annually elected head and four councillors kept accounts and arranged employment for paupers by placing them as servants to city residents or assigning them to crafts within the home. The other cofrades alternated household duties, working for an hour or more in the morning and an hour at night.

Giginta offered the plans of the Lisbon Misericordia as a model for poor houses throughout Spain. He carefully drew a design for the Casas, emphasizing the practicality of their construction in order to appeal to government bureaucrats. At the same time he was able to incorporate enough Christian symbolism into the reformed houses to encourage pious donors. Each Casa was to be of light and inexpensive material, divided into four sections, in the form of a cross, for men, women, boys and girls. The paupers would contribute to their own support by working in the Casa at a task which suited their skills. The blind would work with iron, the crippled in tailoring, women would weave cloth or make ribbons, lace, buttons, and garments. Giginta hoped that master artisans in the cities would be willing to donate time to teach crafts to the paupers. Children would be taught to read, write and count.

But Giginta did not prevent paupers from supporting their Casa in the traditional manner through begging. Paupers would beg in the morning, at noon, and again at the hour of dinner when they could take advantage of meal-time opportunities, 'going two by two through the streets asking in a loud voice in the name of Christ's mercy'. The most pitiable paupers in the homes, he advised, should go a-begging to solicit alms on behalf of the others. Giginta understood that beggars fared well at religious events and so he recommended that they all solicit alms on holy days and participate in sacred processions. Paupers should also accompany funerals and carry their customary torches for the dead to take advantage of opportunities to obtain new clothes.[97]

Giginta was an able campaigner for his cause. After sending copies of the proposal to the Cortes of Castile, he sought to persuade the president of the Royal Council of the value of his welfare scheme.[98] In *Tratado de remedio de pobres*, he presented to the president a propaganda piece written in the form of a dialogue. Valerio, his protagonist in the treatise, supported common homes for the poor, while Mario opposed the plan. Valerio led the discussion by criticizing popular sentimentality concerning the poor. Some people, he complained, rhapsodized that 'the finest music for God and for our souls both within and outside churches is the begging of the poor, accompanied by our commiserating and succoring them...' Continuing the poetic imagery, he quoted with feigned sincerity the notion that 'the best church ornament is the sight of paupers, who one can say are the living stones of temples, being helped'. Valerio believed that this excessively idealized image of the poor conflicted with the actual treatment of paupers by society. The appearance of beggars merely caused the rich to turn their heads, if not flee in disgust and fear. Paupers were by no means always cherished as religious sentiment would have it. They were also cursed and kicked and ignored. To Valerio, the poor would be far better off in homes of their own than serving as ornaments for those who were more fortunate.

Mario responded along traditional lines, arguing that one could not enclose the poor in good conscience because that would violate the true spirit of charity as well as the natural liberty of paupers. A poor house deprived the people of their freedom; it was an invention that neither God nor his disciples ordered. His objections allowed Valerio to present one of the most attractive features of the proposed Casas de Misericordia. Paupers would be allowed to come and go as they wished after their work was done, 'because humans need diversion and recreation, especially those who are accustomed to leading a life of complete liberty and who cannot discipline themselves readily'. What is interesting in the reformer's response is his recognition that paupers had a right to move about freely. He rejected the assumption of other welfare reformers that the state possessed the prerogative to institutionalize beggars in order to protect the health and safety of the commonweal.

Mario then reminded the eager reformer of the unsuccessful attempts to regulate begging by Zamora and neighboring cities. 'Look, more than 30 years ago, some parts of Castile wanted to do this very thing, and they had to discard it because the famous theologian Domingo de Soto opposed it, saying it was a project against one's conscience.' Valerio's response to this challenge revealed that the new reforms were conceived in a much more conservative manner than the city ordinances of the 1540s. He contested that Soto's treatise had been written to confront the 'impious' order that some towns established 'more to liberate the rich of inconveniences and nuisances than to adequately provide for the indigent'. He contrasted the Casas de la Misericordia with the reforms of Zamora, saying (with only partial accuracy) that the latter had rejected non-residents and had enclosed residents against their wills, 'like prisoners'. Forbidden to beg, these paupers no longer stood as objects for the mercy of the population.[99] His Casas de la Misericordia on the other hand would respect the traditional rights of paupers and take advantage of the Christian sentiment of mercy.

Giginta's plan was essentially a compromise between the ideas of

Domingo de Soto and Juan de Medina in allowing the indigent to beg and move about among the people and yet work for their welfare when possible in their own home.[100] His moderate views gained the attention of Zamoran officials, who in 1581 asked Giginta to aid them in erecting a new home for paupers in the city. The reformer sent on a copy of his proposal with the admonition that their institution 'not resemble a school or anything like a prison, but rather an orderly home of good Christian handicraft workers'. He mentioned that his program had been accepted by municipal governments in Granada, Toledo and Madrid in spite of some local opposition, and he suggested that the council hold a general procession, as was done in Madrid, to ascertain the reaction of residents to the new project.[101]

Had Giginta's project been able to stand alone, it might have met more success, but it quickly became involved in a more radical attempt by the church and the central government to centralize administration of hospitals in the realm. For over a century, various clergymen and town officials had been calling for a reduction in the number of hospitals to simplify distribution of poor relief.[102] They considered confraternities directly responsible for inadequacies in their current health care system. Procuradores denounced confraternities for spending too much of their corporate charity on festival banquets,[103] and the church complained that their pursuit of the acts of mercy was so undisciplined that they made poor relief woefully inefficient. To prevent further accretion of private charitable programs, synodal constitutions prohibited new confraternities from forming without episcopal permission. Organizations that did not submit to the rule were forced to pay large fines to the church, which distributed the payments to hospitals and paupers, the assumed victims of unregulated charitable activity.[104] The Council of Trent heard complaints about the recalcitrance of Spanish confraternities in the face of ecclesiastical attempts to co-ordinate their poor relief activities. During the early sessions of Trent, the apostolic preacher of Andalucia, Juan de Avila, accused them of betraying their opportunities to perform good deeds for the poor by incurring heavy expenses at festivals and by distributing among themselves alms intended for the poor. He recommended that the church merge confraternal charitable institutions into one or two hospitals per city and extend to local prelates control over their finances.[105]

On this matter, secular authorities in Spain were in agreement with the church hierarchy. Many times in the sixteenth century magistrates in Zamora and Valladolid had attempted to limit the number of confraternities and hospitals in order to facilitate inspection of premises.[106] In 1581–83 the Crown decided to join the movement for reform. Philip II circulated a royal provision to all major Castilian towns and cities requesting that each hospital and confraternity send him a report of its financial resources, its founders and its charitable obligations. The king explained that he intended to redirect these resources to one or two hospitals in every town. He declared that a great amount of money currently was being wasted on personnel and that many small hospitals did not have the facilities or income to care properly for the sick. Under the present system, moreover, he stated that it was difficult for episcopal visitors to ascertain that cofrades respected the wills of founders and donors and carried out their pious duties.[107] This concern was indicative of a growing authoritarian movement across Europe. Civil and religious leaders were attempting to inspect the consciences of the community.

When the ordinary of the Zamoran bishopric and officials of the municipal council received the request for a survey of the city's hospitals, they immediately gave their support to the policy of consolidation.[108] Zamora's city fathers envisioned unifying the medical care of the 13 smallest hospitals whose combined rents amounted to 856 624 bushels of grain every year. Since the hospital of San Ildefonso treated primarily plague victims and those with other contagious diseases, they excluded it from the proposed amalgamation. Upon investigation of city facilities, it became apparent that only one hospital, the Sotelo, had sufficient space and facilities to incorporate all the health care services of Zamora. Originally the Sotelo had been designed to admit 20 paupers, although at times as many as 70 patients were accommodated in its rooms. It alone had land on which to expand and an adequate water supply for many more patients.

But this planned centralization of Zamora's hospitals encountered serious obstacles when brought to the attention of residents. At the outset administrators of the Hospital of Sotelo refused to amalgamate its services with those of other hospitals. The mayordomo and patrons, who included a representative of the monastery of San Francisco, a canon of the cathedral, and Francisco de Sotelo, cousin of the founder, vowed to block the reform. They decided to send Francisco de Sotelo to ask the Crown not to violate the will of the hospital's founder by transforming its original purposes. He prepared to argue that the foundation left by Alonso de Sotelo was sufficient to care for the poor in its charge.[109]

Zamora's smaller hospitals gave the city council their own reasons for preserving their individual identities. The Misericordia claimed that it provided useful and unique services in burying the poor. Others claimed that the bequests supporting their hospitals carried with them obligations to hear masses, which would be difficult to honor under one system. In making out the survey, moreover, councilmen recognized that some hospitals had no rents at all. They were supported only by the charity of cofrades, a source of income which would dissolve with the abolition of the private confraternities. Taking these factors into consideration, the city ultimately decided not to unify its hospital facilities. Zamora maintained its confraternal system into the mid-eighteenth century.

Several town governments near Zamora succeeded, if only temporarily, in limiting the number of their hospitals despite resistance by cofrades. Upon receiving the Crown's instructions, the city fathers of Salamanca agreed to reduce 19 hospitals to two, leaving one within the city for paupers and the infirm, and another outside the walls for people with contagious diseases.[110] Special concessions were made nevertheless to preserve the symbolic expression of the acts of mercy. Officials allowed the confraternity of Nuestra Señora de Rocamador, located near the stone bridge, to continue its traditional hospitality to pilgrims by transferring to a separate ward in the new general hospital of Santísima Trinidad. There cofrades of Rocamador acquired jurisdiction over 50 pine wood beds reserved for pilgrims. They assumed charge of the property and finances of the pilgrimage ward and designed their own rules. They were given complete autonomy in allocating places to pilgrims as long as no more than two hostellers were put to a bed. Councilmen also allowed flagellants of the Vera Cruz to maintain its almshouse in the monastery of San Francisco, where it customarily performed ritual acts of distributing bread and money to paupers as well as blankets to widows. Reformers tried to assure donors of Salamanca that the newly reorganized hospital system would not obstruct observance of masses and prayer services on behalf of their souls.[111] For these purposes the Santísima Trinidad would commission seven priests to say weekly masses in the name of welfare contributors, and the city's confraternities would continue their purely devotional exercises in their own churches and chapels.

It took the city council in Medina del Campo until 1587 to consolidate its hospitals after a long battle with local charitable corporations. The council attempted not only to dissolve most of the small confraternal hospices but also to divert the rents of brotherhoods without hospitals for use by the General Hospital. Out of over 60 confraternities of craftsmen in the city, the council elected to preserve six whose acts of mercy were considered particularly valuable. It also exempted from the process of consolidation the confraternities of the Santíssimo Sacramento, representing the city's parishes. For the rest, the new General Hospital in Medina del Campo absorbed all their charitable activities and processed them into bureaucratic relief programs. It provided clothing, medicine, surgical and convalescent services for the sick; it extended lodging to pilgrims; and it raised foundlings and orphans.[112]

The movement to centralize hospitals advanced in other areas of Castile as well. In 1584, the five hospitals of the town of Villalpando that survived an attempt at consolidation a century earlier united to form the General Hospital, or Sancti Spiritus, at the insistence of the bishop of Leon.[113] Philip II ordered Madrid's 15 institutions to merge into two major hospitals, the General Hospital and the hospital of Antón Martín serving patients with contagious or incurable diseases. But in the king's capital, reform did not proceed smoothly; only six of the hospitals were in fact eliminated while the others continued to operate.[114] More impressively, in Sevilla 76 out of 112 hospitals merged into the hospitals of Espíritu Santo and Amor de Dios.[115]

Within a decade, cities with centralized relief agencies and those with traditional private forms of welfare confronted the real test – the test of the comparable effectiveness of their respective systems. In the 1590s, the tragic decline of Spain as a major European power began. The economy seriously weakened, increasing the ranks of the unemployed and creating extensive indigency problems. The most severe outbreak of the bubonic plague since the Black Death of the fourteenth century struck northern Spain and was moving down the peninsula, bringing with it an influx of refugees from Asturias and Galicia.[116] The battle between public and private relief joined once again. In the early stages of decline, one could hear the Cortes of Madrid announcing that the reduction of hospitals had not been useful. Representatives of the three estates petitioned that consolidated hospitals be returned to their previous condition. They called upon the Spanish people to found new hospitals, a request that several individuals and confraternities promptly proceeded to fulfill.[117]

As private beneficence appeared to gain the upper hand, one last dedicated reformer, Cristóbal Pérez de Herrera, attempted in these difficult years to sustain the languishing movement to rationalize poor relief. Primary physician in the court of Philip II and Philip III,[118]

Pérez de Herrera called for a national program to establish workhouses. Perceiving that a major weakness in the reform schemes of his predecessors was that many urban areas did not co-operate and that those paupers who were turned down in one town merely travelled to another, he proposed that every city in the realm implement reforms at the same time. To enforce such a scheme, the physician realized that he had to gain the support of the Crown's ministers. By 1592, he won over Friar Diego de Yepes, confessor to the King, and Rodrigo Vázquez Arce, President of the Royal Council. He submitted his first discourse, 'Del amparo y reformación de los fingidos vagabundos', to the Cortes on 13 April 1595.[119] The reaction was immediate and favorable. On 20 April the Cortes petitioned Philip II to implement Pérez de Herrera's plans and repeated the request in February the next year. In January 1597, the President of the Royal Council sent instructions based on Pérez de Herrera's reform to fifty towns and villages in the kingdom to co-ordinate their programs.[120]

The policy that Pérez de Herrera advocated was a mixture of practical ingenuity and moral asceticism. Using the Aristotelian metaphor of society as comparable to the human body, his therapy was to get all its members working in harmony. Each city should erect a special workhouse to instruct the poor in trades in order to facilitate a general recovery of the economy.[121] Once the economy was recuperating and the poor learned good work habits, Pérez de Herrera speculated that it would not be difficult for able paupers to find employment. Some would return to their previous jobs, while a number of men would serve the king in war. Others would act as household servants and the remainder might go into the countryside to farm.

The physician-reformer also believed that once false beggars were usefully employed, there would be no lack of funds for the sustenance of the truly poor. Even former beggars would give charity graciously, for they 'know well what it was like to be poor'. Other people, convinced now that they were giving to the worthy Christian poor, would donate generously. Within Pérez de Herrera's workhouses, as in Giginta's Casas de Misericordia, paupers would be asked to do meaningful chores. (One avid supporter of the poor houses called them 'Palacios del Desengaño' because those paupers who feigned illnesses and disabilities were miraculously cured when they found that they must work.[122]) They would be allowed to collect their own alms as well, a policy that undoubtedly would have pleased the anti-reformer Domingo de Soto. The poorhouse beggar would carry sacred insignia around the neck, including a portrait of a cross, an image of the Virgin and a rosary, in addition to the arms of the city in which he was licensed to beg.[123] Again, religion was conceived of as at the service of the state.

Pérez de Herrera's concern to employ paupers in 'meaningful work' was representative of the practical reforms of the *arbitristas*, writers who proposed solutions to the troubles afflicting the nation in the late sixteenth and early seventeenth centuries. These social reformers perceived that the economic problems of Spain were exacerbated by manpower deficiencies which the employment of the poor would alleviate.[124] Pérez de Herrera planned to use the poor in industry and recommended that foundlings and orphans learn mathematics rather than Latin 'to become, not clerics or men of letters, but architects, engineers, and artillery men'.[125]

So many times pleas for reform like his had gone out. So many times they had ended in failure. By the end of the sixteenth century urban governments finally refused to entertain another scheme, too weakened for the experiment again. Zamora's city council briefly considered setting up a large hospice for beggars late in 1597, meeting with the ecclesiastical estate to determine whether or not the city possessed sufficient facilities and financial resources for an almshouse. They decided that the expenses of such a building was prohibitively high due to the impoverished condition of city residents, and feared that a large home for paupers would simply attract more non-residents. 'Since we are situated near Galicia and Portugal, if we had an almshouse here, such a large quantity of paupers would gather that we would never be able to support them.'[126] Instead the city narrowed its focus and sought to provide for poor residents by distributing bread to parishes and soliciting charity at homes of private individuals. Although contributions followed and city fathers praised the generosity of residents, physicians lamented that still beggars were sick with hunger. Men were dying in the streets, creating such hazardous and unsanitary conditions, the physicians warned, that residents might well worry of plague in the summer. In response, the municipal council divided the city into four sections and appointed a constable for each to ensure that the homeless remained in institutions and that the very ill secured hospitalization. It ordered the constables to send able-bodied vagrants away with a few coins and a pound of bread, and to 'do it gently'.[127] The bishop of Zamora described the year of 1598 as one of much hunger, remembering a day when 1000 paupers came to his door for alms. He claimed not to have sold a single bushel of wheat that year, giving it all away to the poor along with over 8000 ducats of charity. In 1599, plague took the lives of many of the people in his jurisdiction, causing a drop in rents and smaller harvests. In the year 1600, the bishop noted that there was a slight increase in the supply of wheat but pessimistically warned that 'there is no escape from the scarcity'.[128]

Valladolid experienced similar problems of food shortage and rampant hunger in its countryside, and like Zamora, its government made half-hearted attempts to provision the needy. In 1597, the city council estimated that more than 300 paupers without homes were circulating in the city and produced for each of them an insignia to wear while begging.[129] In fear of plague, the council tried to accommodate paupers in existing confraternal hospitals. When, in the spring of 1599, they were forced to expel many healthy non-resident paupers for lack of rooms, they transformed the suburban hospital of San Lázaro into a General Hospital for non-residents.[130] By mid-summer the General Hospital was filled to capacity with 280 paupers, and the city's brothel converted into a hospice for more homeless people. At least 800 paupers sheltered in Valladolid's hospitals at the end of 1599. And yet neither the new General Hospital, with all the funds that the city was capable of generating, nor the old confraternities could attend to the needs of all the poor.[131] Beggars clamouring 'that they had come due to the sterility of the year, from the mountains and from Asturias and Galicia and other parts', wandered through the streets but found that the charity had been exhausted.[132] Physicians provided medical services without reimbursement. Welfare services in Valladolid, as in Zamora, failed in these calamitous years.

It is doubtful whether either the reformed system of poor relief or the traditional confraternal system could have provided adequately for the needs of a country experiencing such extraordinary afflictions as those of the late sixteenth century in Spain. Contemporaries did not agree on where to place the blame. Despite the many failures of confraternal charity, centralized poor relief generally was not considered an improvement. Many townsmen disliked the new order, calling reformers and poorhouse administrators 'impious almsgivers'.[133] A poorhouse opened in 1598 to confine Madrid's mendicants did not survive more than a few years. There it was argued that if paupers are prevented from begging in the open air as is their custom, 'they will become anxious and restless, believing themselves to be in jail and apt to become sick for lack of exercise and ventilation'.[134]

Institutionalization of the poor was attempted again by the Spanish government in the eighteenth century but encountered the same opposition. Eighteenth-century welfare reformers deplored the 'extravagant' popular opinion that paupers should not be deprived of their liberty. Campomanes looked back uneasily to earlier times when Spaniards ruined, with their 'sophistic and futile worries', the plans for welfare reform enacted in Zamora, and he fretted over the prospects for success of his program to extend Casas de Misericordia throughout the peninsula.[135] These and other efforts to confine beggars in hospices received little co-operation from townspeople who looked upon the institutions as 'houses of abomination'.[136]

In the course of the sixteenth century, Spaniards regarded the efforts made by the cities of Zamora, Salamanca and Valladolid to prohibit begging and institutionalize paupers as inimical to the nature of mercy and social justice. Without popular sympathy, not even the Crown could enforce the costly welfare projects, dependent still on voluntary contributions. The confraternities had no desire to subsume their acts of mercy into centralized relief programs and steadfastly refused to eliminate ritual banquets and festivals in order to direct more funds to poor relief. By the end of the century, the state was forced to concede the traditional social practice of private almsgiving, asking the 'good people' in individual parishes to support their own poor. Although Spain had begun to reform welfare along lines similar to northern European cities such as Ypres and Mons, it diverged from these models in the course of experimentation. Local confraternities, private individuals and convents recovered from the authorities major responsibility for succoring the poor. 'What is done in other countries is not necessarily a good example for us', Domingo de Soto had warned the king in a commentary on the character of the Spanish people, 'because there the citizens are more inclined to the common good and remain more obedient to existing law than we.'[137]

Differences between Hispanic and trans-Pyrenean cultures intensified with Spain's retention of medieval forms of poor relief. As northern European cities moved into the modern period experimenting with welfare techniques, their treatment of the poor increasingly differed from that of Zamora and its neighboring towns which kept the confraternal system intact. Poor relief reform ruptured the traditional European commonwealth of charity. While medieval Europe once had been bound by a universally shared code of Christian ethics that served a common charitable system, sixteenth-century Europe was split into two entirely different welfare codes. The old one was based on two castes of rich and poor, the new on a more complex social hierarchy that included, most importantly, an assertive middle class. The fact that Spain did not adopt the new welfare approach reflects both its greater attachment to the cultural expressions of the past and its simpler social structure.[138] No-one stood between rich and poor in Spain – not the government, nor the middle class, nor 'undeserving' or 'able-bodied' men. The channels of charity remained open in this society.

Did Spanish paupers suffer from the conservation of confraternal charity? If we consider the evaluations made by scholars on welfare conditions in other parts of Europe, we might well harbor some doubt. For outside Spain, measures to discipline and repress the indigent increased distressingly throughout the sixteenth and seventeenth centuries. Disenchantment with the poor grew as people rejected the idea that the life of poverty contained within itself spiritual value. Not only was public begging frowned upon in most of these middle-class societies but people caught soliciting for life's material necessities were often severely punished. Local governments in England and France enforced fines for almsgiving, the pillory for begging, and threatened those who would not work with banishment, whipping, branding and the galleys.[139] Plans to confine the poor permanently in workhouses and correction homes, euphemistically called by the traditional term 'general hospitals', spread throughout seventeenth-century France and Holland and finally into England in the early eighteenth century.[140] The poor no longer possessed an integral place within the community. Beggars and vagabonds were suspected of crime and violence and held responsible for failures in the economy. The affluent classes considered the indigent a socially marginal group that ought to be separated from the community.

Centralized poor relief gave both religious and civil authorities greater control over the private lives of citizens. Among communities experiencing intense confessional rivalries, poor relief administrators often used food distributions as a form of religious pressure and moral discipline. In the early seventeenth century, rectors in Lyon required a catechism lesson and attendance at mass from poor men receiving bread. In Nîmes after 1651 both Catholics and Protestants used money to encourage conversion or prevent abjuration. Paupers were deprived of aid for reasons of adultery, blasphemy or marriage with anyone from another faith.[141]

The tendency of seventeenth-century European welfare was to isolate beggars physically and morally in order to condemn their way of life. This new practice differed greatly from that of late medieval confraternities which had involved regularly inviting paupers and beggars to participate at their feast-day tables. Michel Foucault has interpreted the harsher treatment of the poor as the triumph of bourgeois and capitalist intentions to secure a 'normal' world in which all potentially dangerous or undesirable individuals such as the indigent, sick, idle, retarded and handicapped, would be isolated from contact with society.[142] This new sentiment directly conflicted with traditional Catholic views that personal contact was indispensable to the proper functioning of social welfare. Without the presence of paupers to make visible the spiritual teaching of poverty and humility, it had always been feared that the wealthy would discontinue donations.

In Spain, where the traditional evaluation of the poor and feeble as representatives of Christ persisted longer, charitable institutions of the early modern period demonstrated little of the concern to confine and ostracize beggars. The absence in Spain of alternative relief measures to control the needy was not due to lethargy, for ambitious new programs were initiated even if quickly discarded. Nor did the country lack practical means to enforce public welfare. The royal government in Castile encouraged reforms and offered its bureaucracy to administer welfare programs already designed by north European governments. Rejection of the new techniques was a conscious decision made by testators and almsgivers who insisted on delivering their money personally, thereby ensuring the failure of voluntary general hospitals.

Only a few of the practically-minded *arbitristas* in Spain would admit of the suggestion once made by Juan de Medina that the best act of mercy for public beggars was physical punishment.[143] It is true, however, that treatment of the poor became somewhat harsher in the course of the sixteenth century. The expulsion of non-resident beggars from urban areas in the last decades contrasted with generous attempts in Zamora during the 1540s to assign wealthy residents to individual paupers, or in Toledo to place paupers in private households to ensure their maintenance.[144] Prohibitions on begging and confinement in almshouses nonetheless were enforced only temporarily during periods of extreme financial stress. In more prosperous times, Spanish authorities left almsgiving to the discretion of individuals. They rejected ideas of northern reformers that welfare ought to be taken from private initiative and transferred to authorities because as Martin Bucer once said, 'it is hard for one man to know all, and things be more easily spied out by those who are appointed for this purpose'.[145] Domingo de Soto argued instead that charitable givers should not even attempt to scrutinize the physical and moral qualities of those in need. This attitude was articulated more widely in the common projection of an unsparing and clement spirit of mercy upon the Virgin Mary, the Spanish representative of Christian virtue. In the centuries-old debates btween Justice and Mercy posed by theologians and dramatized by the public in religious plays, Mercy generally triumphed over the narrower preoccupations of Justice.[146]

Travellers to Spain in the early modern period remarked on the differences between welfare practices in their own countries and those of the Iberian peninsula. Joseph Townsend was amazed at the extent of charitable services provided in Oviedo, the capital of one of the poorer regions of Spain. He exclaimed that little more could have been done to assist the indigent than that which was already performed at the city's *hospicio* where 280 men, women and children were comfortably accommodated. Residents' charity also supported infants in the hands of wet nurses and provided prelates and monasteries with outdoor relief to the poor. Yet Townsend felt troubled by all this charity, which he constantly referred to throughout his travels in Spain as 'mistaken generosity'. He once dared to ask the Asturian bishop if he were not doing paupers a disservice by offering alms so readily and perhaps depriving them of incentive to work. 'Most undoubtedly', the prelate responded, 'but then it is the part of the magistrate to clear the streets of beggars; it is my duty to give alms to all who ask'.[147] Poor relief in Leon-Castile displayed an expansive view of brotherhood similar to that evoked in the earliest Christian writings on fraternal love. In principle, charity was not to be denied for reasons of immorality or improper behavior. How dramatically this approach differed from that of public welfare institutions which made a conscious effort to distinguish between 'deserving' and 'undeserving' poor!

Welfare in Castile also dismissed genteel concern to avoid contact with dirt, disease and stench. These conditions for the truly pious were the physical trials that helped them transcend the comforts of the flesh. The hospital, the street gutter and the brothel were flash points from which the presence of God emanated as clearly as from the rural shrine. Confraternities sought to encompass unpleasant and sinful areas of the urban environment by turning them into charitable causes.

Cofrades of Nuestra Señora de la Piedad y Pobres de la Cárcel in Zamora regularly visited the local jail to perform their holy work, and those of the Misericordia sought out the poor and sick in the streets. It was not the custom, even among aristocrats, to turn away from urban squalor to exhibit delicacy of temperament. It is indeed difficult to imagine a more inclusive or more expedient welfare system in the period than that which named the Cofradía de Nuestra Señora de la Consolación y Concepción to police a local prostitution house in Valladolid and extract part of the proceeds for urban charitable programs.[148] At a time when Protestant cities were forcibly closing brothels,[149] the parish confraternities of Spain adopted gentler methods to discourage prostitution. The Cofradía de la Santa Caridad in Toledo provided small amounts of money to prostitutes for purchasing food during Holy Week to enable them to stop practicing their occupations. The women were also indoctrinated in Christian precepts with the hope that they would abandon their ways entirely.[150] All across Spain, prostitutes as well as prisoners, beggars and *conversos* were allowed to form their own confraternities to enjoy the benefits of spiritual brotherhood.[151]

Confraternal welfare embraced a variety of needs, revealing a relatively high level of social tolerance. It sought to aid diverse elements of the population and reform the moral habits of the poor and unfortunate through compassion, almsgiving, and, whenever opportunities arose, through religious instruction. In this the confraternities presented a marked contrast to the more frequently drawn picture of inquisitorial intolerance in Spanish society during the period of the Catholic Reformation.

If the strength of religious belief was the basis for rejecting the harshest disciplinarian welfare schemes that blamed the poor for their conditions with punishment and confinement, then it helped Spain avoid a form of injustice practiced elsewhere in the west. But the question raised by Juan de Medina as to whether it were not better for the poor to have a welfare system that made more efficient use of material resources than one that maximized society's compassion remained a valid consideration for the sixteenth century as it still does today. It is difficult to ascertain, however, if the centralized relief programs of northern Europe, designed to allocate resources efficiently, provided for the poor better than Spain's decentralized system, primarily because we lack accurate indices of poverty. Northern Europe, moreover, was experiencing unprecedented economic prosperity at the end of the sixteenth century while Spain was undergoing severe economic recession, so that the number of paupers in the respective areas did not depend exclusively on the organization of poor relief facilities. Experienced sixteenth-century vagabonds who roamed both northern and southern Europe may have formed an opinion on the matter of the relative effectiveness of the two systems, but unfortunately it has not been recorded.

Without a doubt, few of the means of support available to the indigent in Spain in the late sixteenth century were satisfactory. Unless paupers belonged to their own confraternities, in which they were treated as equal partners in programs of mutual assistance, the relief that they received was highly competitive, seasonal, and burdened with obligations to return spiritual favors. And yet those Spanish reformers who criticized the confraternal system did so because they felt that it was too lenient and too inefficient – an uncompromising complaint. While they argued cogently that traditional concern for the spiritual welfare of benefactors was not necessarily in the best interest of the poor, the alternatives that they offered, designed to protect almsgivers from 'undeserving' beggars and to stimulate the economy for the middle class, were no more in their favor. The social esteem that medieval charity bestowed upon the poor in considering them intercessors with God, early modern public welfare took away by condemning them for their economic dependency. The choice between the welfare agencies of the medieval moral economy and of the modern profit economy was not a happy one for the poor, for neither system was intended to do more than alleviate the worst ills of poverty.

4 The Catholic Reformation and Tradition

Among the most important issues currently confronting historians of the early modern period is the degree to which the two Reformations, Protestant and Catholic, affected the religious lives of the common people in Europe. It is a matter that has engendered intense debate ever since the publication in 1971 of Jean Delumeau's survey of the literature in Catholic Reformation history. In his book, Delumeau raised to unprecedented heights the stature of the Reformation's contribution to western civilization, arguing that sixteenth-century religious movements succeeded in evangelizing the majority of the European people for the first time in the history of Christianity. The thesis rests on the premise that the common people of the Middle Ages were only vaguely informed of the precepts of the gospel and that their spiritual world-view more closely approximated to pagan than orthodox Christian beliefs. Keith Thomas had argued along similar lines that the English Reformation was responsible for replacing the medieval notions of a world animated by magical forces with a more modern view of a universe controlled by divine providence.[1]

This extremely positive evaluation of the role of the Reformations, with its implicit condemnation of medieval heterodoxy, has been criticized by many social historians. Those sympathetic with the 'longue durée' approach to history are skeptical that such a complex process as the Christianization of Europe could have been achieved in the course of two centuries given the organizational structures of the Catholic and Protestant churches. To date, most of the discussion among historians rests on speculation and professional instinct, although a few scholars have set out to test the Delumeau thesis in local studies. By re-creating the conditions of pre-Reformation religious activities in the countryside, where the vast majority of the population lived, they hope to see more clearly any change that might have been brought about later as a result of official church policies. Gerald Strauss made the first step in this direction by exploring indoctrination programs of Lutheran reformers in sixteenth-century Germany. After careful evaluation of evidence in official visitation reports he was compelled to conclude that the reformers failed to eradicate superstitious beliefs and rituals among the peasantry, and he challenged the idea that Protestant reforms reached the masses.[2]

115

Scholars of Catholic countries are just beginning to pay attention to the problem. They seek to find evidence of either acceptance or rejection of Tridentine reforms by the populace. Sara Nalle has affirmed that in the decades following the Council of Trent, the laity in the province of Cuenca recited common prayers more accurately and more often responded with the correct answer to questions on creed posed by the Inquisition than they had in earlier years.[3] In his study of the diocese of Lyon, Philip Hoffman notices less advancement. He is convinced that the Counter Reformation made an impact only in urban areas and demonstrates that even here reforming clergy experienced constant difficulties and setbacks in trying to discipline folk religion.[4] Further investigation into local histories will undoubtedly yield a more detailed and subtle perspective on the evolution of popular religious culture from the medieval to the modern period. In evaluating medieval religion, we must keep in mind that definitions of what it meant to be 'Christian' changed over time and avoid applying exclusively Tridentine standards to this earlier period. Undoubtedly many pious medieval theologians would have been anathemized had the church of their time held to the rigorous definitions of orthodoxy authorized later at Trent.

A second and related problem that confronts scholars of the early modern period is whether Tridentine reforms in particular broke with traditional religious practices or merely purified old customs and ways of thinking among the laity. In the process of reforming abuses, did Trent create a new Catholic culture? Or did Tridentine policies result in a more or less complete reaffirmation of medieval Christianity? Clues to both these historiographical issues are revealed in the interaction of Counter Reformation policies on popular culture in Zamora. In seeking to control lay piety, church fathers at Trent reached out to every episcopal see in Christendom. Zamora, like the others, was pulled into its reforming grip.

When theologians met at Trent to discuss the means by which they might restore Catholic unity to Europe, they wrestled with two conflicting concerns. On the one hand, well-placed criticisms by Catholics as well as Protestants of ignorance and moral laxity in the church convinced them of the need for purification of the religious life. Radical ideas among Protestants, on the other hand, such as 'faith alone' and the 'priesthood of all believers' seemed to threaten the very essence of Catholic belief and drew from the Council's leaders a strong negative reaction. They responded to Protestant innovations in theology by reaffirming tradition on questions of faith and doctrine. In administrative matters, however, they moved in new directions, and it was here that Trent exerted influence upon the dioceses to transform the character of popular piety.

Church fathers realized that weakness in the understanding of doctrine and abuses in ritual practices called for substantial reform of pastoral services. Their first objective therefore was to extend closer ecclesiastical supervision over lay religious activities and improve instruction in church doctrine by strengthening ties of pastors with parishioners. This effort brought them directly into conflict with confraternities which, since the late fifteenth century, had offered extensive opportunities for lay participation and occasional management in liturgical functions. Until required to say daily masses in the seventeenth and eighteenth centuries, parish priests normally had performed only one or two masses a week for their congregations.[5] It was rather the confraternities, with their private oaths to observe masses on holidays and on anniversaries of members' deaths, that had taken the initiative to institute and attend regular eucharistic celebrations. The confraternities scheduled masses on their own, financed them with their private funds, and appointed their own ordained cofrades as presiding officers. Since these members frequently came from the mendicant orders, confraternal services caused continual tension with parish pastors in the cities.

Other services performed by confraternities competed with parochial activities as well. They maintained their own chapels, chaplains, and images. They called for rogations in times of need and filled the streets with processions in honor of patron saints. Confraternities not only regulated the frequency with which their members made confessions, they also constituted the public or semi-public social groups in which restitution for sins was made after absolution by priests.[6] They assumed responsibilities, moreover, that in a later period were reserved for parish priests, such as carrying extreme unction to the dying and announcing deaths to the public by ringing bells.

So many confraternities operated in Spanish society that the church found it impossible to supervise thoroughly their activities. At mid-century, a parish priest in Toledo complained bitterly that 'with so many brotherhoods, the laymen are in such firm control that they order the priests around as if they were day-laborers'.[7] Despite repeated attempts by local episcopal supervisors to regulate corporate pursuits by inspecting statutes,[8] the organizations eluded their control. The ecclesiastical estate in Spain complained to Pope Paul

IV in 1556 that confraternities violated clerical authority and provoked numerous private scandals.

> We have received much harm and poor example from the confraternities which are called San Juan de Letrán and Sancti Spiritus and from diverse others that have been instituted in some bishoprics and cities and villages in these realms. Many persons of sinful personal habits and others who owe many debts enter these confraternities wishing to protect themselves with ecclesiastical jurisdiction. And with these privileges and exemptions, such persons evade our authority to punish, and do not pay their debts. In addition, they bury [their members] with tall crosses without calling the parish priest, and administer the sacraments to whomever asks for them as well as to cofrades. We beg that such privileges and concessions of exemptions to laypeople and clerics of these hospitals and confraternities be revoked.[9]

The universal brotherhood of believers in Spain posed almost as great a threat to Catholic clergymen as the universal priesthood conceived by Protestants, a situation which confraternities indeed seemed to approach by administering sacraments and arranging local worship services.[10] Closer supervision of confraternities was therefore of utmost concern to Tridentine reformers eager to extend episcopal authority over lay religious life.

The last sessions of the Council of Trent in 1562 and 1563 passed legislation on confraternities and hospitals aimed at reducing confraternal independence as well as purifying the moral behavior of lay members and improving the financial and medical quality of welfare.[11] The Council issued new disciplinary codes that required confraternities regularly to account for their activities to episcopal authorities. It asserted that bishops were executors of all pious dispositions, both those made in last wills and those instituted by the living. To ensure observance of charitable deeds and spiritual obligations requested by benefactors, bishops were given the right to inspect all lay confraternities and hospitals except those under immediate protection of monarchs.[12]

Trent also rendered confraternities and hospitals liable for financial obligations and authorized ordinaries to audit their accounts annually. With the intention of improving care of the indigent and freeing administrators from obsolete foundation rules, Tridentine policy allowed administrators to channel charitable funds in directions that best served the needs of the poor provided that they observed as closely as possible the original purposes of the endowments. Decisions to divert funds to areas other than those specified by donors required the approval of bishops. The law demanded further that ecclesiastical administrators rigorously dispense charity and medical assistance in hospitals received as benefices, and limited to three the number of years that any one person could administer the same hospital, in order to reduce corruption.[13]

On 7 December 1604, Pope Clement VIII issued *Quaecumque*, the last piece of legislation attempting to put an end to the independence enjoyed by medieval confraternities. This constitution reasserted some of the Tridentine legislation and outlined more carefully the role of the ordinary in supervising confraternal activity. *Quaecumque* prescribed that the ordinary must examine, correct, and approve corporate statutes and ratify all spiritual favors and indulgences conceded to religious alliances before they could be published.[14] It further limited lay control over charitable matters by allowing ordinaries to determine the method whereby confraternities received bequests, and, most importantly, it indicated uses for which this charity could be employed. Although benefactors retained the right to stipulate the acts of mercy that they wanted exercised, their wishes could be altered if the donations might be applied more efficiently to other welfare services. The effect of the decree *Quaecumque* was to abrogate the traditional inviolability of testators' wishes and subject almsgiving to direct clerical supervision.

With this piece of legislation the Counter Reformation church had in its hands a tool to transform the character of the corporate religious structure in Europe. It ordered that two or more confraternities pursuing identical purposes could not be newly erected in the same place in order to distribute services more equally and prevent feuding between rival confraternities.[15] This meant, of course, that laypeople no longer would be free to erect confraternities at their own discretion. Ultimately the decree forced the confraternal system to conform more closely to official preferences than it had in the medieval period.

Counter Reformation measures to control confraternities were enforced more promptly in Castile than in other areas of Europe.[16] Philip II accepted the Tridentine decrees with minor revisions less than two weeks after their official ratification by Pope Pius IV on 26 January 1564. He circulated the decrees among the Castilian clergy in several printed editions during the spring and summer of 1564, and the following year provincial councils convened in Salamanca, Santiago, Toledo, Zaragoza, Valencia and Granada to review the decrees for the education of prelates. The Crown's instructions to Castilian prelates regarding episcopal visitation of confraternities varied only slightly from original Tridentine prescriptions. Ordinaries were required to ascertain regularly that masses and pious obligations were being fulfilled, but they were not allowed to inspect account books relating to property and other purely financial matters. This reservation, intended to protect royal jurisdiction, was nevertheless frequently ignored by prelates suspicious that confraternal expenditures in secular affairs were taken from funds intended for pious purposes.

Synodal constitutions drawn up in Salamanca in 1570, in Zamora in 1586, and in Astorga in 1595 reiterated Tridentine requirements that all confraternities secure licenses from local ordinaries. An official survey in 1771 concluded that all but five of Zamora's 113 confraternities were approved by religious authorities.[17] In accordance with Trent's aims to strengthen parochial jurisdiction, Zamoran ecclesiastics immediately nominated priests to preside over confraternal religious services in order to reduce the role of the regulars, particularly the Franciscans and the Dominicans. The confraternity of Nuestra Señora del Portal, newly erected in 1564, was required to accept the parish priest or chaplain of San Salvador de la Vid to say its masses.[18]

Zamoran ordinaries examined confraternal account books every few years to regulate expenditures and ensure proper disposal of pious bequests. They carefully recorded the number of masses that confraternities were required to perform and noted delinquencies in their obligations. Their efforts, however, were not always adequate to ensure observance of liturgical services. Writing with a certain acquiescence, the inspector for the years 1678 to 1684 noted that the confraternity of Todos Santos had failed to observe 250 masses during the period.[19] In the seventeenth century, negligence in attending to the Liturgy was usually attributed to serious decline in membership and diminished income that made it difficult for confraternities to pay priests for services. To ensure that the impoverished brotherhood of the Ovejeros observed its 70 annual masses, the cathedral chapter ordered that its mayordomo deposit 3000 *maravedís* with the priest of the church of San Leonardo for that purpose.[20] At times ordinaries agreed to consolidate a number of masses which had accumulated over the years into collective eucharistic rites to curtail expenses and alleviate cofrades burdened with frequent attendance. In 1622, for example, they cut back the number of masses required of the confraternity of the Misericordia in order to direct more funds toward hospital and funeral services.[21] To save resources, some confraternities were ordered to reduce the number of requiems that they promised for the souls of members who died. In one of the more blatant measures of discrimination against women in the Counter Reformation period, Nuestra Señora de la Consolación was asked to eliminate masses altogether for the souls of female cofradas.[22] Ordinaries also ensured that wax supplies were sufficient for religious services, processions and vigils; and they required mayordomos to read statutes at least twice yearly for members.

Along with financial difficulties, Zamoran confraternities suffered recruitment problems as a result of an overall population drop of 27 per cent in the city between the years 1619 and 1637.[23] Aristocratic confraternities were no less affected by the downward trend than those of commoners. The ordinances of the Cofradía de San Ildefonso noted in 1623 that the number of cofrades fell from its customary level of 70 to 33, and ascribed the cause to 'the ruination of many of the principal families of this city as well as the little devotion of its present inhabitants'.[24] Ordinances of Nuestra Señora de la Candelaria stated in 1650 that demographic losses caused a decline in donations and bequests that forced the confraternity to protect its remaining rental income by restricting membership to eleven laymen and eight clerics.[25] The noble confraternity of San Juan de Acre which ran a small hospice and distributed alms to the poor within its neighborhood suffered such serious membership problems in the seventeenth century that its welfare services were curtailed severely. Between 1637 and 1639, the confraternity had only three members. It operated with two cofrades in 1644, five in 1654, and only one in 1661. Its goods were formally reclaimed by the church in 1751.[26]

Counter Reformation measures also sought to tighten moral discipline over the laity, a goal rigorously pursued in Zamora. According to clergymen, the worst abuses of confraternities arose during common meals and feast day celebrations when cofrades squandered their money on food and drink and indulged in merry making. Synodal constitutions in Zamora forbade confraternities to celebrate communal meals in sacred places, and individual visitation reports prohibited confraternities from spending excessively for lunches and banquets.[27] They explicitly prohibited brotherhoods from financing social events with funds directed toward pious causes and required that all such expenses be paid privately by cofrades. The church then began to levy fines on brotherhoods that spent alms and bequests on food and drink. And it came down harshly on the Holy Week custom of consuming *meriendas* before penitential parades and stopping for pastries and wine at stalls set up along processional routes. Such snacking constantly interrupted the pace and interfered with the solemnity of the events, ecclesiastics muttered, to say nothing of violating Lenten fasting requirements.[28] Synodal constitutions of Astorga in 1595 protested that some confraternal devotions were nothing more than old superstitions and explicitly prohibited members from submerging images and relics in streams and rivers to solicit rain.[29] Confraternities were soon punished as well for 'dishonourable dancing'.[30]

One would have noticed, walking through the seventeenth-century Castilian city, a mood distinctly more subdued than in earlier times. Public criers stopped proclaiming celebrations on the eve of festivals, and drummers no longer called cofrades to gather at communal banquet tables. The joyous parades, frolics and bull-runs through the streets quietened into rosary devotions and prayer vigils. Even the mourners – those ever-present reminders of death – made further concessions to austerity by carrying fewer candles in funeral corteges.[31] The new sober mood extended as well to the most private recesses of the worshipper's mind at prayer. For the church hierarchy was leading an effective campaign to advance its decisions on dogma by encouraging certain types of contemplative devotions among the public. In response to Protestant rejection of several of the sacraments, for instance, the Council asserted that all seven sacraments were crucial to salvation and promoted new confraternities in their honor. The most successful of the new groups was the Santíssimo Sacramento dedicated to revering the eucharist.

The proliferation of confraternities dedicated to the Santíssimo Sacramento dates from 1538, when the Dominican Tommaso Stella founded a confraternity in honor of the host in the church of Santa María della Minerva in Rome. The special duties of its members were to attend masses, receive the eucharist on special holidays and accompany the Sacrament when carried to the sick. Pope Paul III approved these activities shortly thereafter, granting it numerous indulgences and privileges and explicitly calling it a model for other confraternities.[32] In 1542 the church in Spain procured a bull from the Pope that affirmed the indulgences in order to encourage creation of similar confraternities among the Spanish populace.[33] The earliest confraternities of the Santíssimo Sacramento in Zamora date from

1545, and by the end of the century they were installed in almost every parish in the city. The Spanish episcopacy appealed to the Santíssimo Sacramento to instruct the laity in the doctrine of transubstantiation by organizing communal practices that gave expression to the real presence of Christ in the host. One of its main responsibilities was to parade the viaticum through the streets when carried to homes of the sick, ensuring that it was covered with fine brocade canopies and surrounded with lighted torches. The air of pageantry was enhanced by the custom, frequently remarked upon with unease and not a little contumacy by foreign travellers in Spain, of passersby suddenly falling on their knees and striking their breasts as a gesture of contrition whenever the Sacrament passed their way on the streets.[34]

Several other arch-confraternities designed by the Counter Reformation hierarchy specifically elucidated Catholic doctrine. The church affirmed that souls in purgatory continued to demand aid from the living and encouraged confraternities of the Souls in Purgatory, called *Las Animas* in Spain, to collect alms and prayers on behalf of souls. In seventeenth-century Zamora the Animas became almost as popular as the Santíssimo Sacramento among the parishes, where they were closely supervised by rectors. Cult utensils such as the plates that members circulated at mass to collect charity were molded with hungry nude figures extending hands upward in supplication of alms, the currency by which they obtained redemption.[35]

The arch-confraternities of the Holy Name of Jesus spread orthodoxy in a variety of ways within parish communities. In France, those established in the late sixteenth century took on the appearance of vigilante clubs ready to take up arms to defend the faith against Protestants,[36] but their usual function was to cultivate personal devotion through prayer, examinations of consciences, penitences, and visitations to tabernacles. The Dominican monastery in Zamora established the Dulce Nombre de Jesús in 1575 to praise God and ensure that his name was not taken in vain. Similar confraternities later emerged in the countryside where, in the absence of challenges from heretics, they crusaded to prevent women and children from swearing in the name of Christ. The Santo Nombre de Jesús in the village of Muelas near Zamora would permit no villager who blasphemed to become a member, expelling women who cursed or called upon the devil while imposing fines on male members for similar offenses.[37]

The confraternity of the Christian Doctrine instilled orthodoxy at a more intellectual level. In the 1540s both cathedral canons in Zamora and a group of lay cofrades in Valladolid organized educational services for the dissemination of Catholic doctrine to children. Their schools and similar ones across Europe were officially recognized as arch-confraternities in 1607 when Pope Paul V, in the bull *Ex credito nobilis*, accorded them formal titles and privileges.[38] The confraternities endeavored to spread knowledge of Catholic doctrine to homeless children while providing food and shelter as well as technical skills and handicraft.

All these new advocacies diverted attention from traditional holy patrons that had been chosen by the community. A shift away from native cults in which Mary had acquired a leading role, toward devotions that gave greater recognition to Christ in particular, has been noted in many parts of Europe after the Reformation. Protestant communities, of course, set out to eliminate veneration of Mary and the saints altogether and to relate exclusively with God. But Catholic communities also began to focus on the God-head. In Troyes for example devotions to Christ became so popular that only two confraternities dedicated to Mary continued to attract large numbers of affiliates in the middle of the sixteenth century.[39] In Zamora, a similar iconographical revolution occurred in the aftermath of Trent. Confraternities transferred allegiance away from indigenous cults toward officially recommended devotions. In this process the patrons who suffered the greatest loss of favor were the saints, dropping from 37 per cent of all advocacies in the sixteenth century to 22 per cent in 1771.[40] Those who were most likely to survive Counter Reformation changes were health-bearing patrons such as San Roque, San Antonio, San Blas, and, particularly among women in the countryside, Santa Agueda, protectress against breast diseases.

Dedications to the Virgin Mary also dropped, from 36 per cent of all Zamoran confraternities in the sixteenth century to 26 per cent in 1771.[41] Although Mary managed to maintain her pre-eminent position among eighteenth-century confraternities, prevailing by 10 per cent over devotions to Christ, her image as the invincible defender of the needy nevertheless was challenged seriously by the new Catholic theology. Reform-minded Catholics as well as Protestants felt that medieval veneration of Mary had exceeded her merits. Erasmus of Rotterdam, whose ideas found enthusiastic support among enlightened clerics in mid-sixteenth century Spain,[42] presented the most famous criticism of mariolatry. He composed a letter attributed to the Virgin in which she vigorously protested the tendency of suppliants to rely exclusively on her for spiritual assistance. The letter was addressed to the Protestant Glaucoplutus, expressing relief and gratitude that he aided Luther's struggle to 'convince the world that it is a thing altogether needless to invoke saints'.[43] She felt that her role as intercessor had reached unreasonable proportions, as if her son were still an infant in her arms who did not dare deny her anything for fear that she might refuse him her breast.

Erasmus's complaint that Jesus never became an adult within the context of medieval piety did not fall on deaf ears, for during the Counter Reformation artistic tastes turned from the iconography of the radiant young mother holding Christ as a baby in her arms to the Pietà image of a sorrowful mother bracing the somewhat unwieldy figure of the mature, martyred redeemer across her lap. By focusing on sufferings of the Virgin, Tridentine reformers sought to re-direct attention to the crucial event of Christian theology, the redemption of Christ. They hoped to avoid presenting Mary in a role that would detract from the glory and authority of her son. Church fathers divested Mary of the potency of her nurturing reputation by condemning the 'indecency' of artwork that showed her offering milk from her breasts to the infant Christ.[44] Equally restrictive was their assertion that the most popular of all the confraternities' iconographical images, the Mother of Mercy, whose insignia was carried by the Misericordias, was unorthodox. Trent charged that paintings and sculptures of the madonna shielding humanity under her cloak from the injuries of *fortuna* and the wrath of God implied the Virgin's sovereignty in deciding the fate of men on earth, and attempted to ban these reproductions.[45]

To correct heterodox Marian beliefs among the laity, the Catholic hierarchy encouraged devotions to the Virgin that properly situated her status beneath Christ. In 1564 the Jesuit order began setting up Congregations of the Virgin Mary designed to educate the faithful in Marian dogma, commit members to professing the Creed as enunciated by the Council of Trent, and regulate attendance at confession and mass.[46] The Dominicans promoted confraternities of the rosary to express devotion to Mary through repetition of prayer cycles and contemplation of the fifteen mysteries. The leading Counter Reformer, Pope Paul V, gave the monastic order of the Servites permission to spread the cult of Our Lady of Sorrows by setting up new confraternities under her patronage. The confraternities were designed to meditate regularly on the Virgin's seven sorrows. 'Christ Lost by His Mother', 'Christ betrayed by an Apostle', and the 'Deposition from the Cross', were experiences that emphasized her emotional submission to the ordeals of Christ and, like the rosary devotions, made her part of the crucifixion.[47]

The Spanish motif of the Mother of God contemplating the Passion was the most highly developed in Europe.[48] The Virgin without the Christ-child, suffering in solitary silence, set the tone for the Spanish Catholic Reformation. In late sixteenth-century Zamora cofrades began to demonstrate particular enthusiasm for the new symbol of Nuestra Señora de las Angustias. The statue of her image in the parish church of San Vicente depicted a bereaved Mary whose tears spoke the same language of cleansing and renewal as the bleeding of the flagellants.[49] In seventeenth-century Valladolid, a penitential brotherhood commissioned the naturalist sculptor Gregorio Hernández to design a new figurine of Mary for its Easter processions. Hernández's iconographical theme of the *Soledad*, the Virgin of Solitude agonizing over the Passion, spread quickly throughout Spain. Like the sorrowful statuary of the Angustias in Zamora, the Soledad was created to inspire deeper public devotion by cofrades keenly aware of the emotionally stirring power of pathos in religion. Other seventeenth- and eighteenth-century appellations of the Virgin in the region of Leon-Castile recalled images of sorrow as well as new doctrinal themes. The Mater Dolorosa, the Consolation, the Immaculate Conception and the Incarnation replaced medieval depictions of Mary in attractive natural settings within the localities. The new Marian devotions expressed a standardized, sober and orthodox piety adapted to Tridentine christology with less emphasis on her curative and consoling powers.

As the Marian cult increasingly evoked sorrowful themes, the figure of her martyred son Christ gained favor as patron of confraternities. The adoption of Christ by urban confraternities brought to fruition the ascetic strain of late medieval peasant spirituality. As the earlier Marian confraternities in the city had emulated the merciful and nurturing character of their patron saint by performing acts of charity, the new Christo-centric confraternities imitated the Passion and Crucifixion by disciplining the flesh, fasting, and walking barefoot through the streets. The Christian narrative tale enacted by the populace now moved from the childhood of Christ lying in the arms of Mary to his adulthood followed by his death and resurrection.

The penitentials had been common in Italy and Germany since the thirteenth century but failed to gain the attention of Spaniards until two centuries later. The first Spanish penitentials appeared at the very end of the fifteenth century, bearing the insignia of the cross and calling themselves the Cofradías de la Santa Vera Cruz. The date at which the Santa Vera Cruz began to practice self-flagellation is disputed by confraternities in Spain today. The preaching of St Vincent Ferrer (1350–1419) provoked the earliest known disciplinary processions in Spain, although no permanent societies dedicated to mortification of the flesh appear to have been formed at that time.[50] A confraternity organized by Genoese in Valencia in 1487 may have incorporated scourging methods long practiced in Italy, while a Sevillian confraternity named the Vera Cruz discussed corporate flagellation practices in statutes of 1538 which purport to have been modelled on a confraternity of the Vera Cruz in Toledo.[51]

Zamoran confraternities have claimed the distinction of being among the first flagellant groups in Spain and, indeed, the first identified primary source certifying their activities comes from the villages of the province. The earliest confraternities called the Santa Vera Cruz appear in the town of Benavente in 1482, and in the tiny villages of Moradora in 1489 and Perdigón in 1497.[52] A few years later, documentation testifies that the Santa Vera Cruz had spread to the city of Zamora. In 1501, the city council referred to one among urban residents and later citations associate it with the monasteries of San Francisco and Santo Domingo.[53] The information provided in these records does not mention penitential acts. The only identifiable religious activity is the patronization of a hospital for 'unfortunate paupers' by the Vera Cruz in Benavente.

Statutes drawn up in 1524 by the Vera Cruz in the northern Zamoran village of Villalpando are the first to identify self-mortification clearly as a permanent devotional practice.[54] Every Maundy Thursday, the statutes claim, cofrades performed flagellation exercises in honor of Christ. At the monastery of San Francisco where the Vera Cruz held its meetings, cofrades gathered at 5 p.m. on Maundy Thursday with certificates substantiating the fact that they had taken confession which permitted them to participate with a clear conscience in the memorial penitential procession. Inside the refectory, cofrades put on their penitential tunics, took a small repast, and listened to a sermon by one of the Franciscan preachers. After these preliminaries, they formed a procession of two main groups, the cofrades of penitence who flagellated themselves and the cofrades of light who carried torches. The mayor, holding the organization's pendant, led the holy parade into town with the abbot bearing the first cross close behind. Deputies maintained order and regulated the pace of the procession as young boys with torches sang soft monotonous litanies. At the end behind a second cross surrounded by clerical cofrades, the brothers of penitence whipped themselves on the back in slow rhythmic movements with an 'honorable and orderly' demeanor. After filing past the major churches of town, the procession returned to the cloister of the monastery where the abbot washed the self-inflicted wounds in wine.

The flagellation instruments of the brothers were designed to reproduce Christ's own experiences. Cofrades of the Vera Cruz of Argujillo wore tunics open over the shoulders, with scapularies or shoulder straps and hoods of linen that completely covered their heads. Their feet and legs were bared. The tips of their scourges were wiped with wax 'in order that they can draw blood'.[55] The blood spilled was substantial, and it was no accident that most of the flagellators were young men in their teens and twenties with the physical strength necessary to endure the rigorous exercise. A Portuguese observer of Holy Week in Valladolid in 1605 swore that some of the 1400 flagellants of one Holy Week confraternity tore more than a pound of coagulated blood from their flesh, which he thought scandalous and horribly cruel compared with more moderate practices in Lisbon.[56]

The flagellators covered their heads with hoods of linen, giving an eerie appearance to the processions that continues to challenge the imagination of scholars and modern-day spectators of Spanish Holy Week. Philippe Ariès believes that the special dress of the penitents derived from their attention to burying the dead. He surmises that the hooded garments constituted a special type of clerical dress for the laity which were adopted initially at private mourning ceremonies and later worn in the streets during public processions.[57] According to John Henderson, the white-colored fabric of so many confraternal uniforms imitated baptismal robes to signify cofrades' new-found innocence of sin through repentance.[58] But it is Robert Harding who presents the most convincing interpretation. He proposes that penitential garments concealed social distinctions and expressed ideals of brotherhood and spiritual equality in emulation of early Christian ascetics.[59] Sixteenth-century statutes of the Castilian penitentials strongly suggest that the hooded outfits were designed to erase the personal identity of cofrades and make them unrecognizable to the public. Statutes of the Vera Cruz of Villalcampo (1534) which required cofrades to wear special disciplinary shirts explicitly prohibited them to reveal 'known signs'. In a regime of status and privilege, social recognition was a form of domination. The hoods guaranteed that

Kastilianischer Büßer (Geißler)

Castilian penitent (flagellant)

Penitente (flagelante) castellano

4.1 A Castilian flagellant on Holy Thursday
'In this manner those of Castile expiate their sins on Holy Thursday.'
[Source: *Das Trachtenbuch des Christoph Wieditz von seinen reisen nach Spanien (1529) und den Niederlanden (1531/32)* (Berlin: Verlag von Walter de Gruyter & Co., 1927), Laminas LVI]

Büßer in Saragossa

Penitents in Saragossa   Penitente en Zaragoza

4.2 A flagellant from Zaragoza
'In this manner the men of the kingdom of Zaragoza punish themselves in penitential devotion.'
[Source: *Das Trachtenbuch des Christoph Wieditz von seinen reisen nach Spanien (1529) und den Niederlanden (1531/32)* (Berlin: Verlag von Walter de Gruyter & Co., 1927), Laminas LVII]

flagellators conducted their exercises in a spirit of humility rather than pride.[60] That the concept of spiritual equality is key to understanding the meaning of cofrades' appearance is reinforced by another universal dress code. Penitents were not allowed to carry any sort of hand weapon, an instrument designed, of course, to intimidate or harm others. Violence was to be directed exclusively at their own bodies, for they were assuming the penalty of man's aggressive nature.

Concerning the conscious goals of penitents, the written statutes are absolutely clear. The Vera Cruz of Argujillo (1588) explained that by personally re-enacting Christ's trial, members were sharing in the pain of redemption. On Holy Thursday, 'we proceed barefoot, in remembrance of the cruel nailing, and we go pouring blood from our bodies, in memory of the blood Our Lord shed that day ... and we go scourging the shoulders, because by doing this, we are crowned with blessings of glory with the Good Authors'.[61] Bearing upon their bodies the punishment for sin, they sought to merit the salvation that Christ offered mankind.

It was in keeping with the manner in which the illiterate populace expressed their beliefs that the penitents dramatically imitated in their own lives the experiences of Christ on earth. Their organizations were especially popular in rural areas of Leon-Castile,[62] where scourging and re-enactment of the crucifixion took on special ferocity. And those which were erected in cities claimed the largest lower-class membership of all urban confraternities.[63] A wide variety of handicraft industry was represented in Zamora's Vera Cruz, including a particularly large contingency of cloth workers, who were members of the least organized and most poorly paid trade. Residents with Jewish backgrounds also joined these open societies. Ten of the 57 cofrades attending a reunion of the Vera Cruz in 1524 were recognized as 'judíos conversos'.[64] It was in the penitential brotherhoods that plebeian movements coincided with Tridentine emphasis on Christ's redemption to form a particularly powerful current of Catholic devotion.

Gradually the passion recapitulations of the Vera Cruz became more ostentatious in props if not in acting. Penitents converted village streets into journeys to Calvary, shouldering together papier mâché and canvas representations of Christ's trial on platforms as wide, it was said, as small houses.[65] Groups within a village co-ordinated episodic re-enactments of the crucifixion for each day of Holy Week. In these pre-Easter celebrations the austerity imposed on other confraternities was set aside, making participation in the penitentials highly attractive to the upper classes. The plain dress of the medieval penitents was replaced by more formal outfits, even among the traditional Vera Cruz which attached white frill collars to its black tunics in the early seventeenth century.[66] Aristocratic confraternities designed velvet robes with ornate conical hats to distinguish their processions. In some parts of Europe, particularly in France, the penitentials became almost exclusively aristocratic in composition by the seventeenth century[67] and in Zamora several had to struggle to maintain their contact with commoners. The confraternity of Nuestra Señora de las Nieves y Jesús Nazareno in Zamora's parish of San Juan de la Puerta Nueva responded in 1651 to the increasing prestige of its cult by tightening membership requirements and admitting no additional scribes, government officials or other notables in order to associate with the 'humble people'.[68]

The new cult became extremely popular, especially in Old Castile, where the main problem of the church was to restrain zealous young men from too frequent self-flagellation. It finally forbade cofrades from public scourging on saints' days and limited mortification exercises to Holy Week, the day of the Cross in May, and during rogations in times of urgent need such as outbreaks of pestilence or famine. By the end of the sixteenth century, 22 confraternities of the Vera Cruz could be found in the province of Zamora,[69] while in the south of the peninsula so many appeared within a few years that the church decided to prevent the public from erecting any more. A synodal statute of Guadix y Baza in the province of Granada ascertained that flagellation was just becoming extensive at mid-century when it prohibited, in 1554, the formation of confraternities of the 'Santa Cruz, called the *disciplinantes*' which had recently initiated flagellation on Holy Thursdays.[70]

Everywhere the flagellants became so numerous that they had to adopt new more creative titles to distinguish themselves. The Santísimo Crucifixo joined the Vera Cruz in both of Zamora's mendicant convents, while advocacies of Nuestro Señor de la Resurrección, Nuestro Señor de la Cruz del Quadrado, and Nuestro Señor de la Transfiguración took root in the parish churches. The size of each passion brotherhood expanded as well. Those from Zamora grew from about 50 members in the early sixteenth century to several hundred by the end of the century, while confraternities in Valladolid incorporated up to 2000 members in the age of the baroque.[71]

Until the late sixteenth century, when the church tightened supervision over members, women participated with men in penitential activities. Women represented the virtue of mercy along with Mary, and in this role they were not allowed to flagellate. Their task was to carry torches and candles to solace victims. These 'cofradas de luz' walked in procession illuminating dirt and cobble stone streets for barefoot flagellants. Some of them imitated Veronica by wiping the blood and sweat-stained faces of men with large veils. It was also customary for them to circulate with their faces covered in their own informal processions around the city's churches to visit the stations of the Cross and re-enact the visual experiences of Mary. But their active participation in the theater of sorrow was brief. Toward the end of the sixteenth-century, Philip II, in fear that women who hid their identities might be encouraged to behave immorally, ordered that they uncover their faces at all events,[72] and thereafter the confraternities also began to require that women sit at separate tables in silence during feast-day banquets.[73] The puritanical zeal of the Counter Reformation gradually alienated male and female roles in the religious drama by discouraging women from engaging in penitential piety entirely. By the seventeenth century, only men could be found among the passion confraternities. Distrust and fear thus challenged women's place in the Christian saga of redemption. Women were relegated to positions of spectators, where they indulged their own passive, perhaps irreligious, but always life-affirming fascination with flagellation exercises. Every man knew, so an eighteenth-century account of penitential processions tells us, that the outfit he wore and the physical exertion of flagellation were especially effective means of displaying his masculinity to female crowds. 'It is known that this is one of the forms of courtship most appreciated by young women ... and it is already a well-worn observation that the majority of weddings are performed on Holy Thursday and the day of the Cross in May', when the penitentials came out into the streets.[74] At these climactic moments in the Christian liturgical year, the populace played out the two great themes of western philosophy, embodied by *eros* and *thanatos*, in close if discordant pageantry.

At times it seemed that *thanatos* might prevail through repressive domination and zeal, for the penitentials became increasingly favored by testators to accompany their remains in funeral processions. The diligent Isabel Flórez of Zamora, for example, summoned for her funeral march in 1599 four penitential groups in addition to her parish confraternity and a rosary devotion.[75] The *disciplinantes* rapidly gained respect in the eyes of municipal authorities for their severe expiatory methods of soliciting divine favor. They were called upon to accompany funerals of important officials and noblemen, to protect the health of kings and queens, and, despite Trent's discouragement of pagan rites, to supplicate good weather. The Vera Cruz of Villalpando agreed in its statutes that if the magistracy of the town called upon it for help in any 'tribulation' such as famine or pestilence, all cofrades would gather upon the ringing of its church bell and decide together if they would put themselves through the scourging process for the welfare of the rest of the community.[76]

It is interesting to speculate on why flagellation has appealed so strongly to the Spanish people, particularly to the peasants and handicraft workers who first adopted the practice. The initial appearance of penitential exercises in rural villages may have been related to the severe economic conditions in which many of the Castilian people lived in the medieval period. Those who suffered daily in the weary sun-stoked plains of Castile may have found this valiant endurance of intensely painful scourges the most convincing way to reach and propitiate God, for they had learned to associate ill-fortune with their own moral failures. By inflicting pain on their bodies, cofrades simulated punishment for sins which deepened their sense of repentance and convinced the public of their sincerity to God. Self-mutilation provoked physiological exhaustion which may have released guilt-feelings and led cofrades to believe that they were securing God's mercy for the community. Flagellators were the people's heroes. By the late sixteenth century, the very period of Spain's tragic collapse as a major power in Europe, public penance was being taken up with strenuous emotion by urbanites all across the peninsula who now shared with peasants a temperament of sorrow and mourning. The flagellation movement was the populace's most poignant cultural testament to the decline of Spain.

Once cofrades began to mortify the flesh, it was difficult to restrain them and some clergymen worried that the penitents were usurping the power of the church to elicit divine grace, although most ecclesiastics approved of the passion devotions and gave them support. Since the beginning of the Reformation, the church had been trying to draw attention to the act of redemption and create a proper balance in popular devotions by diverting advocacies away from the saints to Christ and his sorrowing mother. The penitentials approached this goal more closely than any other type of Counter Reformation confraternity. In assessing the original achievements of the Counter Reformation in the history of Christianity, therefore, the penitentials' call for public reflection on the crucifixion was undoubtedly the most outstanding.

In their own ways, the other new confraternities – the Doctrina Cristiana, the Santíssimo Sacramento, the Animas and the rosary devotions – worked with the penitentials to usher in the Spanish baroque era. The clerically-sponsored religious groups were designed especially to encourage orthodoxy among the laity. They set out to teach Christian precepts with catechisms, to deepen understanding of the doctrine of transubstantiation, and regulate attendance at Holy Communion and Penance. These official devotions called attention to the authority of the church in delivering the sacraments, and replaced locally inspired cults that once had molded popular piety in their own unique ways. In relation to the elaborate lattice of confraternal devotions under favored local saints in the Middle Ages,[77] the early modern period presented a more standardized and homogenous pattern of advocacies.[78]

The baroque age also witnessed an unprecedented extension of clerical control over lay piety. Trent increased the hierarchy's disciplinary powers over the internal affairs of the confraternities and gave local pastors and ordinaries authority to enforce punitive measures against cofrades who failed to maintain peace and comply with corporate rules. Traditionally members had assumed complete responsibility for observing communal obligations by promising at initiation ceremonies to fulfill all requirements or incur mortal sin. After Trent, the church annulled such spiritual penalties and charged ordinaries to impose monetary penalties when statutes and other corporate standards were violated. The new policy helped the cathedral chapter in Zamora implant its vision of moral and financial austerity over lay activities.

This change supports John Bossy's thesis that the post-Tridentine church attempted to impose unity over Christendom from above through tighter clerical supervision while the medieval church allowed independent expression of beliefs.[79] Bossy argues that the Counter Reformation church attempted to replace particularist interests, like kin groups and autonomous confraternities which acted in their own way as peace-keeping forces in society, with clerically-controlled institutions. The sacrament of baptism, for example, had been used in the medieval period by parents to extend kinship ties for the welfare of their children. The post-Tridentine church tried to reduce this source of private support by limiting the number of god parents at baptisms and offering parish catechetical programs for young people to fulfill educational responsibilities traditionally held by family members.[80] Likewise, the reforming church sought to make new use of the sacrament of penance. In the early Middle Ages, penitents confessing their sins customarily made open restitution with their neighbors as part of the cleansing process, a practice that served the important function of reducing social tensions. Around the thirteenth century, the church began to encourage penitents to concentrate on reconciling their behavior with their inner consciences rather than with the people around them by cultivating private discussions with confessors. Not surprisingly, Trent supported private confessions which served to enhance the authority of priests in the absolution of sin.[81]

In a similar manner the post-Tridentine church attempted to replace traditional confraternal activities that had operated to harmonize relations in the community with parochial services that drew allegiance to ecclesiastical authority. In this respect the difference between the medieval cult of the Host of Corpus Christi and the Counter Reformation devotion to the Santíssimo Sacramento is particularly striking. The feast in honor of Corpus Christi was authorized in a papal bull in 1264 and its cult spread gradually throughout Europe in the fourteenth and fifteenth centuries. In urban areas, Corpus Christi day was celebrated with elaborate processions in which the entire community participated. Clerics, municipal officials and townspeople, each strictly placed in order of dignity and authority, accompanied the consecrated host as it was carried through village thoroughfares after masses.[82] In Zamora, the clergy and the aristocracy lined up in procession either according to titles within their estates or according to confraternities. Commoners collected by confraternity or by trade. Beginning at 6 a.m. the community assembled into its proper stations at the cathedral for a parade down the main street to the plaza of San Juan, the center of civic activities. Each trade brought its own game or invention as it was sometimes called, which was a float carrying costumed figures or mechanical devices that moved and played tricks. At the plaza of San Juan, each craft set into motion its special display before city council members, who judged the spectacle and awarded prizes of satin and damask cloth or money. Throughout the day religious plays and farces took place in the square of San Juan or in front of the cathedral. Musicians, jugglers, dancers, and grotesque figures meandered among the crowds and a huge *tarasca* or *dragon*, symbolizing Satan, sauntered in and out of the streets goading children until sometime in the course of the day it was subdued, presumably by the overpowering spiritual presence of the Holy Sacrament.[83]

In contrast to these gay and animated celebrations of Corpus Christi, the cult of the Santíssimo Sacramento implemented by the

Counter Reformation church was somber and restrained. The parishes did not join together in city-wide festivities, but honored the Sacrament with private prayers and vigilances. Piety left the streets for the sheltered altars of parish churches. The power of the host, once externalized in the subjugation of demons among the community, revealed itself only privately to individuals at tabernacles or in sickbed.

Several scholars, such as John Bossy, Bartolomé Bennassar and Marc Venard, have expressed serious doubts that the Counter Reformation church's efforts to control lay piety strengthened the allegiance of the masses to Catholicism.[84] Bossy and Venard suggest that Tridentine victories weakened the very life source of the church by cutting off the innumerable local roots of popular faith. Their evaluations provide an interesting perspective on Jean Delumeau's thesis that European society finally became 'Christianized' in the early modern period through the educational policies of the Catholic and Protestant Reformation churches. If discussions in recent Reformation historiography leave us with the ambivalent impression that the faith of the populace became less intense as it became more standardized, they serve the useful purpose of reminding us that the spread of orthodox beliefs and behavior need not necessarily imply an increase in the strength and vitality of faith, characteristics which are, in any event, very difficult to measure.[85] Both Bossy and Venard speculate from the growth of secular attitudes in the eighteenth century that the post-Tridentine church failed to tap the inner spirit of believers. Their conclusions may well be true, although more specific causal connections between the rise of secularism and reduction of popular sources of piety still must be established.

Considerable evidence exists in Zamora to indicate that however we choose to assess the value of plebeian forms of worship in sustaining devotion to Christianity, Trent never succeeded in extinguishing these local sources. In fact, if we delve beneath the surface of the imposed institutional homogeneity of the city's confraternities, it becomes apparent that Trent's influence on popular piety was actually quite modest. Although the people's confraternities drew closer to official notions of orthodoxy, they insisted upon their traditional independence in matters of salvation. Above all they did not relinquish to the church hierarchy the responsibility that they had always claimed over the destiny of their members' souls. Despite Trent's vigorous attempts to assume for the clerical order essential control over transmitting grace and pardoning sins, the confraternities continued to operate as if these spiritual powers resided in the community. This is true especially of that strong-willed and irrepressible order of *disciplinantes* which bypassed entirely the sacramental system of the church in recovering grace for the faithful through expiation of the flesh. These passion confraternities effectively shaped and co-opted Tridentine directives on worship of Christ to late medieval penitential devotions practiced by the Santa Vera Cruz. It was these indigenous penitentials rather than Tridentine arch-confraternities that attracted the interest of the faithful in the baroque period and that persist even today in inspiring religious enthusiasm. In Castile, penitential devotions have succeeded where other new devotions have failed to involve the public, especially young men, in church ritual. Their role in stimulating piety has been important as well in the Hispanic colonies of the New World. There they assisted the missionary orders in spreading the gospel to Hispano-Indian populations.[86] Contemporary Latin-American religion still exhibits the penitential character of late sixteenth-century Castilian spirituality. The achievements of these passion confraternities attest to the tenacity of local religious cults to survive the centralizing directives of the Vatican and demonstrate that the Counter Reformation was not exclusively a ministerial movement.

At no time in the two centuries following Trent did the Spanish populace turn away from their private prayer co-operatives. Rather than rely on the parochial system of masses for the dead, they continued to place trust in brotherhood programs designed to deliver souls to heaven. Indeed membership in confraternities throughout Spain did not contract significantly in the course of the seventeenth and eighteenth centuries. In 1771, when the central government ordered surveys of all confraternities in the country with the intention of appropriating their endowments for public welfare programs, the number of organizations still operating exceeded 25 000. The totals by province and in proportion to population are listed in Figure 4.3.

These surveys taken by the Council of Castile were utilized by the Council's treasurer, Pedro Rodríguez Campomanes, to calculate that the Crown of Castile possessed 19 024 confraternities while the Crown of Aragon had 6557.[87] Although some provinces have been left out of the list, like Galicia, Guadalajara, Madrid, Cuenca, Salamanca, Jaen and Granada, and one or two of the returns are incomplete, such as Soria and possibly Extremadura, it reveals an interesting pattern of confraternal density in the second half of the eighteenth century. The number of confraternities was highest in the

Table 4.3   Confraternities in Spain in 1771

Provinces	Number of confraternities	Total Population in 1787[88]	Number of confraternities per 1000 population
Zamora	1034	73 890	13.99
Toro	1049	91 532	11.49
Valladolid	1886	192 661	9.79
Palencia	950	111 143	8.55
León	1612	248 168	6.50
Segovia	1066	165 805	6.43
Toledo	1887	327 583	5.76
Burgos	2468	460 395	5.36
Aragon	3253	614 070	5.30
Navarra	1166	224 549	5.19
Avila	587	113 762	5.17
Alava	364	70 710	5.15
Soria	785	169 403	4.63
Cordoba	730	231 139	3.16
Guipúzcoa	315	119 128	2.64
La Mancha	509	204 436	2.49
Catalonia	1949	801 602	2.43
Viscaya	233	114 863	2.03
Murcia	668	332 474	2.01
Sevilla	1096	738 153	1.48
Asturias	380	345 833	1.10
Valencia	764	771 881	0.99
Extremadura	287	412 041	0.70
TOTALS:	25 038	6 935 221	3.61

Average Number of Persons per Confraternity: 277

Source: *Archivo Histórico Nacional, Sección Consejos Suprimidos. The surveys are as yet uncatalogued, but can be found with the aid of the archivists under their respective provinces.*

central provinces of Leon-Castile, and lowest in the coastal regions, a distribution probably characteristic as well of earlier periods.

In Zamora where exact statistics are available for comparing confraternities before and after the Counter Reformation, it is evident that their number varied very little between the two periods. Zamora had 113 confraternities in 1771,[89] a relatively slight decline from the 150 which had operated in the mid-sixteenth century, especially in light of the general population decline from 2150 households to 1926

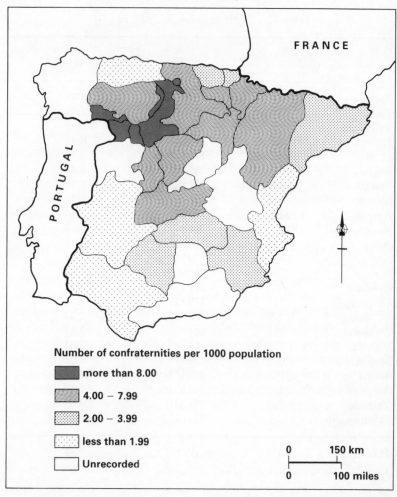

4.4 Incidence of confraternities in relation to populations of Spanish
    provinces in 1771

in the later period. Proportionately, confraternities dropped from one
for every fourteen households in the city in the sixteenth century to
one for every seventeen households two centuries later. Other cities
also appear to have preserved their traditional corporate structure
reasonably well. Toledo for example had 194 confraternities in 1771, a
figure which compares well to its 143 in the sixteenth century. For its
size, the village of Toro maintained the highest number, with 84

confraternities in 1771; Burgos had 77.[90] These cases indicate that the reforms initiated by the Council of Trent did not significantly alter the density of the corporate structure of Spanish society.

CONCLUSION: THE PSYCHOLOGY OF CONFRATERNAL PIETY

To evaluate the place of the Catholic Reformation in the history of Christianity, therefore, we must not exaggerate the novelty of its contributions to popular faith. This is true whether we consider Trent's reforms or native revivalist movements like the disciplinantes. Profound similarities existed between late medieval and early modern devotions which indicate that the Counter Reformation did not significantly transform the attitude of the Spanish populace toward the sacred.

The manner in which cofrades practiced acts of penitence during the sixteenth and seventeenth centuries, emulating and re-enacting the deeds of Christ, was not unlike their use of the acts of mercy begun in earlier times. Both expressions of piety evoked Biblical imagery in personal physical gestures. Penitential activity reconstructed the life of Christ to share directly in his experiences. The disciplinantes began their Holy Week solemnities with communal banquets commemorating the Last Supper and re-enacted episodes of the crucifixion in their theatrical processions by carrying crosses and mortifying the flesh. They acted out redemption scenes to preserve the memory of the original Messianic moment and revitalize its significance in the minds of actors and spectators. The Vera Cruz of the village of Argujillo practiced penitential acts, it explained, because 'every faithful Christian ought to retain in his memory, and write with very bitter and painful passion on his [conscience?]', the fact that Christ suffered and died to redeem our sins.[91] The terminology employed by the Vera Cruz in this eighteenth-century statement clearly indicates the purpose served by dramatic ritual in Catholicism. Re-enacting religious deeds was a way of recording history, of making the Christian past come alive in the mind without the aid of the written word. It was an old medieval technique that the more literate society of the modern period recognized as a form of 'writing'.

Beyond the practical function of stimulating memory, the religious rituals of confraternities served supernatural purposes. Penitential acts, like merciful acts, were performed with the intent of eliciting divine grace for sinners. The Catholic church maintained that self-punishment satisfied divine justice and strengthened Christians against evil by fortifying their wills with the merits of Christ.[92] Thus imitation of historical deeds was not merely a commemorative act, but also an instrumental act. Like charity, memorial drama conferred grace *ex opere operantis*, by reason of the good pious sentiments of those who performed it.[93]

The efficacious results attributed to the dramatization of Biblical history can be most fully perceived in the celebration of the Last Supper, the Christian ceremonial act that received more extensive and deliberate examination than any other sacred rite in the sixteenth century. A matter of contention between Protestants and Catholics, the meaning of the Sacrament was carefully defined by both groups. By comparing their distinctive interpretations of this holy service, we can gain greater insight into their understanding of religious ritual in the form of charity and penitence as well.

A critical issue in the sixteenth-century liturgical controversies related to the eucharist's commemoration of the sacrifice of Christ. Traditional theology formulated in the second century held that the mass recalled before God the sacrifice of Christ and thereby renewed for communicants its redemptive value.[94] The official Catholic position was founded specifically on the interpretation by the early church fathers of Christ's words, 'do this in *remembrance* of Me,' expressed originally in the New Testament by the Greek word *anamnesis*. To the early fathers, the term *anamnesis* implied more than mere mental recollection, as might be suggested by its English translation 'remembrance,' or 'memorial'. The Anglican Benedictine liturgist Dom Gregory Dix explains that for the early church, *anamnesis* had the meaning of '"re-calling", or "re-presenting" before God an event in the past, so that it became *here and now operative by its effects*'.[95] The celebration of the eucharist by the priest 're-enacted' the historic event of Christ's redemption in a way that did not again sacrifice Christ, but 're-presented' the same original sacrifice at a different time. Whenever the mass is celebrated, says a scholar of medieval drama, 'the original sacrifice is made present again (not commemorated) in all its original efficacy'.[96] As ritual, the mass existed outside of time, playing out the life, ministry, crucifixion and resurrection of Christ in the eternal present.

In a strict sense, that which was recreated at mass was not the *occasion* of Christ's sacrifice, for the body and blood were offered but not immolated again. Rather the *effects* of Christ's sacrifice were renewed, and it was with this interpretation in mind that Catholic theologians spoke of the power of the Liturgy to bring about remission of sins, divine grace and eternal life. When Thomas Aquinas referred to the propitiatory effects of the passion flowing through the Holy Sacrament for the remission of sins, he expressed Catholic belief in the power of ritual to elicit grace directly from God for the benefit of the community as a whole.[97]

The idea that the Liturgy produced immediate saving grace for communicants fertilized the popular notion that by increasing the number of masses attended or arranged for one's soul, a person could gain a greater amount of grace.[98] Anxiety over the fate of the soul after death compelled individuals to multiply masses for repeated divine intercessions. This was not the least of the eccentricities that convinced Protestants of a need to reinterpret church liturgy. Both Luther and Zwingli rejected the idea that the eucharistic service remitted sins, arguing that the death of Christ alone saved mankind. Protestant theologians interpreted the *anamnesis* of the Last Supper as a subjective 'calling to mind' of Christ's death and resurrection, and rejected the idea that Christ's body and blood were sacrificed once again before God. Luther believed that the eucharist was neither an oblation nor a re-enactment of Christ's sacrifice at another point in time. He emphasized that the one and only sacrifice was Calvary.[99] Zwingli also argued that the eucharist did not actually renew Christ's sacrifice but metaphorically commemorated it.[100] Despite differences among reformers in the precise interpretation of eucharistic theology, they all divested the Lord's Supper of its mediatory significance as a sacrificial offering and made it purely an expression of communal thanksgiving for a promise of salvation already gained in the past.[101]

Protestant theology also stripped the acts of mercy and penitence of their propitiatory character.[102] In attempting to abolish belief in the efficacy of external forms of piety and deepen the internal life of the spirit through private Bible reading, reformers ridiculed the use of the acts of mercy to exercise morality. John Calvin found the medieval church's presentation of the acts as models of behavior for the laity shortsighted and responsible for inculcating the idea that only these particular gestures were called for by Christ as demonstrations of brotherly love. In his commentary on Matthew's passage, he lambasted the way in which the acts were used by Catholic divines. 'It is foolish for monks and pinhead disputants of that sort', he chided, 'to invent six works of mercy (as Christ mentions no more): as if even children could fail to understand that in synecdoche, *all* the duties of love are being praised.'[103] Calvin's annoyance with the rigidity of popular manifestations of the spirit of charity reflected more than his highly cerebral approach to religion; it reflected a culture in which these particular ritual acts were losing their symbolic meaning.

It was in Catholic societies, where the acts of mercy retained their traditional function as channels of grace, that they endured in social custom. Catholic clergymen continued to interpret the acts as archetypes of Christian love and defended their didactic value. In a primarily non-literate society, the theatrical performance of stereo-typed gestures helped fortify moral behavior through a sort of kinesthetic stimulation of the memory. Portraits of the saints engaged in holy work also assisted identification with model forms of behavior. On this matter, Saint Teresa de Jesús gives her assent. Creative as she was in her mystical visions, she admitted her dependence on images to elicit pious feelings. 'I had so little ability to represent things in my mind, except for what I could see. Unlike other persons who can see things in their minds whenever they pray, I could gain nothing from my imagination ... for this reason I was such a friend of images.'[104] Visual representations carried Christ's message to the simple people just as the Bible carried the Word to the educated. This we have seen in Zamora, where the theatrics of almsgiving sought to sustain the economic order according to the Christian code of morality. By repeatedly enacting the same scriptural gestures of charity, rich and poor played out together the theme of brotherly love that they hoped to infuse into their daily lives.

In light of the Catholic laity's persistent use of ritual to strengthen the faith as well as the hierarchy's adherence to medieval didactic methods of disseminating doctrine and morals to the public, we must question again the extent to which the Catholic Reformation signified a change in medieval piety. In Zamora we noted that the church succeeded in drawing medieval confraternities into a more tightly woven structure with strong ties to the parishes. It succeeded as well in directing more confraternities toward officially-advocated types of devotions and away from the native Marian cults. And yet we also notice, beyond these formal institutional changes, that the actual expression of piety by the populace remained quite traditional. Lay people continued to rehearse dramatically the historical narrative of their religion. Their acts of penitence, no less than their acts of mercy, expressed religious ideals through gestures of the body. Cofrades asserted, as they always had done, that external actions reveal the inner spirit and bring one closer to sanctification. The complex arena of Christian symbolism lost none of its meaning as they re-enacted Biblical history and morality. Thus baroque piety in Spain is remarkable not so much because it expressed a more orthodox and penitential faith than that of the Middle Ages, but because it renewed and prolonged the forms of consecrated behavior that had existed among the commonfolk for centuries.

This attachment to the paradigms of the Middle Ages contrasted with Protestant attempts to rid the religious life of external forms. For the populace, Catholic espousal of ritual and Protestant anti-ritualism was one of the most important differences between the two religious communities. Movement away from ritual did not begin in Spain until the late eighteenth century, when a small group of reformers influenced by the Enlightenment began to distrust formulaic religious acts, considering them a façade that hindered the development of a more personal spiritual life.[105] The attitude prevails today that ritual does not express genuine religious commitment.[106] Among the 'learned' in particular, only the anthropologists consistently recognize that symbolic behavior is an intensely rich experience that can express, deepen, and re-affirm communal values. Looking back to traditional European culture, it is only with their conscious appreciation that ritual is meaningful rather than empty that we begin to understand the longevity of certain sacred performances within popular piety.

Notes and References

ABBREVIATIONS

ACZ	Archivo de la Catedral de Zamora
AG Simancas	Archivo General de Simancas
AHN	Archivo Histórico Nacional
AHPZ	Archivo Histórico Provincial de Zamora
AMZ	Archivo de la Mitra de Zamora
CSEL	*Corpus Scriptorum Ecclesiasticorum Latinorum*
DDC	*Dictionnaire de droit canonique*

INTRODUCTION

1. Emile Durkheim, *Les formes élémentaires de la vie religieuse: le systèm totémique en Australie* (1912) translated by Joseph Ward Swain, *The Elementary Forms of Religious Life* (New York: Free Press, 1965).
2. Ibid., p. 16.
3. In *Religion and the Rise of Capitalism* (London, 1912).
4. E.g., Ingeborg Weber-Kellermann, *Deutsche Volkskunde zwischen Germanistik und Sozialwissenschaft* (Stuttgart, 1969).
5. Gabriel Le Bras, 'Statistiques et histoire religieuses. Pour un examen détaillé et pour une explication historique de l'état du catholicisme dans les diverses régions de France', *Rev. d'Histoire de l'Eglise de France* (October 1931) pp. 425–49; *Introduction à l'histoire de la pratique religieuse en France* (Paris: Presses universitaires de France, 1942–5); and *Etudes de sociologie religieuse* (Paris: Presses universitaires de Paris, 1955).
6. Keith Thomas, *Religion and the Decline of Magic* (London, 1971); Natalie Z. Davis, *Society and Culture in Early Modern France* (Stanford, 1975); Carlo Ginzburg, *Religioni della classi popolari, Quaderni Storici*, XLI (May–August, 1979) and *The Cheese and the Worms. The Cosmos of a Sixteenth-Century Miller*, translated by John and Anne Tedeschi (Baltimore, 1980); Richard C. Trexler, *Public Life in Renaissance Florence* (New York, 1980); William A. Christian Jr., *Local Religion in Sixteenth-Century Spain* (Princeton, 1981); and Thomas A. Brady, Jr. *Ruling Class, Regime and Reformation at Strasbourg 1520–1555* (Leiden, 1978).
7. Aron Ja. Gurevich, review of Jacques Le Goff, *La naissance du Purgatoire* (Paris, 1981) in *Journal of Medieval History*, IX (1983) 71–90; and 'Oral and Written Culture of the Middle Ages: Two "Peasant Visions" of the Late Twelfth–Early Thirteenth Centuries', *New Literary History*, XVI (Autumn 1984) 1, 51–66.

8. Lionel Rothkrug, 'Religious Practices and Collective Perceptions: Hidden Homologies in the Renaissance and Reformation', *Historical Reflections*, vii 1 (Spring 1980); and Roland Bainton, *Here I Stand! A Life of Martin Luther* (Nashville & N.Y., 1950).

9. Herbert Grundmann, *Religiöse bewegungen im mittelalter; untersuchungen über die geschichtlichen zusammenhänge zwischen der ketzerei* (Berlin, 1935); Jacques Toussaert, *Le Sentiment religieux en Flandre à la fin du moyen age* (Paris, 1963); Cinzio Violante, *Studi sulla cristianità medioevale* (Milan, 1972); R. Manselli, *La religion populaire au moyen âge* (Montreal–Paris, 1975); and Oronzo Giordano, *Religiosità popolare nell'alto medioevo* (Paris, 1979).

10. Benedicta Ward, *Miracles and the Medieval Mind. Theory, Record and Event, 1000–1215* (Philadelphia, 1982) p. 76.

11. Rothkrug, 'Religious Practices and Collective Perceptions', 64–5.

12. Jean Delumeau, *Catholicism from Luther to Voltaire*, originally published in 1971 by Presses universitaires de France; English edition, 1977.

13. Durkheim, *Elementary Forms of Religious Life*, p. 6.

14. G. Le Bras, 'Les confréries chrétiennes. Problèmes et propositions', *Revue historique de droit français et étranger* (Paris, 1940–1) 324.

15. John Bossy, 'The Counter-Reformation and the People of Catholic Europe', *Past and Present*, 47 (May 1970) 51–70.

16. For example, León Lallemand, *Histoire de la Charité* (4 vols, Paris, 1910); W. K. Jordan, *Philanthropy in England 1480–1660* (London, 1959); A. R. Hands, *Charities and Social Aid in Greece and Rome* (Ithaca, New York, 1968); M. Mollat, *Etudes sur l'Histoire de la Pauvreté* (Paris, 1974); William R. Jones, 'Pious Endowments in Medieval Christianity and Islam', *Diogenes*, cix (Spring 1980).

17. Teófanes Egido, 'La cofradía de San José y los niños expósitos de Valladolid', *Estudios Josefinos*, 53 (Valladolid, 1973) 77–100; and 'Religiosidad popular y asistencia social en Valladolid; Las Cofradías Marianas del s. XVI', *Estudios Marianos*, xlv (Salamanca, 1980) 197–217. Pedro Carasa Soto, 'La asistencia social y las cofradías en Burgos desde la crisis del Antiguo Régimen', *Investigaciones Históricas*, iii (1982); Marie-Claude Gerbet, 'Les confréries religieuse à Caceres de 1467 à 1523', *Mélanges de la Casa de Velázquez*, vii (1971) 75–113.

18. Wm. J. Callahan, 'Confinement and Poor Relief in Eighteenth-Century Spain', *Hispanic American Historical Review*, 51 (1971); 'Corporate Charity in Spain: The *Hermandad del Refugio* of Madrid, 1618–1814', *Histoire Social*, ix (1976) 159–186, and *La Santa y Real Hermandad del Refugio y Piedad de Madrid, 1618–1832* (Madrid, 1980). And María Rosa Pérez Estévez, *El problema de los vagos en la España del siglo XVIII* (Madrid, 1976).

19. J. Delumeau, *Catholicism*, pp. 129–153; and Le Bras, *Etudes*. See also J. Gedille, D. Julia and M. Venard, 'Pour un repertoire des visites pastorales', *Annales, Econ. Soc. Civ.* (1970) 561–6.

20. G. Meersseman, 'Etudes sur les anciennes confréries dominicaines',

Archivum Fratrum Praedicatorum, xxii (1951) 54–55.
21. P. O. Kristeller, 'Lay Religious Traditions and Florentine Platonism', *Studies in Renaissance Thought and Letters* (Rome, 1956) p. 105.
22. J. J. Scarisbrick points out that women in English religious guilds were frequently full members and they sometimes held official positions: in *The Reformation and the English People* (Oxford: Basil Blackwell, 1984) p. 25.
23. Le Bras, 'Les confréries chrétiennes', p. 310.

1. THE CONFRATERNAL STRUCTURE OF ZAMORA

1. AHPZ, Desamortización, *Caja* 108.
2. Augustine, *The City of God*, book 21, chapter 27. See also Hugh of Saint Victor, *On the Sacraments of the Christian Faith (De Sacramentis)* book 2, part 16. English version by Roy J. Deferrari, (Cambridge, Massachusetts: Medieval Academy of America, 1951).
3. Augustine, *Enchiridion*, 110. Assistance offered by the living was efficacious only for moderate sinners however, according to Augustine. Those who committed mortal sins were incapable of being saved. 'When, then, sacrifices either of the altar or of alms are offered on behalf of all the baptized dead, they are thank-offerings for the very good; they are propitiatory offerings for the not very bad; and in the case of the very bad, even though they do not assist the dead, they are a species of consolation to the living.'
4. John Bossy's study of the social consciousness of the mass examines the process whereby communicants offered prayers and charity for the benefit of souls in purgatory during services. 'Essai de Sociographie de la messe, 1200–1700', *Annales, E.S.C.*, xxxvi, (1981) pp. 44–70.
5. Claudio Sánchez-Albornoz, *Despoblación y repoblación del Valle del Duero* (Buenos Aires, 1966) p. 253.
6. Amando Represa, 'Génesis y evolución urbana de la Zamora medieval', *Hispania*, cxxii (1972) 528–30.
7. Juan de Villuga, *Repertorio de todos los caminos de España* (Medina del Campo, 1546), several copies of which are in the Biblioteca Nacional in Madrid, in the section *Libros Raros*.
8. Bartolomé Bennassar, *Valladolid au siècle d'or* (Paris, 1967) p. 80.
9. The land of the province of Zamora was similar in fertility to that of other regions in Spain. The sedimentary soils bordering the Duero were particularly rich for agriculture, and only the region of Sayago contained extremely poor soil, suitable solely for sheep-grazing or forestry. To the north of the city, the Tierra del Pan supplied cereals and some meat; to the east, the Tierra del Toro provided wines as well as cereal and meat; and the southern Tierra del Vino provided wine, wheat, legumes and fruits. Except during times of scarcity, Zamora was self-sufficient in subsistence items. But such times of scarcity, usually produced by inadequate rainfull, occurred regularly. José Antonio Alvarez Vázquez has calculated that almost every three years residents sought permission from the cathedral chapter to engage in petitionary

processions for rain due to serious droughts. (José Antonio Alvarez Vázquez, 'Diezmos y agricultura en Zamora, 1500–1840' [Doctoral thesis, University of Salamanca, 1977] pp. 55–9.)

10. *leg*. 18, doc. 2, August 1230; *leg*. 15, doc. 16, 10 May 1250.
11. Amando Represa, 'Génesis', 534.
12. Some of the merchants were French: AMZ, no. 1419, *leg*. 13=(D–3), no. 26.
13. Luis G. de Valdeavellano, *Curso de Historia de las Instituciones españolas* (Madrid, 1977) p. 268. Chroniclers of the Reconquest in the eleventh century noted that the Moors, for administrative purposes, carefully segregated workers into districts according to craft. Some of these crafts advanced to the stage of guild organization, with selected men of the profession enforcing government regulations on production, prices, and weights. They also inspected handicraft techniques and working conditions. See Julius Klein, 'Medieval Spanish Gilds', *Facts and Factors in Economic History* (Cambridge, Mass., 1932) p. 164 and 168. Although voluntary fraternal organizations of craftsmen did not emerge in the Muslim towns in Spain, nor in Africa before the thirteenth century (see S. D. Goitein, *Studies in Islamic History and Institutions* [Leiden, 1966], pp. 267–70), the practise of segregating crafts may have given craftsmen the impulse to form guild corporations.
14. G. Meersseman, 'Etudes sur les anciennes confréries dominicaines', *Archivum Fratrum Praedicatorum*, xxii (1951) pp. 275–93; and 'Pénitents ruraux communitaires en Italie au XIIᵉ siècle', *Revue d'histoire ecclésiastique*, xlix (1954) pp. 343–90.
15. Population figures come from the AG Simancas, Expedientes de Hacienda, *leg*. 205; 'Relación de los vecinos', 1561.
16. Teófanes Egido, 'Religiosidad popular y asistencia social en Vallodolid: Las Cofradías Marianas del s. XVI', *Estudios Marianos*, xlv (Salamanca, 1980) 198; and Linda Martz, *Poverty and Welfare in Habsburg Spain* (Cambridge, 1983) p. 159.
17. Sara Tilghman Nalle, 'Religion and Reform in a Spanish Diocese: Cuenca, 1545–1650' (PhD dissertation, Johns Hopkins University, 1983) p. 255. The ratio for the city of Toledo taken from Linda Martz's study is affirmed by William Christian as representative of the entire region of Toledo in *Local Religion in Sixteenth-Century Spain* (Princeton, N.J., 1981) p. 149.
18. Benedetto Varchi, *Storia fiorentina* (Florence: Salani, 1963) pp. 9 and 36. Population figures come from David Herlihy and Christiane Klapisch-Zuber, *Les Toscans et leurs familles* (Paris, 1978) p. 183, using a coefficient of 6.21 for 9527 hearths.
19. Natalie Davis, 'The Sacred and the Body Social in Sixteenth-Century Lyon', *Past and Present*, 90, 51.
20. Monika Zmyslony, *Die Bruderschaften in Lübeck bis zur Reformation* (Kiel, 1977); and Edith Ennen, *The Medieval Town* (New York, 1979) p. 200. Population statistics for Lübeck are cited in Ennen, p. 188. Her estimation of the population of Hamburg is for the mid-fifteenth century (p. 88). Over 100 confraternities existed in Northamptonshire in the early sixteenth century, with fourteen in Northampton. Lincolnshire

had 120 confraternities with five in both Stamford and Louth. Leicester had seven. J. J. Scarisbrick, *The Reformation and the English People* (Oxford, 1984) p. 28. In 1619, Lima, Peru, with a population of approximately 9500, supported 46 lay confraternities. See Olinda Celestino and Albert Meyers, *Las cofradías en el Perú: Región central* (Frankfurt, Main, 1981) p. 117.

21. AHPZ, *leg.* XXX, no. 20.
22. Three quarters of the residents in the neighborhood of the cathedral of Zamora were identified as paupers in a census of 1618. AHPZ. *leg.* XXX, no. 20. For Valladolid, see Bennassar, *Valladolid*, p. 439.
23. AMZ, no. 66, dated 19 April 1338.
24. AMZ, Archivo de los Ciento, *Ordenanzas de la Cofradía de los Racioneros*, late sixteenth century.
25. AMZ, Archivo de los Ciento, *Constituciones de la Cofradía de los Ciento*, 1588.
26. AMZ, Archivo de los Ciento, *Constituciones de la Cofradía de Santa María la Antigua*, no. 1.
27. In 1591, the 147 secular priests in the city shared with the regulars at least 158 positions in clerical confraternities, while the city's 86 noble families shared 269 openings in aristocratic organizations. AG Simancas, Dirección General del Tesoro, *Inv.* 24, *leg*, 1301.
28. Most of them joined plebeian brotherhoods in addition to those of their own estate.
29. AHPZ, Protocolos, no. 719, *fol.* 247.
30. The *maravedí* was the smallest unit of account in the Castilian monetary system. Its approximate value was one-sixth of a 1980s US cent; 375 *maravedís* equalled a ducat.
31. Fees required by noble confraternities varied more than those of commoners, ranging from 300 to 1000 *maravedís* in the sixteenth century.
32. AHPZ, Protocolos, no. 263, *fol.* 63; and no. 267, *fol.* 339.
33. AHPZ, Protocolos, no. 153, *fol.* 340.
34. AHPZ, Protocolos, no. 574, *fol.* 402v. And AHPZ, Protocolos, no. 575, *fol.* 332v.
35. These were the Cofradía de Nuestra Señora de la Caridad and Nuestra Señora de la Anunciación, commonly known as 'Valdés'. Teófanes Egido remarks on a similar phenomenon in Valladolid. Four aristocratic confraternities incorporated purity of blood statutes there, while the majority were open to people of diverse races, classes and professions; in 'Religiosidad popular', p. 203.
36. A. Sicroff, *Les Controverses des statutes de 'pureté de sang' en Espagne du XV au XVII siècle* (Paris, 1960) pp. 20–32 and 95; and Antonio Domínguez Ortiz, *La clase social de los conversos en Castilla en la Edad Moderna* (Madrid, 1955) vol. III, pp. 9–17.
37. Ronald Weissman, *Ritual Brotherhood in Renaissance Florence* (New York: Academic Press, 1982) pp. 212–13; and Natalie Zemon Davis, 'City Women and Religious Change', *Society and Culture in Early Modern France* (Stanford, 1975) p. 75.
38. Widows made up 24% of all households in Zamora in 1561 and 18.6

percent in 1599. AG Simancas, Hacienda, *leg.* 205. Widows constituted high percentages of the poor in other Castilian cities: 83% of all the poor in Medina del Campo; 60% in Segovia; and 38.6% in Valladolid. Bennassar, *Valladolid*, p. 436.

39. In Spain, women enjoyed full legal rights to dispose of property, and they were among the most important grantors of land to the confraternities. According to the Visigothic codes of the early Middle Ages, women in Spain had the same juridical rights as men over their properties. Upon the death of their husbands, they recovered full ownership of dowries from their husbands, and inherited one half of the goods acquired during the marriage, in addition to goods directly willed to them. See Law XVI of the *Leyes de Toro*, 1505; and Claudio Sánchez-Albornoz, 'La mujer española hace mil anos', in *España y Islam* (Buenos Aires, 1943) pp. 116–18.

40. The French philosophes and physiocrats, of whom Denis Diderot was the most articulate, led the first critical discussions about corporate society. See especially Diderot's article on 'Art' in the *Encyclopedie*. In Spain, see Rodríguez de Campomanes, *Apéndice a la educación popular*, III, iii–cclxx.

41. AHN, *Sección Clero, Carpeta* 3584, no. 15, 6 August 1440.

42. Archivo Parroquial de San Lázaro, no. 47.

43. Archivo Parroquial de San Torcuato, *Libro* 18, Accounts of the Cofradía de San Juan Bautista, 1613–32.

44. On the guilds in Zamora, see María del Carmen Pescador del Hoyo, 'Los gremios de Artesanos en Zamora', in the *Revista de Archivos, Bibliotecas, Museos* (Madrid) LXXV (1968–1972) pp. 183–200; LXXVI (1973) pp. 13–60; and LXXVII (1974) pp. 67–101.

45. Bernard H. Moss, *The Origins of the French Labor Movement: The Socialism of Skilled Workers, 1830–1914* (Berkeley and Los Angeles, 1976); E. P. Thompson, *The Making of the English Working Class* (London, 1963).

46. William H. Sewell, Jr. *Work and Revolution in France*, (Cambridge, 1980) pp. 77–113.

47. R. W. Southern, *The Making of the Middle Ages* (New Haven, 1953) p. 248. Stories of the miracles of the Virgin show that she did not withhold her aid from thieves, vagabonds and miscreants of any sort. See, for example, the codices of the *Cantigas de Santa María* in the Escorial; Jesús Montoya Martínez, *Las colecciones de milagros de la Virgen en la edad media: el milagro literario* (Granada, 1981) pp. 152–3; and Johnannes Herold, *Miracles of the Blessed Virgin Mary*, edited by Eileen Power (London, 1928).

48. For a critical examination of the thought of several Salamancan theologicans, see Karl Deuringer, *Probleme der Caritas in der Schule von Salamanca* (Freiburg, 1959).

49. Proceedings of the public vow of the Immaculate Conception, recorded in Luis Calvo Lozano, *Historia de Villalpando y su tierra.* (Zamora, 1981) pp. 126–9.

50. Ibid.

51. AMZ, Uncatalogued. *Estatutos y Ordenanzas de la Cofradía de*

Nuestra Señora de la Anunciación, page 1.

52. On the strict requirements of virginity for woment to enter the ranks of sainthood in the Middle Ages, see P. Bröwe, *Beitrage zur Sexualithik des Mittelalters* (Breslau: 1932); and André Vauchez, *La Sainteté en Occident aux derniers siècles du moyen âge* (Rome: 1981) pp. 442–5.

53. *Ordenanzas de Nuestra Señora de San Antolín y del Señor Santiago de la Cuidad de Zamora. Año de 1503* in E. Fernández-Prieto, *Nobleza de Zamora* (Madrid, 1953) pp. 33–45.

54. Pierre Duparc places the origins of confraternities of the Holy Spirit before the Carolingian age, although the oldest texts which he uses mentioning the Holy Spirit date from the thirteenth century. Pierre Duparc, 'Confréries du Sant-Esprit et communautés d'habitants au moyen-âge', *Revue historique de droit français et étranger*, 4th series, 36 (1958) p. 350; The Hospital order of friars of the Holy Spirit was founded in the mid-twelfth century in Montpellier, after which time it spread throughout Europe. Joseph Duhr, 'Confréries', *Dictionnaire de Spiritualité ascétique et mystique* (Paris, 1953) p. 1472.

55. Early church fathers interpret the term *paracletus*, as used in the gospels of John, the only place where it appears in the Bible, as 'advocate, intercessor and comforter'. (Origen, *de Princ.* II. vii. 4; Chrysostom, *Hom. in Joh.* lxxv; Augustine, *Tractate IX*, 'On the gospel of John', p. 65, and *Tractate XCIV*, p. 367. The term 'consoler' was used by Hugh of San Cher in the mid-thirteenth century, in *Com. on John*, on XV:26, ('"Paracletus": id est consolatur'); and Nicolas of Lyra in the fourteenth century, *Com.* on John XIV:16, ('id est consolatorem').

56. Archivo de la Catedral de Salamanca. *Constituciones Synodales* of 1570, *fols* 27 and 28, *Const.* 51 and 53; and AMZ, *Libro* III, *tít.* XVII, *Constituciones Synodales* of 1584, *Const.* 18.

57. AHPZ, Municipal, *Libro de Actas* (12) 17 April 1589. On the growth of the cult of the Virgen de los Remedios, see B. Porres Alonso, 'Advocación y culto de la Virgen de los Remedios en España', *Hispana Sacra*, xxiii (1970) pp. 3–77.

58. ACZ, *Libro* 94. *Libro de los Acuerdos de la Cofradía de Nuestra Señora del Socorro*, *fol.* 22.

59. E. Fernández-Prieto, *Nobleza de Zamora*, p, 429.

60. AHPZ, Municipal, *Libro de Actas* (14) 27 July 1599.

61. AHPZ, Municipal, *Libro de Actas* (90) 10 May 1563, and (10) 12 November 1571, fols 119v–121.

62. Confraternities across Europe governed themselves with remarkably similar democratic forms, changing little over the centuries. The thesis of Ronald Weissman which associates confraternal democracy in Florence with the ideology of the republican city-state (see his *Ritual Brotherhood*) seems less compelling in the context of the general phenomenon of confraternal republicanism, in absolutist as well as in democratic states. These multitudinous cells of republicanism, offering direct participatory government to so much of the population in medieval and early modern Europe, and their role in and influence on

political theory and experience has yet to be fully acknowledged and explored.

63. Archivo parroquial de San Frontis; *Libro* 38, *Ordenanzas* of 1630.
64. Canon 691 in the *Corpus Juris Canonici*.
65. Church councils of the early Middle Ages decreed that those who failed to distribute bequests in alms according to the wishes of the dead would be excommunicated; and the Justinian Code confirmed rights to the will of the dead (*Codex Justinianus*, 1, 3, 45); the sentiments of conciliar decrees were repeated by Canonists, see Gratian's *Decretum*, Canon 9, 'Qui oblationes', and Canon 11, 'Clerici vel saeculares'; and Huguccio, *Summa ad Dict.*, 88, canon 5. The *Siete Partidas* enforced the fulfillment of testamentary works in *partida* 6, *tít.* 10, *leyes* 1–6.
66. The church was heartily opposed to this practice, arguing that lay people did not have the right to designate what did and did not constitute a mortal sin. Throughout the late Middle Ages it attempted to eradicate these confraternal oaths.
67. Proving negligent on many occasions. *Ordenanzas*, AMZ, Archivo de los Ciento, *Constituciones de la Cofradía de los Cientos fols* 26–28; the Cofradía de San Nicolás sent the *mayordomo* and his four assistants to inspect its property, Fernández-Prieto, *Nobleza de Zamora*, p. 384.
68. AMZ, uncatalogued civil process against the Cofradía de Nuestra Señora de la Caridad, 1581. Disputes in 1494 are recorded in the ACZ, no. 1450, *leg.* 36=(L–4); no. 15.
69. Valdeavellano, *Curso de Historia de las Instituciones españolas*, p. 247. Sánchez-Albornoz's study of church cartularies in the tenth and eleventh century anticipates the conclusions made by his student, Valdeavellano, in *Despoblación y repoblación del Valle del Duero* (Buenos Aires: 1966) pp. 284–9 and in *El régimen de la tierra en al reino Asturleonés hace mil años* (Buenos Aires, 1978) pp. 19–57, where he stresses the spiritual motivations behind the hundreds of donations to monasteries which he has examined. Other scholars argue, however, that much land was turned over to secular princes and counts from peasant proprietors whose main concerns were to secure protection against dynastic and baronial warfare and violence. Documentation to support the latter thesis is not cited, but by its nature is less likely to have survived. See Robert Smith, 'Spain', chapter VII of *The Cambridge Economic History of Europe*, vol. I, edited by M. M. Postan (Cambridge, 1966).
70. In the *Catastro del Marqués de la Ensenada*, a register of property, salaries, and other income of individuals and religious institutions in the provinces of Castile, compiled in the mid-eighteenth century, we have the opportunity to calculate the amount of land held by the various religious institutions, including confraternities and hospitals.
71. The early church fathers recommended that one-third to one-half of one's estate, 'the share of the soul', be given for pious purposes, as donations to church institutions or alms to the poor, and these were frequently administered by confraternities. Augustine directed that bequests in alms should not exceed a son's share if children survived. Gratian returned to Augustine's position, although other canonists

argued that Augustine's intention had been to dissuade but not to prohibit donations larger than an inheritor's share. Roman law imposed definite minimal limits on inheritances for children (*pars legitima*) of one-half to one-third of estates. See Michael M. Sheehan, *The Will in Medieval England* (Toronto, 1963) pp. 8, 123, and 127. In 1505, Spanish secular legislation restricted the amount that could be bequeathed for the welfare of one's soul to one-fifth of one's estate (*Leyes de Toro, leyes* 12 and 32); and according to Moralists (not stated in Canon Law), testators could leave up to one-third of the 'legítimo', and the 'mejora', (usually used to favor one son in a system in which primogeniture was not encouraged) to the church for pious causes so long as it would not harm descendents. Natural law required that parents give to their children only that which they needed. If they left more than one-third to the church, and inheritors took it to court, the will of the civil judges prevailed.

72. Property holdings of the cathedral chapter in Zamora and its management of lands is explored in detail in José Antonio Alvarez Vázquez's thesis, 'Diezmos y argicultura en Zamora', already cited. In 1546, Bishop Antonio de la Aguila confirmed that the church in Zamora was worth more than 5000 ducats, ranking twenty-fifth in wealth among peninsular cathedral churches. AG Simancas, *Patronato Eclesiástico*, No. 1.

73. AHPZ, *Libro de Actas* (14), *fol*. 330, 22 August 1588.

74. *Ordenanzas de la Cofradía de San Nicolás*, in E. Fernández-Prieto, *Nobleza de Zamora*, p. 387, *tít*. XIX.

75. 'porque mejor se junten', AMZ, uncatalogued, *Ordenanzas de la Cofradía de Nuestra Señora de la Anunciación, fol*. 8v, 1531. For locating the statutes of this confraternity, commonly called 'Valdés', I am grateful to Father Ramon Fita Revert, personal secretary to the Bishop in Zamora.

76. *Ordenanzas de la Cofradía de San Nicolás*, in Fernández-Prieto, *Nobleza de Zamora*, p. 383. *tít*. IX and X.

77. AMZ, Archivo de los Ciento, *Ordenanzas de la Cofradía de Nuestra Señora de la Visitación*.

78. AMZ, Archivo de los Ciento, *Ordenanzas de la Cofradía de los Racioneros, fol*. 3, *tít*, 3 and *fol*. 10, *tít*. 11.

79. *Ordenanzas de la Cofradía de San Nicolás*, in Fernández-Prieto, *Nobleza de Zamora*, p. 390, *tít*. 31.

80. Archivo Particular de Don Enrique Fernández-Prieto, *Orden* 1891, no. 7, *Estatutos de Nuestra Señora del Rosario y Purificación*, 1544; *tít*. 13 and 14.

81. AMZ, Archivo de Santa María de la Horta, Santo Tomás, no. 17. The ordinances of Santo Cristo are from the eighteenth century.

82. Archivo Particular de Don Enrique Fernández-Prieto, *Estatutos de la Cofradía de Nuestra Señora de San Antolín*.

83. *Ordenanzas de la Cofradía de San Antonio Abad*, 1591, transcribed by José del Carmen, and published in 1928; a copy of which was kindly given to me by the current mayordomo.

84. *Ordenanzas de San Nicolás*, 1538, in Fernández-Prieto, *Nobleza de*

Zamora, p. 386.

85. AMZ, Archivo de los Ciento, *Ordenanzas de la Cofradía de Nuestra Señora de la Antigua; Estatutos de la Cofradía de la Vera Cruz*, in Luis Calvo Lozano, *Historia de la Villa de Villalpando y su Tierra* (Zamora: Diputación Provincial, 1981).

86. Archivo Parroquial de San Frontis, *Libro* 38, *Ordenanzas de 1630*.

87. AMZ, Archivo de los Ciento, *Ordenanzas de la Cofradía de los Racioneros, fol.* 17v.

88. AMZ, Archivo de Santa María de la Horta, Tomás Apostal, *Libro* 16, *Ordenanzas de la Cofradía de San Cucufate*, 1509.

89. *Ordenanzas de la Cofradía de San Nicolás*, in Fernández-Prieto, *Nobleza de Zamora*, pp. 391–2.

90. AMZ, Archivo de los Cientos, *Ordenanzas de la Cofradía de Nuestra Señora de la Antigua*, 1566.

91. AMZ, Archivo Santa María de la Horta, Santa María de la Horta, no. 41(1) *Ordenanzas de la Cofradía de Santa María de Tercia y Santa Catalina* 1552, ordinance no. 10.

92. *Ordenanzas de Nuestra Señora de San Antolín...*, in Fernández-Prieto, *Nobleza de Zamora*, and the *Estatutos de la Cofradía de la Santa Cruz*, in Luis Calvo Lozano, *Historia*, statutes of 1580, pp. 240–1.

93. *The New Catholic Encyclopedia*, 'Meals, Sacred'. And Emile Durkheim, *The Elementary Forms of Religious Life*, trans. by Joseph Ward Swain (New York: Free Press, 1965) p. 378.

94. Cofrades of San Ildefonso dined on fruit of the season, partridges and roast hens, breasts of fowl in rice, lamb, beef, and bacon finished off with more fruit, pastries, and white wine from Madrigal or Medina del Campo. Three smaller repasts were interspersed throughout the year, consisting of lighter foods such as pastries and fruits. It was a wealthy confraternity which could fare well, and was by no means representative of most fraternal meals. The poor confraternity of San Cucufate ate much more frugally on fruit and trout. AMZ, *Ordenanzas de la Cofradía de San Ildefonso*, p. 518.

95. Ibid.

2. THE CHARITABLE ACTIVITIES OF CONFRATERNITIES

1. Pierre Chaunu, *Le Temps des deux réformes de l'Eglise* (Paris: Fayard, 1975) p. 172. Gabriel Le Bras has said that late medieval confraternities were oriented less toward the practise of the sacraments and more toward the liturgy and acts of mercy and piety. *Introduction à l'histoire de la pratique religieuse en France* (Paris, 1942–45) vol. 1.

2. The duties of almsgiving were by no means a peculiarly Christian phenomenon. All major world religions have shared a similar evaluation of charity, including the idea that charity propitiates the gods. Edward Westermarck, *The Origin and Development of the Moral Ideas* (London, 1906), chapter 23 on 'Charity and Generosity'. For a discussion of the attitudes of the early church fathers to charity, see Boniface Ramsey, O.P., 'Almsgiving in the Latin Church: The Late

Fourth and Early Fifth centuries', *Theological Studies*, XLIII, 2, (June 1982) 226–59.

3. Tomás de Trujillo, *Libro llamado Reprobación de Trajes y abusos de juramentos con un tratado de limosnas* (Estella, 1563) 225.

4. AMZ, *Ordenanzas de San Ildefonso*, of 1503, p. 522.

5. Augustine, *Enchiridion*, Chapter 19:67–9, in CSEL, XLIV, 48; English edition in *The Library of Christian Classics* (Philadelphia, 1955), VII, pp. 378–81.

6. *Enchiridion*, Chapter 19:72.

7. Augustine, *In. Ep. Ionn.* 8:9, in Migne, *Patrologia Latina*, XXXV, col. 2040.

8. Those which repeated Augustine and were adopted as formal acts of charity were: to relieve the poor, to clothe the naked, to visit the sick and to bury the dead. *The Rules of St. Benedict*, chapter 4: 'The Tools of Good Works'.

9. *Monumenta Germaniae Historica*, ed. George Pertz, (1835) *Legum, tomus* 1, *Karoli Magni capitularia*. 802. 'Admonitio Generalis', lines 16–29.

10. Michel Mollat, *Les Pauvres au Moyen Âge: étude sociale* (Paris, 1978) pp. 112–13.

11. Alfonso X. *Las Siete Partidas*, *Partida* 1, *tít*. XXIII, *ley* IX.

12. They paralleled here the seven sacraments, the seven theological and cardinal virtues, the seven cardinal sins and the seven gifts of the Holy Spirit (wisdom, understanding, counsel, fortitude, knowledge, piety and fear of the Lord.)

13. Juan Ruiz, Arcipreste de Hita, *Libro de buen amor* (Madrid: Espasa Calpe, 1974) pp. 257–63.

14. ['Hope and faith you will lose
    when before God
    you stand, wait and see

    with great generosity
    offer acts of charity
    that your will be pure

    The greatness of charity
    is that it fulfills all needs
    and he who receives it not shall pass Heaven by.]

    Pedro de Verague, *Doctrina de la discreción* in Florencio Janer (ed.), *Biblioteca de Autores Espanoles* (Madrid: 1864) LVII, pp. 373–8.

15. 'El catecismo de Albórnoz', in *Studia Albornotiano* (Cartagena, 1972) II, p. 225. The verse is also included in the *Summa Theologica* of Thomas Aquinas, Part. II, Q. 32, Art. 2.

16. AHPZ, Protocolos, no. 80, *fol*. 348.

17. AHPZ, Protocolos, no. 80, *fol*. 249.

18. AHPZ, Protocolos, no. 130, *fols* 239–44v.

19. Victor Turner, *Dramas, Fields and Metaphors* (Cornell, 1974) p. 249.

20. ACZ, *leg*. 18, doc. 2; *leg*. 17, no. 1; and *leg*. 12, no. 14.

21. AMZ, *Ordenanzas de San Ildefonso*, p. 512; AMZ, Archivo de los

Cientos, *Ordenanzas de Nuestra Señora de la Antigua* of 1566, page 3.

22. According to official censuses in the AG Simancas. Hacienda, *leg*. 205.

23. Fundamental studies of the history of hospitals in Spain are: Fermín Hernández Iglesias, *La beneficencia en España* (Madrid, 1876); Antonio Rumeu de Armas, *Historia de la Previsión Social en España* (Madrid, 1944); María Jiménez Salas, *Historia de la Asistencia Social en España en la edad moderna* (Madrid, 1958); and the articles deriving from a conference in Portugal, compiled in *Actas das los Jornandas Luso-Espanholas de Historia Medieval* (2 vols, Lisbon: 25–30 September 1972). For Europe in general, and especially France, see the recent study by Michel Mollat, *Les Pauvres au Moyen Age, étude sociale* (Paris, 1978).

24. There is no available evidence that the merchants formed a confraternity in the twelfth century. ACZ, no. 1419, *leg*. 13, no. 26. In the mid- to the late-fifteenth century, the confraternity of Nuestra Señora del Caño took jurisdiction over the hospital.

25. ACZ, *leg*. 16, no. 46.

26. A detailed study of the origins of the word 'falifa' by Manuel García Blanco attributes it to Arabic origins; this usage appeared first in the thirteenth century, and by the fourteenth century the new meaning of a pledge of clothing was common in these parts of Spain. Manuel García Blanco, *La lengua española en la epoca de Carlos V* (Madrid, 1967) pp. 135–67.

27. AHPZ, Protocolos, no. 118, *fol*. 143.

28. ACZ, *leg*. 239.

29. AHPZ, Protocolos, no. 36, *fols* 320–1; 17 September 1546.

30. *Estatutos de la Cofradía del San Ildefonso*. p. 531; and Archivo Particular Fernández-Prieto, *Libro de los Acuerdos de la Cofradía de San Ildefonso de los Cavalleros* 1582–1611.

31. Archivo Garci-Grande, *Libro de Cuentas de la Cofradía de San Ildefonso*, 1520. In 1520, the hospital was supplied with 26 blankets, six feather mattresses, four sleeping mats and three sheets.

32. The wood of the guayaco tree began to be shipped to Spain from the island of Hispañola in 1508 for treatment of syphilis. André Soubirán and Jean de Kearney, *El Diario de la medicina* (Barcelona, 1980) pp. 184–5; J. A. Paniagua, Clínica del Renacimiento', in P. Laín Entralgo (ed.), *Historia Universal de la Medicina*, vol. IV (Barcelona, 1973) p. 100; P. Laín Entralgo, *Historia de la Medicina moderna y contemporánea* (Barcelona, 1954) p. 49; H. Haeser, *Lehrbuch der Geschichte der Medicin*, vol. II (Jena, 1881) pp. 82–3, and vol. III, pp. 246–7, and 290–3. And Robert S. Munger, 'Guaiacum, the Holy Wood from the New World', *Journal of the History of Medicine* (Spring 1949) pp. 196–229.

33. Archivo Particular Fernández-Prieto, *Libro de los Acuerdos de la Cofradía de San Ildefonso*; 1582–1611.

34. AHPZ, Municipal, *leg*. 21, no. 58; 8 August 1586.

35. AHPZ, Diputación, *leg*. 63.

36. Archivo de la Universidad de Santiago. Archivo de los Reyes Católicos, Serie 3, Libro 1, *Libro de la Real Cofradía de Santiago*,

1503–04; and *leg.* 63, no. 27. Donations increased to a sixth of a ducat to cover building and repair costs, nos 42–48.

37. Ibid. *leg.* 63, nos 28, 42–8.
38. Ibid., *Sección* 6, *libro* 1. *Libro de cabildos de la Real Hospital.* fol. 26v. Little is known about the medical treatment provided in the hospital. Generally, only patients with non-contagious diseases were allowed into the hospital. Medicine bought at the fairs in Medina del Campo was used, and barber-surgeons performed bloodletting and cleaned and shaved pilgrims as they entered. In 1557, a severe outbreak of the plague in the city compelled the hospital to accept children stricken with buboes, considered symptoms of a contagious disease. The children were treated with medicaments and purged in a manner done 'without sticks'. Ibid., *libro* 2.
39. AMZ, Archivo de Santa María de la Horta. Santa María de la Horta, no. 41 (1).
40. *Ordenanzas de la Cofradía de la Vera Cruz de Villalcampo* in Luis Calvo Lozano, *Historia*.
41. Archivo parroquial de San Frontis, *Libro* 33.
42. Antonio Rumeu de Armas, *Historia de la previsión social en España* (Madrid, 1944) pp. 587–97, and pp. 242–4 on security against dangers of maternity.
43. Marjorie Nice Boyer, *Medieval French Bridges: A History* (Cambridge, Massachusetts: Medieval Academy of America, 1976) p. 31. Mircea Eliade discusses the universal use of the concept of bridges in *The Sacred and the Profane, The Nature of Religion*, translated by Willard R. Trask, (New York and London, 1959) pp. 181–3.
44. St Bernard, *Sermo de Aquaeducto. In Nativitate Beatae Mariae Virginis*, in Migne, *Patrologia Latina*, vol. 183, col. 1013–14.
45. Alexandro Anglico, Dr. *Tratado muy útile de las obras de misericordia*, translated from the Latin by Pero González de la Torre (Toledo, 1530) *fol.* 6.
46. AHPZ, Desamortización, *Caja* 138.
47. For the distribution of hospices along the road to Santiago in Burgos, see the article by Pedro Carasa Soto, 'La asistencia social y las cofradías en Burgos desde la crisis del Antiguo Régimen', *Investigaciones Históricas*, vol. III (University of Valladolid, 1986) pp. 179–229. Hospitals and hospices dependent on confraternities in Leon, Astorga, Zamora, Salamanca, Cuidad Rodrigo and Palencia are examined by José Sánchez Herrero, 'Cofradías, Hospitales y Beneficencia en algunas diócesis del valle del Duero, siglos XIV y XV', *Hispania*, cxxvi (January–April 1974) 34.
48. The attribution of pious motives to bridge-building in the twelfth century accelerated bridge construction after a period of relative abandonment in the central Middle Ages according to Marjorie Nice Boyer, *Medieval French Bridges*, p. 31. One of the earliest bridge confraternities appeared in 1084 in France, near Bonpas, over the Durance river. 'Confréries', DDC (Paris, 1935–65) col. 142. In England, Stratford-upon-Avon had two brotherhoods of bridges, that of the Holy Cross and of the Assumption. See J. J. Jusserand, *English*

Wayfaring Life in the Middle Ages (London, 1961) p. 32.

49. The bulls were republished in 1806 in Valladolid in 'Bulas y Brebes de diferentes sumos Pontífices, las que contienen varias concesiones y gracias en favor del santuario y cofrades de Nuestra Señora de Carballeda'. For graciously providing me with copies of the bulls and ordinances of the Cofradía de los Falifos in Rionegro del Puente, I thank Don José Prieto Carro, of the village of Rionegro.

50. *Constituciones de la Cofradía de Nuestra Señora de la Carballeda*, published in Valladolid, no date; approved by the council of the confraternity in 1785 and by Carlos III in 1787. Introduction, *fols* 2v and 3; chapter 11, *fols* 10 and 10v; and the bulls, pp. 3, 15 and 16.

51. *Constituciones de Nuestra Señora de la Carballeda*, *fols* 5v and 6; chapter 13, fol. 11; chapters 21 and 22, *fols* 14 and 14v. In Madrid, the Hospital de los niños expósitos, or la Inclusa, began to take in children by 1572 after devoting itself to convalescents. In 1600, the Asilo de los niños Desamparados was also established in Madrid for children. Jacques Soubeyroux , 'El encuentro del pobre y la sociedad: asistencia y represión en el Madrid del siglo XVIII', *Estudios de Historia Social*, 20–1 (1982) 21.

52. In the last decade of the sixteenth century, 5000 *maravedís* would have been equivalent to the value of 10 bushels of wheat.

53. Archivo Municipal de Salamanca, uncatalogued, *Libro del recibo i gasto de los niños expósitos de la cofradía de San Joseph y Nuestra Señora de la Piedad*.

54. Teófanes Egido, 'La cofradía de San José y los niños expósitos de Valladolid', *Estudios Josefinos*, 53 (Valladolid, 1973) 83–5 and 95–9; and Archivo Municipal de Valladolid, *Libro de Actas*. 23 July 1597, *fol.* 245.

55. ACZ, *leg*. 255. *Libro de Niños expósitos*.

56. ACZ, *leg*. 18, no. 24.

57. *Ordenanzas de la Cofradía de San Nicolás*, in Fernández-Prieto, *Nobleza de Zamora*, p. 397.

58. Ibid., p. 397.

59. AMZ, *Ordenanzas de la Cofradía de Nuestra Señora de la Anunciación*, or Valdés, *fols* 40v and 41v; and ACZ, *leg*. 239 and 208.

60. AMZ, Documentación Valdés. *Libro de Acuerdos*, *fol*. 83v. 2 December 1638. By the end of the eighteenth century, the total amount of property owned by the confraternity of San Nicolás brought in 2845 bushels of wheat and barley in yearly income. AHPZ, *Desamortización, Caja* 102, no. 8.

61. AMZ, *Ordenanzas de la Cofradía de Nuestra Señora de la Anunciación*, *fols* 29–29v, and 37.

62. AHPZ, Protocolos, no. 353. *fol*. 253.

63. AHPZ, Diputación, *leg*. 69.

64. Ibid.

65. AMZ, Archivo parroquial de Santa María de la Horta, Santa Lucía, No. 29. Archivo parroquial de San Ildefonso, No. 19. And AHPZ, Protocolos, no. 348, *fols* 172 and 185v; no. 331, *fols* 241–242; and no. 287, *fols* 3v–4.

66. Pablo de Espinosa, *Teatro de la Santa Iglesia metropolitana de Sevilla* (Seville, 1635) 71.

67. Ellen Friedman, *Spanish Captives in North Africa in the Early Modern Age* (Madison, 1983); and James William Brodman, *Ransoming Captives in Crusader Spain: The Order of Merced on the Christian-Islamic Frontier* (Pennsylvania, 1986).

68. AMZ, Archivo parroquial de Santa María de la Horta, Archivo de San Julián (4). ACZ, *leg*. 19, no. 6.

69. AHPZ, Protocolos, No. 69. *fols* 502–508v; and ACZ, *leg*. 19, no. 6.

70. AG Simancas, Consejo y Junta de Hacienda, *leg*. 240, no. 22. Archivo Municipal de Valladolid, *Libro de Actas*, 4 August 1586, *fols* 407v. See also Ruth Pike, *Penal Servitude in Early Modern Spain* (Madison, 1983) pp. 63–5, on other confraternities dedicated to distributing alms, food and clothing to prisoners.

71. Salamanca, Archivo del Ministerio de Sanidad y Seguridad Social. *Cofradía de Caballeros (XXIV) Viente y Quatro, de las Reales Carceles de esta cuidad* (Salamanca, 1915).

72. The point at which burying the dead entered the ranks of religious duties is obscure. It had been highly valued in ancient cultures, but was not cited in Matthew's description of holy works. St Augustine recognized it as a charitable act, and medieval commentaries on Matthew's passage since at least the thirteenth century added the burial of the dead to the list. It was named as an act of mercy in the cartulary of Mas-d'Azil in 1093, and Jean Beleth, a Parisian theologian and liturgist, cited it in his description of the acts in his *Summa de Ecclesiasticus officiis* of the late twelfth century. Nicolas of Lyra, *Biblia Latina*, and Hugonis de S. Chara, *Biblia Latina*. Jean Beleth, *Summa de Eccclesiasticis officiis*, chapter 77 in *Corpus Christianorum*, vol. XVI (Tunholti, 1976). Philippe Ariès believes that burying the dead as an act of mercy was a product of the late Middle Ages. *L'homme devant la mort* (Paris, 1977) pp. 184–5.

73. Hippolyte Hélyot, *Histoire des Ordres Monastiques* (Paris, 1719) vol. VIII, pp. 262–3; and Maurice Bordes, 'Contribution à l'étude des confréries de pénitents à Nice aux XVIIe–XVIIIe siècles', *Annales du Midi: Revue Archeologique, Historique, et Philologique: Revue de la France Meridionale*, xix 139 (July–December 1978) 384.

74. Fernando da Silva Correia, *Origen e formação das Misericórdias portuguêsas: Estudios sôbre a História da Assistência* (Lisbon, 1944).

75. AMZ, *leg*. 1097, No. 1; Archivo parroquial de San Lázaro, no. 1; and Archivo parroquial de San Juan de la Puerta Nueva, *Libro* 12. In Lima, Peru, the Confraternity de la Caridad y Misericordia performed essentially the same functions, burying the dead, caring for paupers, attending to the sick and dowering orphans. See Olinda Celestino and Albert Meyers, *Las cofradías en el Perú: Región central*, p. 116.

76. AHPZ, Protocolos, no. 128, *fols* 223–3v.

77. AHPZ, Protocolos, no. 264, *fol*. 130.

78. AHPZ, Protocolos, no. 449, *fol*. 155.

79. AMZ, Libro 66, *Ordenanzas de la Vera Cruz de Villalcampo*, *fols* 165–5v.

80. AMZ, Libro 66, *Ordenanzas de la Cofradía de Vera Cruz de Argujillo*.
81. Archivo de la Universidad de Santiago. Archivo de los Reyes Católicos, *leg.* 63, no. 32, *fols* 4, 8, and 8v.
82. AMZ, Archivo de los Ciento, *Ordenanzas de la Cofradía de los Ciento*, *fols* 23v–24; *Racioneros*, *fol.* 15; and *San Nicolás*, in Fernández-Prieto, *Nobleza in Zamora*, *fol.* 389.
83. AMZ, Archivo de los Ciento, *Constitutiones de la Cofradía de los Ciento*, *fol.* 25.
84. AHN, Clero, *leg.* 8373, testament of 1478.
85. Th. Klauser, 'Das altchristliche Totenmahl nach dem heutigen Stande der Forschung', *Theologie und Glaube*, xx, (1928) 599–608; A. Parrot, *Le refrigerium dans l'Au-delá* (Paris, 1937); A. Stuiber, *Refrigerium Interim. Die Vorstellungen vom Zwischenzustand und die fruhchristliche Grabeskunst* (Bonn, 1957). P. A. Fevrièr, 'A-propos du repas funeraire: cult et sociabilité', *Cahiers archeologiques* xxvi (1977) 29–45; M. Meslin, 'Convivialité ou communion sacramentelle? Repas mithriaque et Eucharistie chrétienne', *Paganisme, judaisme, christ-ianisme … Mélanges offerts à Marcel Simon* (Paris, 1978) 295–306. For the practise of *refrigerium* in the early Middle Ages and legislation regulating it, see Oronzio Giordano, *Religiosità popolare nell'alto medioevo* (Bari, 1979) pp. 67–71.
86. Augustine, *Confession*, VI, 2; and J. Quasten, 'Vetus superstitio et nova religio. The Problems of *refrigerium* in the ancient Church of North Africa', *Harvard Theological Review*, xxxiii (1940) 253–66.
87. Augustine, *Epistularium*, XXII, 6, CSEL, xxxiv, pp. 58–9.
88. The eleventh-century Council of Coyanza limited participation at funeral ceremonies and offertory meals to clerics, paupers and 'the weak', and prohibited banqueting by the laity around sepulchres. Alfonso García Gallo, *El Concilio de Coyanza* (Madrid, 1951) pp. 24–5, 318–19. Biblioteca Nacional de Madrid. *Constituciones Syno-dales de Avila*, *fol.* 110v, capitulo 12; and AMZ, *Constituciones Synodales de Astorga*, *const.* XVI capitulo 6.
89. N. Hoyos Sancho, 'Luz a los muertos', *Las Ciencias*, xxiv (1959) p. 933; and Violet Alford, *Pyrenean Festivals* (London, 1937) p. 262.
90. L. Hóyos Saínz, 'Folklore español del culto a los muertos', *Revista de Dialéctologia y Tradiciones Populares*, 1 (Madrid, 1945) pp. 30–53.
91. Mikhail Bakhtin, *Rabelais and his World*, trans. Helene Iswolsky (Cambridge, Mass., 1968; originally published in Moscow, 1965) pp. 79–80; see also Arnold van Gennep, *Manuel de Folklore Français contemporain*, 1 (Paris, 1946) p. 777; Claude Dolan-Leclerc, 'Cortège funebre et societé au XVIe siècle à Aix-en-Province: Le presence des pauvres', *Le sentiment de la mort au Moyen Age* (Montreal, 1979) p. 107; Deschamps, *Les Confréries au moyen âge* (Bordeaux, 1958) p. 96; P. Ariès, *L'Homme devant la mort*, p. 33; J. Huizinga, *Homo Ludens: a study of the play-element in culture* (Boston, 1955); and Harvey Cox, *The Feast of Fools; a theological essay on festivity and fantasy* (Cambridge, Mass., 1969).
92. Michel Foucault, *Les Mots et les choses*, first French edition, 1966 by Editions Gallinard; published in English as *The Order of Things* (New

York, 1971).
93. *Summa Theologica*, Part 1, Q. 1, Art 9.
94. *Summa Theologica*. Part 111, Q. 61, Art 1.
95. Frances Yates, *The Art of Memory* (Chicago, 1966) chs III and IV.
96. As twentieth-century society moves away from the written word toward multi-media for the reception of messages, the role of images in molding behavior is undergoing critical examination by psychologists and sociologists. Feminist scholars are particularly aware of the power of images to form public opinion and stimulate individuals' identification with stereotypes. See for example Susan Griffin's criticism of commercial presentations of images of women in *Pornography and Silence* (New York, 1981).
97. Yates utilized Aquinas as the principal proponent of medieval memory images for the teaching of Christian doctrine. She analyses his comments in *The Art of Memory*, pp. 74–81.
98. The fundamental studies of church liturgy are Dom Gregory Dix, *The Shape of the Liturgy* (1st edn, Glasgow, 1945); and Dom Cyprien Vagaggini, *Il senso teologico della Liturgia* (1st edn, 1957; 2nd edn revised and augmented, 1958). See also M.-D. Chenu, 'The Symbolist Mentality', in *Nature, Man, and Society* (Chicago, 1979); originally published in 1957 as *La théologie au douzième siècle*.
99. According to the twelfth-century sacramentalist, Hugh of Saint-Victor, ' … symbolum, collatio videlicet, id est coaptatio visibilium formarum ad demonstrationem rei invisibilis propositarum.' ('a symbol is a juxtaposition, that is, a coaptation of visible forms brought forth to demonstrate some invisible matter'.) *Expos. in Hier, cael.*, iii, ad init (*PL*, CLXXV, 960D); The Council of Trent defined the sacraments as 'symbols of sacred things, and visible forms of an invisible grace', in Session XII, ch. III.
100. AHPZ, Municipal, *Libro de Actas* (11) 21 Jan 1589.
101. AG Simancas, Consejo Real, *leg.* 203, *fol.* 4.; and Calvo Lozano, *Historia*, pp. 126–9.
102. AHPZ, Municipal, *Libro de Actas*. (2) 21 June 1512, 7 May 1513, and 27 June 1519; (6) 22 Aug 1541; and (8) 19 July 1563 and 21 July 1563.
103. Archivo Histórico Provincial de Valladolid. *Libros de Actas*. Distributions are noted in (11) 18 June 1512; 25 May 1517, *fol.* 51; 24 July 1551, *fol.* 45; 25 June 1582, *fol.* 697v; 20 June 1584, *vol.* 70; 21 June 1585, *fol.* 215; 11 September 1585, *fol.* 255; 20 June 1586, *fol.* 379v, and 27 August 1586, *fol.* 421v.
104. Archivo parroquial de San Frontis, *libro* 28. San Antonio Abad; and AMZ, *Libro* 66, *Ordenanzas de la Cofradía de la Vera Cruz de Argujillo*. AHPZ, Protocolos, no. 69. *fol.* 14, 2 May 1541; AMZ, *Ordenanzas de San Ildefonso*, p. 520; and AMZ, Archivo de los Cientos *Ordenanzas de los Racioneros*, p. 7.
105. Benedicta Ward, *Miracles and the Medieval Mind* (Philadelphia, 1982) pp. 145–50 on the cult of Rocamadour; and Jean Rocacher, *Rocamadour et son pèlerinage. Etude historique et archéologique* (Toulouse, 1979).
106. In Zamora, the confraternity of Nuestra Señora de Rocamador merged with the Misericordia in the sixteenth century; in Valladolid, Nuestra Señora de Esgueva was associated with Rocamador, as was the

confraternity of Rocamador in Salamanca. Archivo Histórico Provincial de Valladolid. Diputación, *legs* 28 and 133. Archivo Municipal de Valladolid. *Caja* 13, no. 14; and *Libros de Actas* 31 October 1543, *fol.* 295v; 9 September 1528, *fol.* 130v; and 6 April 1554, *fol.* 349. Meersseman, 'la Vierge', p. 15; and M. Villar Y Macías, *Historia de Salamanca*, vol. III, *cap.* XIII, p. 127.

107. Marie-Madeleine Antony-Schmitt, *Le culte de saint-Sebastien en Alsace* (Strasbourg, 1977).

108. Lima, Peru, established a Cofradía de las Carceles in 1569, whose members included three lawyers 'of great learning and conscience' who took turns every four months in defending the imprisoned. Olinda Celestino and Albert Meyers, *Las cofradías en el Perú: Región central* (Frankfurt, Main, 1981) p. 117. See also John K. Chance and William B. Taylor, 'Cofradías and cargos: an Historical Perspective on the Mesoamerican civil-religious hierarchy', *American Ethnologist*, February 1985.

109. Luís L. Cortés y Vázquez, 'La Leyenda de San Julián el Hospitalerio y los caminos de la Peregrinación Jacobea del Occidente de España', *Revista de dialectología y tradiciones populares*, VII (Madrid, 1951) pp. 56–83.

110. Clifford Geertz, *The Interpretation of Cultures* (New York, 1973) pp. 95 and 119.

3. WELFARE REFORM: ATTEMPTS TO DISPLACE CHARITY

1. In recent years, the term is associated with Michel Foucault. He applies it to what he sees as the pre-eminent cultural transformations occurring in civilizations. Essentially, an epistemic change involves a new way to encode knowledge. See his *The Order of Things* (New York, 1971); originally published in France as *Les Mots et les choses*. The traditional Catholic approach to charity corresponds precisely to Foucault's notion that before the seventeenth century, people assumed that knowledge was extended by 'similitudes' or imitation through resemblance.

2. Clifford Geertz, 'Religion as a Cultural System', in Michael Banton (ed.), *Anthropological Approaches to the State of Religion* (London, 1968). See also Mary Douglas, *Natural Symbols* (New York, 1973), and *Purity and Danger* (London, 1966); Victor Turner, *Dramas, Fields, and Metaphors, Symbolic Action in Human Society* (Ithaca, N.Y., 1974), and *The Ritual Process: Structure and Anti-structure* (Chicago, 1969); Marshall Sahlins, *Culture and Practical Reason* (Chicago, 1976).

3. *Ordenanzas de la Cofradía de Nuestra Señora de San Antolín*, in Fernández-Prieto, *Nobleza in Zamora*, p. 34.

4. José Antonio Maravall, *Estado moderno y mentalidad social* (Madrid, 1972) 239.

5. Tomás de Trujillo, *Tratado de la limosna* (Estella, 1563) p. 225.
6. Fray Gabriel de Toro, quoted in María Jiménez Salas, *Historia de la asistencia social en España en la edad moderna* (Madrid: Consejo Superior de Investigaciones Cientificos, 1958) p. 24; and Mateo Alemán, *Guzmán de Alfarache*, ed. V.AA.II., p. 175.
7. Margaret Wade Labarge, *Medieval Travellers* (New York and London, 1982) pp. 199, 203–8.
8. AHPZ, Protocols, no. 37, *fol.* 270. Testament of Francisco García, 1547.
9. AHPZ, Protocolos, no. 720, *fols* 229, 230. Testament of Juana de la Peña.
10. AHPZ, Diputación, *leg.* 1, Testament of Alonso de Sotelo, 1536.
11. AHPZ, Diputación, *leg.* 65, Testament of Pedro de la Torre, 1626.
12. AHPZ, Protocolos, no. 139, *fol.* 355, Testament of Iñés Delgado.
13. In his doctoral dissertation on the cathedral chapter of Zamora, José Antonio Alvarez Vázquez rejects the idea that ecclesiastical institutions were great centers of charity and poor relief. He portrays its contractual relationships of rents, credit, and debts as a system based on sustaining a regimen of privilege. 'Diezmos y agricultura en Zamora (1500–1840)', PhD dissertation, University of Salamanca, 1977, especially p. 18. The manner in which poverty formed an integral part of the economic system of the pre-industrial age is examined in a broad setting in Catharina Lis and Hugo Soly, *Poverty and Capitalism in Pre-Industrial Europe*, translated by James Coonan (New Jersey, 1979).
14. Marina Warner vividly reconstructs images of the Virgin in the past and analyzes their implications for women in *Alone of All Her Sex* (New York, 1976). Her interpretation is of course highly controversial. Clarissa W. Atkinson provides a somewhat different perspective in 'Precious Balsam in a Fragile Glass: The Ideology of Virginity in the Later Middle Ages', *Journal of Family History*, viii, 2 (Summer 1983) pp. 131–43. For a more positive evaluation of the impact of the virgin ideal on the status of women, see Jo Ann McNamara, 'Sexual Equality and the Cult of Virginity in Early Christian Thought', *Feminist Studies*, iii, 3/4, Spring/Summer 1976, pp. 145–58.
15. *Serm. de generalitate elemosinarum*, in C. Lambot, 'Sermon sur l'aumône a restituer de saint Augustin', in *Rev. ben.* 66 (1956) pp. 149–58; text 156–8.
16. *De Nabuthae* VIII, 40 (*CSEL* 3212, 490). For other views of the early fathers on the recipients of alms, see Boniface Ramsey, 'Almsgiving in the Latin Church: The Late Fourth and Early Fifth centuries', *Theological Studies*, xliii, 2 (June 1982) 230–3. Thomas Aquinas expressed similar views in the *Summa Theologica* (Part II, Q. 31, Art. 2): 'In a sinner there are two things, his guilt and his nature. Accordingly we are bound to succor the sinner as to the maintenance of his nature, but not so as to abet his sin ... '
17. Tomás de Trujillo, *Tratado de la limosna*, pp. 165–6.
18. Biblioteca Nacional de Madrid. Bernardino Sandoval, maestrescuela de Toledo, *Tratado de cuan piadosa obra sea proveer a las necesidades corporales y espirituales que padeçen los presos pobres*; manuscript of

the sixteenth century.
19. AG Simancas. Hacienda, *leg.* 205. Poverty in Zamora was significantly more widespread than in major nearby cities, according to similar surveys compiled in 1561. In Valladolid, 9.54% of the households were considered poor; in Medina del Campo, 8.89%; and in Segovia, 15.74%. The statistics must be correlated with the number of poor who were widows since they frequently lived alone without dependents. Simple conversion of household rates to per capita figures is not entirely accurate, therefore. Widows formed a high percentage of the poor in Zamora (66.4%) and in Medina del Campo (83%), and Segovia (60%), while in Valladolid, widows amounted to only 38.6%. See Bennassar, *Valladolid*, p. 436.
20. Tomás de Trujillo, *Tratado de la limosna*, pp. 209.
21. Salamanca University. *Nuevas Ordenanzas de la Congregación de Pobres Vergonzantes de esta Ciudad de Salamanca.* Originally compiled on 14 August 1595, reprinted in 1803 and published on 29 October 1871. Amleto Spicciani discusses in detail a similar confraternity for the shamefaced in Florence in 'The "Poveri Vergognosi" in Fifteenth-Century Florence', in Thomas Riis (ed.) *Aspects of Poverty in Early Modern Europe* (Firenze, 1981) pp. 119–82.
22. Juan Luis Vives, *De subventione pauperum* (Bruges, 1526), translated into Spanish by Dr Juan de Gonzalo Nieto é Ivarra, as *Tratado del Socorro de los pobres* (Valencia, 1781) p. 133; English translation by Sister Alice Tobriner, *A Sixteenth-Century Urban Report* (Chicago: Social Service Monographs, 2nd ser., 1971).
23. The gruesome details are described by clerics at the Escorial in 1560 in a document urging poor relief reform, L–1–12, fol. 199, no. 15; and by many reformers and *arbitristas*, including Juan Luis Vives, Gonzales de Cellorigo, Navarrete, Ordóñez and Argentí y Líes.
24. Biblioteca Nacional de Madrid. *Las Cortes de Valladolid*, 1523, *Petición* 56. 'Otrosi que mande que no anden pobres por el Reyno, vezinos y naturales de otras partes, sino que cada uno pide en su naturaleza, porque de lo contrario viene mucho daño, y se da causa que haya muchos vagabundos y holgazanes.' ['It is also ordered that paupers beg only within their home towns, for if they wander throughout the Kingdom much harm is done and the number of vagabonds and loiterers increases.']
25. According to averages in the census of 1561. AG Simancas, Exp. de Hacienda, leg. 205. Excluding the suburbs, the percentage of paupers in the urban center of Zamora amounted to 25 per cent. The poverty level of residents in the suburbs was higher than that within the walls of the city.
26. AG Simancas, Patronato Real, Cortes, *leg.* 70, *fol.* 57, 1523–24.
27. AHPZ, Libro de Actas (4).
28. Ibid., 3 July 1531 and 10 July 1531.
29. Ibid., 1 September 1531.
30. Ibid., 20 November 1531, and 8 January 1532.
31. Ibid., 26 November 1535, and 29 November 1535.
32. AHPZ, *Libro de Actas* (5), 21 April 1539.

33. Ibid., 11 March 1540, and 12 April 1540.
34. To protect residents, the city bought grain and sold it for five *reales* less per *carga* (4 bushels) than it paid for it. In the early 1530s, these artificial prices were kept down to two *maravedís* a pound; by spring 1539 the city was forced to raise prices to three and a half *maravedís* a pound, and a year later to five and six *maravedís* a pound. AHPZ, *Libro de Actas* (5) 21 April 1539, 15 May 1540. The city council carefully controlled the buying and selling of wheat within the city, frequently prohibiting bakers to use any but that bought from the public *alhóndiga* in order to maintain prices at a reasonable rate. In January 1540 supplies were so low, however, that it allowed anyone from the territory of Zamora to bring bread into the city and sell it at market prices, ibid. (19 January 1540).
35. AHPZ, *Libro de Actas* (5) 12 April 1540, and 16 April 1540.
36. Ibid., 16 April 1540.
37. AHPZ, *Libro de Actas* (5) 4 June 1540.
38. Sections of the Imperial Poor Ordinance issued by Carlos V at Ghent on 6 October 1531 are printed in Carl E. Steinbicker, *Poor Relief in the Sixteenth Century* (Washington D.C., 1937) pp. 245–8.
39. W. K. Jordan, *Philanthropy in England 1480–1660* (London, 1959), pp. 84–5; F. R. Salter (ed.), *Some Early Tracts on Poor Relief* (London, 1926) pp. 120–6.
40. Ernest Troeltsch, *The Social Teaching of the Christian Churches*, trans. Olive Wyon (New York, 1931) vol. 1, pp. 133–6, and vol. II, pp. 565–8; Otto Winckelmann, 'Die Armenordnungen von Nurnberg (1522), Kitzengen (1523). Regensburg (1523) und Ypern (1525)', *Archiv für Reformationgeschichte*, x (1912–13) 242–80; and Shailer Mathews, 'The Protestant Churches and Charity', in Ellsworth Faus, Ferris Laune and Arthur J. Todd (eds), *Intelligent Philanthropy* (Chicago, 1930).
41. Natalie Davis, 'Poor Relief, Humanism and Heresy', *Society and Culture in Early Modern France* (Stanford, 1975) pp. 17–64; and Brian Pullan, *Rich and Poor in Renaissance Venice: The Social Institutions of a Catholic State, to 1620* (Cambridge, Mass., 1971).
42. Davis, 'Poor Relief, Humanism and Heresy', pp. 55–8. For a more detailed study, see Jean-Pierre Gutton, *La société et les pauvres: l'exemple de la generalité de Lyon (1534–1789)* (Paris, 1971). Many of the new relief programs in northern Europe continued to use traditional imagery of almsgiving in propaganda designed to encourage residents to support the institutions. See Jean-Pierre Gutton, *La société et les pauvres en Europe, XVIᵉ–XVIIIᵉ siècles* (Paris, 1974) pp. 142–4.
43. Pullan, *Rich and Poor in Renaissance Venice*, pp. 361–7, 371–422. In England, W. K. Jordan has analyzed the impulse behind the great outflow of charitable donations by Calvinist gentry and merchants in the sixteenth and seventeenth centuries and found it to be intensely religious in nature. The Calvinist doctrine that good works do not contribute to salvation did not deter men from participating in enthusiastic philanthropy for the good of their souls as well as for the welfare of society. 'The Protestant clergy,' Jordan writes, 'being

Calvinist, could not argue that good works were necessary to grace, but they did hold with a most persuasive and sustained vehemence that good works were an authentic and necessary fruit of grace categorically demanded of His saints by God.' There is little reason to believe that Protestants were any more eager to eliminate the opportunity for exercising virtuous actions than were Catholics (*Philanthropy in England*, pp. 18, 20. 151–239). For a technical review of Jordan's work and the criticisms of other historians, see Charles Wilson, 'Poverty and Philanthropy in Early Modern England', in Riis, *Aspects of Poverty*, pp. 253–79.

44. Gerald Strauss, *Nuremberg in the Sixteenth Century* (New York, 1966) pp. 198–9.

45. Miriam U. Chrisman, *Strasbourg and the Reform; a Study in the Process of Change* (New Haven, 1967) p. 278. She has published a more detailed study of poor relief in 'Urban Poor in the Sixteenth Century: The Case of Strasbourg', *Studies in Medieval Culture*, XIII (1978) pp. 59–67.

46. H. J. Grimm, 'Luther's Contributions to sixteenth-century Organization of Poor Relief', *Archiv für Reformationgeschichte*, t. 61 (1970) pp. 225–9.

47. Otto Winckelmann, 'Uber die altesten Armenordnungen der Reformations zeit (1522–1525)', *Historiche Vierteljahrshrift*, XVII (1914–15) 187–228, 361–400. Paul Bonenfant, 'Les origines et le caractère de la reforme de la bienfaisance publique aux Pays-Bas sous le règne de Charles-Quint', *Revue Belge de philologie et d'histoire*, VI (1927).

48. Robert Kingdon, 'Social Welfare in Calvin's Geneva', *American Historical Review*, LXXVI, 1 (February 1971) p. 67.

49. P. A. Slack, 'Comment: Some Comparative Problems in the English Case', in Riis, *Aspects of Poverty*, pp. 281–5.

50. William J. Courtenay explores the use of token coinage by late medieval clerics and confraternities as a means to aid in discrimination between deserving and undeserving poor. 'Token Coinage and the Administration of Poor Relief During the Middle Ages', *Journal of Interdisciplinary History*, III (1972–73) pp. 275–95. Brian Tierney points out medieval precedents to the reforms of the sixteenth century in *Medieval Poor Law: A Sketch of Canonical Theory and Its Application in England* (Berkeley, 1959). For Reformation appraisals of the value of labor, see Robert Jütte, 'Poor Relief and Social Discipline in Sixteenth-Century Europe'. *Annales, E.S.C.*, 5 (September–October 1980) pp. 25–52.

51. W. K. Jordan, *Philanthropy in England*, p. 75, and F. R. Salter, *Some Early Tracts on Poor Relief*, p. 104. *Cortes de los antiguos reinos de León y Castilla*, vol. II, p. 370.

52. See note 22.

53. Vives, *De subventione pauperum*, pp. 150–4, and Tobriner [Eng. trans.], p. 33.

54. Carl E. Steinbicker, *Poor Relief in the Sixteenth Century*, pp. 96–7, 126.

55. AG Simancas, Estado, E–50, *fol*. 63. Madrid, 7 March 1540.

56. Madrid borrowed 2000 bushels of wheat to succor the poor from the end of 1539 to the end of 1540. Archivo Municipal de Madrid. *Libro de Actas* (II), *fol*. 25, 24 November 1540. AG Simancas, Estado E–50, *fol*. 90, 26 June 1540. Biblioteca Nacional de Madrid. 24 August 1540, Madrid.

57. Biblioteca Nacional de Madrid. 25 August 1540, Madrid, 'Instrucción de las leyes que hablan sobre los pobres'. A copy of the laws are contained in P. Campomanes, *Apéndice a la Educación*, part II, pp. 258–67. See note 135 below.

58. Six leagues was approximately 18 miles, about a day's journey by cart.

59. Reform in Madrid had begun before the publication of the decrees. In the years immediately succeeding, the city developed several different programs to succor the needy. Magistrates supervised collection of grain from the public granary and worked with parish priests and citizens to distribute it to needy residents. In 1544 and 1545 Madrid continued to prohibit non-resident paupers from begging and licensed resident paupers (Archivo Municipal de Madrid, *Libro de Actas* (11) 26 April 1542; 26 June 1542; 30 June 1542; 9 May 1544 (*fol*. 265); and 23 February 1545 (*fol*. 356v)). Information on the situation in Toledo at the time of the publication of the king's instructions is only sketchily provided by existing documents, carefully culled by Linda Martz in *Poverty and Welfare in Hapsburg Spain. The Example of Toledo* (Cambridge: Cambridge University Press, 1983) pp. 119–23. In December 1540 or later, Toledo adopted a new poor law prohibiting begging. In March 1543, Cardinal Tavera attempted to care for beggars in existing hospitals and reorganized parish relief to meet the temporary food crisis, a reform implemented again in 1545–6. In the difficult year of 1546, private persons took beggars into their homes in a concerted attempt to keep them cared for and off the streets (p. 127).

60. AG Simancas, Estado E–47, *fol*. 227v, 23 September 1540.

61. AG Simancas, Estado E–50, *fol*. 203, 16 September 1540; second copy, *fol*. 271.

62. Salamanca University, *Libro de claustro*, 1 March 1540, *fol*. 112; Soto was commissioned to visit the Cardinal of Toledo to buy wheat for the city. See also Vicente Beltrán de Heredia, *Domingo de Soto; Estudio biográfico documentado* (Salamanca, 1960) pp. 80–92.

63. Domingo de Soto, *Deliberación en la causa de los pobres* (Madrid, 1965; originally published in Salamanca in 1545) p. 20.

64. Notes on this session are not recorded in *Libro de Actas* for these years. As early as June of 1540, the council took responsibility over feeding sick paupers in hospitals by begging for charity in their name (*Libro de Actas* (5) 12 June 1540). The single notice of the proceedings, only implied in contemporary sources, appears in the *Historia Cómica de Zamora* (Zamora, 1906), by Enrique Junquera, J. Bugallo Sánchez, and C. Rodríguez Díaz, a copy of which is located in the private library of the family of Ramón Luelmo Alonso of Zamora.

65. Soto, *Deliberación*.

66. Fray Juan de Medina, O.S.B., *De la orden* (Madrid, 1965; originally published in Salamanca in 1545) p. 42.

67. For the Judgment of the Sorbonne, see Salter, *Some Early Tracts on Poor Relief*, pp. 76–9.
68. Salamanca University, *Libro de claustro*, A.U.S. 13, *fol.* 203, 22 February 1544, and *fol.* 268, 12 December 1544, and 28 July 1545.
69. Ibid., *fol.* 300v, 23 February 1544 and *fol.* 301v, 8 March 1544.
70. Medina, *De la orden*, p. 218.
71. Archivo Municipal de Valladolid, *Libro de Actas*, 8 July 1541, *fol.* 122.
72. Ibid., 22 November 1542, *fol.* 242; 31 August 1543, *fol.* 276v; 16 September 1543, *fol.* 278; and 23 April 1544, *fol.* 356v.
73. Ibid., 12 January 1540, *fol.* 9v.
74. Ibid., 7 December 1543, *fol.* 298v.
75. Ibid., 1 September 1544, *fol.* 378v; and Soto, *Deliberación*, p. 21.
76. Medina, *De la orden*, p. 151.
77. Soto, *Deliberación*, pp. 20–21.
78. Soto's work was published on 30 January 1545 at the press of Juan de Junta in Salamanca. At the same place on 20 March 1545 the Benedictine Juan de Medina, or Robles, published his treatise. In 1747, it was republished in Valladolid under the title, *La Charidad descreta practicada con los mendigos y utilidades que logra la República con su recogimiento*.
79. Soto, *Deliberación*, pp. 35, 37, 47, and 111.
80. Ibid., pp. 74, 75, 76, 82, 88, and 94.
81. Ibid., p. 110.
82. Medina, *De la orden*, pp. 158, 159, 190, 191, and 286.
83. Ibid., pp. 272 and 286.
84. Ibid., p. 303.
85. Soto, *Deliberación*, pp. 117, 118, and 121.
86. Ibid., p. 122; and Medina, *De la orden*, pp. 262 and 264.
87. Pullan, *Rich and Poor in Renaissance Venice*, p. 284. For an exciting analysis of the thought of Juan de Medina, see José Antonio Maravall, 'De la misericordia a la justicia social en la economia del trabajo: la obra de fray Juan de Robles', *Moneda y Crédito*, 148 (March 1979) pp. 57–88.
88. By the summer of 1543, magistrates contemplated discarding the relief program and discussed the measure with the prior of San Juan; *Libro de Actas* (6) 19 July 1543. But the reforms continued in force until the summer of 1548; *Libro de Actas* (6) 20 June 1544, 8 June 1545, 8 June 1546; (7) 2 July 1548.
89. Diego de Colmenares, *Historia de la Insigne Ciudad de Segovia* (Madrid, 1640) p. 721–722.
90. Criticisms in northern Europe came from churchmen who objected to their loss of authority over charity. The new prohibitions on begging also posed a possible threat to mendicant orders. For the complaints of friars from Ypres and replies, see J. Nolf, *La réforme de la bienfaisance à Ypres au XVIᵉ siècle* (Ghent, 1915) pp. 40–76, and 119–23. Juan Luis Vives's treatise, 'De subventione pauperum' was written in response to some objections over reforms in the Spanish Netherlands. See Bonilla San Martín, *Juan Luis Vives y la filosofía española de Renacimiento* (Madrid, 1929) vol. II. Catholic magistrates in Ypres

consulted theologians at the Sorbonne as to the orthodoxy of prohibitions on public begging and their conditional affirmation quieted most unrest over the issue. Natalie Zemon Davis associates welfare reformers with laymen and clerics of humanist orientation and notes that opposition was most likely to come from the church hierarchy and the mendicant orders, although divisions by no means always occurred along these lines. 'Poor Relief, Humanism and Heresy', pp. 17–20, 59–62. The most critical voice raised against reforms in northern Europe was that of the Spanish Augustinian, Lorenzo de Villavicencio, *De oeconomia sacra circa pauperum curam a Cristo instituta* (Antwerp, 1564). He pointed to the traditional Catholic poor relief system in Spain as the most perfect manner of caring for the poor. The most sophisticated hospital and nursing services came from societies in which, he argued, poor relief remained religiously conceived and administered, as in Spain (p. 170).

91. An argument cited and criticized by Medina, *De la orden*, p. 297.
92. Quoted by Cristóbal Pérez de Herrera in *Respuestas del Doctor Cristóbal Pérez de Herrera, Protomédico de las Galeras de España, por el Rey nuestro señor, a las objeciones y dudas que se la han opuesto al discurso que escrivió a su Majestad de la reducción y amparo de los pobres*, p. 3, undated manuscript in the Biblioteca Nacional de Madrid.
93. Escorial, L–1–12, no. 9 and no. 10., (1560); 'Que las hospitales generales es buen medio para el remedio de los pobres de la república en común se encarga del sustento dellos.'
94. AHPZ, *Libro de Actas* (10) 2 July 1571; 1 December 1571; 19 December 1572; 12 March 1571; 14 April 1572; 22 June 1573; 17 August 1573; 6 October 1573; 5 November 1574; 28 March 1575; 6 April 1575; 12 May 1575; and 16 May 1575.
95. Archivo Municipal de Valladolid, *Libro de Actas* 9 September 1575, *fol.* 337v; and 21 November 1575, *fol.* 383.
96. Biblioteca Nacional de Madrid. Miguel de Giginta, *Tratado de remedio de pobres* (Coimbra, 1579). Parts of the treatise are printed in the appendix of Fermín Hernández Iglesias, *La beneficencia en España* (Madrid, 1876).
97. Ibid.
98. Giginta published his views in several other treatises as well. *Exhortación a la compasión de los pobres* (Barcelona, 1583), *Cadena de Oro* (Perpinán, 1584), and *Atalaya de Caridad* (Zaragoza, 1587). For an expanded discussion of Giginta's efforts, see Linda Martz, *Poverty and Welfare in Hapsburg Spain*, pp. 67–76.
99. *Tratado de remedio de pobres*, *fols* 13, 17, 27v, 28, 35v, and 36.
100. Copies of his proposal were sent to all the cities and villages of Spain, and earned support of a few of them. Under the sponsorship of Cardinal Quiroga, Toledo founded a beggars' hospital that housed about 600 beggars in 1584. The next year Madrid erected an edifice that held 900 paupers. Granada and Barcelona established their own hospitals immediately; the one in Barcelona survived with difficulties into the eighteenth century.
101. AHPZ, *Libro de Actas* (11) 5 June 1587, and 11 December 1587; and

Municipal, *leg*. 21, No. 39.

102. Hernández Iglesias. *La beneficencia en España*, p. 277.
103. Several times in the course of the sixteenth century Procuradores at Cortes complained about the unregulated activities of both confraternities and guilds. In 1534 at the Cortes of Madrid, they petitioned 'that the kingdom is full of confraternities, and they spend in eating and drinking whatever they possess, and since these and other indiscretions are apt to impoverish the secular estate, we ask Your Majesty that from here on, no more be founded without the express licence of Your Majesty, and that those already established be reduced or abolished, as the Chief Justice and city council, with Provisor, Vicar, or archpriest of the city … see fit'. The Petition was not granted by the Crown. Antonio Rumeu de Armas, *Historia de la Previsión Social en España*, pp. 201–4.
104. Biblioteca Nacional, *Constituciones synodales del Arcobispado del Toledo* by Cardinal Juan Tavera, (1536) *const*. 15, *fol*. 9; and AMZ, *Constituciones synodales*, *Libro* III, *const*. IIII, *tít*. XV. William Christian Jr. discusses sentiments against the proliferation of hospitals in the middle of the century in *Local Religion in Sixteenth-Century Spain* (Princeton, New Jersey, 1981) pp. 168–9.
105. Juan de Avila, *Memorial Primero para Trento*, 1551. p. 32, no. 43, in R.P. Camilo María Abad, S.J., *Dos memoriales inéditos para el Concilio de Trento* (Santander, 1945).
106. AHPZ, *Libro de Actas* (4) 26 November 1525 and 29 November 1535. Archivo Municipal de Valladolid, *Libro de Actas*, *fol*. 184, 23 November 1552.
107. AHPZ, Diputación. *leg*. 91, no. 14, 24 February 1583. 'Votos y parezer del provisor de Zamora y de los S. Patronos del Hospital de Sotelo … '; Municipal, *leg*. 21, no. 39; and Archivo Municipal de Valladolid, *Libro de Actas*, 15 December 1581, *fols*. 636v–637v.
108. AHPZ, Diputación, *leg*. 91, no. 14.
109. Ibid.
110. Archivo Diocesano de Salamanca. Uncatalogued papers of 1581, located for me by Father Benigno Hernández, of the Society of Jesus in Salamanca.
111. Ibid., *fol*. 75v.
112. Alberto Marcos Martín, 'La asistencia social en España: el sistema hospitalario de Medina del Campo en el siglo XVI', *Cuadernos de Investigación Histórica*, II (1978) pp. 341–62. On the consolidation of five hospitals run by confraternities in the village of Muñoz de las Posadas in the diocese of Avila in 1570, see Martz, *Poverty and Welfare in Hapsburg Spain*, pp. 62–5.
113. Archivo Parroquial de Villalpando. No. 66. *Apeó del Hospital, y memoria de Roquemador de este villa*; and Calvo Lozano, *Historia*, pp. 90–2.
114. Jerónimo de Quintana, *Historia de la antigüedad, nobleza y grandeza de la Villa de Madrid* (Madrid 1954, republication of edition of 1629) pp. 99, 445, 447, 448, and 450–3; and Martz, *Poverty and Welfare in Hapsburg Spain*, pp. 81–3.

115. Hernández Iglesias, *La beneficencia en España*, p. 278. Juan Carmona García describes the fierce resistance of Sevillian confraternities and the municipal council to the efforts of the Crown and episcopacy to unify hospitals in *El sistema de la hospitalidad pública en la Sevilla del Antiguo Régimen* (Sevilla, 1979).

116. Bartelomé Bennassar, *Récherches sur les grandes épidémies dans le nord de l'Espagne à la fin du XVIᵉ siècle, problèmes de documentation et de mèthode* (Paris: S.E.V.P.E.N., 1969).

117. The Cortes' plea came in 1592. Hernández Iglesias, *La beneficencia en España*, p. 279. On the failures of the beggars' hospitals in Toledo and Barcelona and the General Hospital in Madrid, see Martz, *Poverty and Welfare in Hapsburg Spain*, pp. 74–6, 83–4, and 85.

118. Dr Cristóbal Pérez de Herrera, *Discursos para el amparo de los legítimos pobres y reducción de los fingidos: y de la fundación y principio de los Albergues destos Reynos, y amparo de la milicia de ellos* (Madrid, 1598). In this treatise, Pérez de Herrera summarizes the discussion of several previous works. It has been recently edited in *Clásicos Castellanos* (Madrid, 1975) vol. 199, with a lengthy sketch of the author's life and activities in poor relief reform by Michel Cavillac. Pérez de Herrera's official title was that of *protomédico*, a position created in 1477 to supervise public health officials and regulate health conditions. *Novísima Recopilación*, lib. 7, *tít.*, 38, *ley* 2; and *lib* 8, *tít.* 10, *ley* 1.

119. *Discursos*, in *Clásicos Castellanos*, pp. xxxv–xxxvi.

120. Ibid., p. 252, and introduction, pp. xxxviii–xxxix. Pérez de Herrera claimed that 800 copies of his treatise were distributed through Spain and its dominions, p. xxxvii.

121. Ibid., pp. xi–xii, 51–59, and 193.

122. Ibid., p. 259, Epilogue: Letter of Alonso de Barros approving the treatise of Pérez de Herrera and recommending his project to the Crown.

123. Ibid., pp. 55 and 184.

124. The *arbitrista*, Sancho de Moncada, referred to parish registers to show that in 1617 there were only half as many marriages as there had been in earlier years.

125. Pérez de Herrera, *Discursos*, pp. 104–09.

126. AHPZ, *Libro de Actas* (13) 18 August 1597; 29 August 1597; and 24 September 1597.

127. AHPZ, Libro de Actas (14) 13 May 1598; 15 March 1599; and 21 August 1599; 8 March 1599; and 30 July 1598. In February 1598, the city prohibited residents from buying more than six loaves of bread at the market, and limited non-residents to buying two 'for the road', to prevent them from reselling it elsewhere, especially in Portugal. (14) 16 February 1598.

128. AG Simancas, Patronato Ecclesiástico, *leg.* 135.

129. Archivo Municipal de Valladolid, *Libro de Actas*, 22 September 1597, *fol.* 287; and 28 November 1597, *fol*, 357.

130. Ibid., 13 October 1597, *fol.* 314; 24 October 1597, *fols* 326v–327; 28 November 1597, *fol.* 356v and 358v; 24 May 1599, *fols* 824v–825; and 18 June 1599, *fol.* 850v.

131. Ibid., 18 July 1599; and 8 Oct 1599, *fols* 922 and 923.
132. Ibid., 28 June 1599, *fol.* 862v; 14 July 1599, *fol.* 875; 8 October 1599, *fol.* 922; 22 November 1599, *fol.* 944v.
133. Pérez de Herrara, *Discursos* p. cxxv.
134. Ibid., pp. 61, 62.
135. Campomanes held up the Zamoran reforms of the 1540s as a model program for all of Spain in the eighteenth century; and Bishop Antonio Jorge Galván of Zamora attempted to reinstitute these reforms enclosing the poor in the city, with more success. The most long lasting and effective of Galván's reforms was the foundation of two maternity wards in the Hospital of Sotelo. Pedro Rodríquez Campomanes, *Apéndice a la educación popular* (Madrid, 1775). *Apéndice II*; pp. CXLV–CXLVII; and CCXVIII–CCXIX: Ministerio de la Governación, *Nuevos apuntos para el estudio y la organización en España de las instituciones de Beneficencia y de Previsión*, part 1, 395; and AMZ, A.P.X. (Antonio Piñuela), *Rebuscos para formar la Historia de Zamora como Antigua Numancia* (1858), a handwritten history of the city.
136. For the persistence of the ideas of Domingo de Soto in the eighteenth century, including these observations, see W. J. Callahan, 'Confinement and Poor Relief in Eighteenth-Century Spain', *Hispanic American Historical Review*, LI (1971) pp.13–14; and Soubeyroux, 'El encuentro del pobre y la sociedad: asistencia y represión en el Madrid del siglo XVIII', *Estudios de Historica Social*, 20–1 (1982) pp. 81–2.
137. Soto, *Deliberación* p. 120. 'Porque son por alla gentes mas inclinados al bien común y que duran mas atados a cualquier ley que nosotros'.
138. Jaime Vicens-Vives, *An Economic History of Spain* (Princeton, N. J., 1969) pp. 335–43; Antonio Domínguez Ortiz, Los extranjeros en la vida española durante el siglo XVII'. *Estudios de Historia Social de España* (Madrid, 1960) IV, ii, 293–426; and André-E. Sayous, 'La Genèse du système capitaliste: la pratique des affaires et leur mentalité dans l'Espagne du XVIe siècle', *Annales d'Histoire Economique et Sociale* (1936) 334–54.
139. Gutton, *La société et les pauvres*, p. 119; the English banished rogues to the colonies, to France, Germany, Spain and the Low Countries in the *Acts of the Privy Council of England*, New Series XXXII; 503–04, (1597 and 1603).
140. Gutton, *La société et les pauvres*, pp. 122–144; and Emmanuel Chill, 'Religion and Mendicity in Seventeenth-Century France', *International Review of Social History*, VII (1962) pp. 400–25. In Italy, see B. Geremek, 'Renfermement des pauvres en Italie (XIVe ... XVIIIe siècles): remarques préliminaries', *Mélanges en l'honneur de Fernand Braudel* (2 vols; Toulouse, 1973). The first workhouse in England was established in Bristol in 1697; Worcester, Hull, Plymouth and Exeter quickly followed its example.
141. Wilma J. Pugh, 'Social Welfare and the Edict of Nantes: Lyon and Nîmes', *French Historical Review* (Spring 1974) p. 352, 355–7, and 362–3.
142. Michel Foucault, *Histoire de la folie à l'âge classique* (Paris, 1972) pp. 92–7.

143. Juan de Medina, *De la orden*, p. 161.
144. Linda Martz, *Poverty and Welfare in Hapsburg Spain*, pp. 123–30.
145. Cited in Heal, 'Hospitality', p. 83, from M. Bucer, *A Treatise how by the Worde of God Christian Mens Almose Ought to be Distributed* ([printed abroad, 1557?] S.T.C. 3965) pp. 6–8; and Peter Martyr Vermigli, *Loci communes* (Zurich, 1563) bk. 2, precept 8, sect. 7.
146. Louise Fothergill-Payne, *La alegoría en los autos y farsas anteriores a Calderón* (London, 1977) pp. 198–9.
147. Joseph Townsend, *A Journey through Spain*, 3 vols (London, 1791) 11:9. More remarks can be found in vol. III, pp. 57–9; 183–4; and 251–2. Comte Alexandre de Laborde (1773–1842) also lavished praise on the generosity of the high Spanish clergy in *Itineraire descriptif de l'Espagne* (Paris, 1808).
148. Valladolid, Archivo Municipal, *Libro de Actas*, 19 May 1542, *fol.* 196v; and 24 February 1552, *fol.* 98v.
149. Vern L. Bullough, *Sexual Variance in Society and History* (Chicago, 1976) pp. 433–4; *Sin, Sickness and Sanity, A History of Sexual Attitudes* (New York, 1977) pp. 140–1; Derrick Sherwin Bailey, *Sexual Relation in Christian Thought* (New York, 1959) p. 206; Nina Epton, *Love and the English* (London, 1960) pp. 68, 91; and Merry Weisner Wood, 'Birth, Death and the Pleasures of Life: Working Women in Nuremberg 1480–1620' (University of Wisconsin-Madison, PhD dissertation, 1979) pp. 271–90.
150. Martz, *Poverty and Welfare in Hapsburg Spain*, pp. 192 and 195. See also Mary Elizabeth Perry, '"Lost Women" in Early Modern Seville: The Politics of Prostitution', *Feminist Studies*, iv 1, (February 1978) p. 211, on acceptance of prostitution by the city fathers of Seville.
151. Ruth Pike, *Penal Servitude in Early Modern Spain* (Madison, 1983) pp. 23, 36–7; and Robert Ignatius Burns, *The Crusader Kingdom of Valencia* (Cambridge, Mass., 1967) p. 206.

4. THE CATHOLIC REFORMATION AND TRADITION

1. Jean Delumeau, *Le catholicisme entre Luther et Voltaire*, (Paris, 1971) English edition, *Catholicism from Luther to Voltaire* (London, 1977) Keith Thomas, *Religion and the Decline of Magic* (London, 1971).
2. Gerald Strauss, *Luther's House of Learning* (Baltimore and London, 1978).
3. Sara Tilghman Nalle, 'Religion and Reform in a Spanish Diocese: Cuenca, 1545–1650' (PhD dissertation, Johns Hopkins University, 1983).
4. Philip T. Hoffman, *Church and Community in the Diocese of Lyon, 1500–1789* (New Haven, 1984).
5. Pierre Chaunu, *Le Temps des deux réformes de l'Eglise* (Paris: Fayard, 1975) p. 156; and A. D. Wright, *The Counter Reformation. Catholic Europe and the non-Christian World* (New York, 1982) pp. 51, xxvi (1957) pp. 275–88.
6. John Bossy, 'The Social History of Confession in the Age of the

Reformation', *Transactions of the Royal Historical Society*, 5th series, 25 (1975) pp. 24–5.

7. Cited in William Christian, *Local Religion in Sixteenth-Century Spain* (New Jersey, 1981) p. 166.

8. Toledan synodal constitutions of 1536 and 1580 warned that confraternities needed to be strictly supervised, but the harshest words about confraternities came from the French church hierarchy. At the Council of Rouen in 1581, confraternities were the object of severe reprimand. 'Les confréries qui se sont établies par pieté, sous le nom de charité, nuisent beaucoup aux fideles, en dérangeant l'ordre ordinaire des églises; elles introduisent dans les esprits un désir inquiet de domination, et une sorte de fanatisme. On elève dans chaque église autel contre autel, on oppose sacrifice à sacrifice, prêtre à prêtre, paroisse à paroisse.' ['Confraternities that are established for pious purposes in the name of charity do much harm to the faithful by upsetting the normal order of church services; they introduce into the heart a restless will to power and a sort of fanaticism. In each church, we see altar strike out against altar, sacrifice confronts sacrifice, priest opposes priest, parish confronts parish.'] Cited in the DDC 'Confrérie', col. 153.

9. AG Simancas, Patronato Real, *Caja* 16, *fol.* 86.

10. Scarisbrick argues that the establishment of Protestantism in England caused a marked shift of the balance of power in religion in favor of the clergy, for, among other reasons, the confraternities that until then had offered wide opportunities for lay control over religious ceremonies disappeared. 'So did the large army of unbeneficed clergy who before were largely under lay control. The new Protestant minister, if he was a zealous servant of the Gospel, was a disciplining, preaching authority-figure. He may not have had the sacramental powers of the old priest, but he expected rank-and-file lay people to be more passive, more attentive, and more regular church goers.' Scarisbrick, *The Reformation and the English People* (Oxford, 1984) pp. 39, 164–70.

11. *The Decrees of the Council of Trent*, Session XXII; see also 'Confrérie', in the DDC.

12. This qualifying clause was added at the request of the Portuguese representative, and exempted the confraternities of the Misericordia in Portugal from episcopal surveillance. See Gabriele Paleotti, *Acta Concilii Tridentini, annis 1562 et 1563 originalia*, edited in Sebastian Merkle, *Concilia Tridentina Diaria* 111/1 (Freiburg-im-Breisgau, 1931) p. 431.

13. Mansi, *Concilia*, XXXIII, col. 185.

14. 'Confrérie', DDC, cols. 156, 171, and 172; and Deschamps, *Les Confréries au Moyen Age* (Bordeaux, 1958) pp. 186–8.

15. Within about one kilometer of each other, with the exception of the Santíssimo Sacramento, dedicated to the eucharist, and the Doctrina Christiana, for educating children in religious precepts.

16. H. Jedin, *Crisis and Closure of the Council of Trent*, translated by N. D. Smith (London, 1967) p. 158. AG Simancas, Patronato Real, *leg.* 22–1, and 22–36 has Phillip II's recommendations to legates of the

provincial councils of 1565–66. The doctoral dissertation of Sara Tilghman Nalle, 'Religion and Reform in a Spanish Diocese: Cuenca, 1545–1650' shows that Tridentine reforms significantly altered parish structures within a couple of decades after their publication. For the slow diffusion of reforms in France, see Jean Imbert, 'Les prescriptions hôspitalières du Concile de Trente et leur diffusion en France', *Revue d'histoire de l'église de France*, XLII (1956) pp. 5–28.

17. AHN, Consejos Suprimidos, *leg.* 7098, no. 29.

18. AMZ, Archivo San Ildefonso, no. 37.

19. AMZ, *Orden* 17, *leg.* 25, no. 5.

20. AMZ, Archivo de Santa María de la Horta, Parroquía de San Leonardo, *leg* 15, visitation of 1598.

21. AMZ, *leg.* 1097, 1.

22. AMZ, *Ordenanzas de la Cofradía de Nuestra Señora de la Consolación*, of the parish of San Bartolomé.

23. José Carlos Rueda Fernández, 'La ciudad de Zamora en los siglos XVI y XVII: estudio demográfico', *Studia Zamorensia*, 2 (1981), using his appendice I, p. 131.

24. AMZ, *Ordenanzas de la Cofradía de San Ildefonso.*

25. Fernández-Prieto, *Nobleza de Zamora*, p. 372.

26. Ibid., p. 401.

27. AMZ, *Constituciones Synodales de 1586, Libro* III, *const.* IV, *tít.* XV; and AMZ, Archivo de Santa María de la Horta, San Julián (4) 1603; and San Leonardo, *leg*. 15, *Visitación de 1603.*

28. Madrid, Real Academia de la Historia. Colección de Jesuitas, t. 105, no. 80, 29 March 1575, letters of the Bishop of Zamora. AMZ, *Orden* 17, *leg.* 25, 2nd part.

29. *Constituciones Synodales de Astorga*, 1595, *const.* 13, *cap.* 7.

30. Salamanca, Archivo Diocesano, uncatalogued papers of 1591.

31. Ibid. *cap*. 6 and 19; Zamora, Archivo parroquial de San Lázaro, no. 48, visitation to the confraternity of the Santíssimo Sacramento of 1607; AMZ, *Orden* 26, *leg*. 30, no. 17, continued the regulations in the eighteenth century. For similar changes in Florence, see Weissman, *Ritual Brotherhood in Renaissance Florence* (New York: Academic Press, 1982) p. 214.

32. Ch. Cordonnier, *Le Culte de Saint-Sacrement* (Paris, 1923) pp. 223–37. See also Giancarlo Angelozzi, *Le confraternite laicali*, p. 42; and 'Confrérie', in the DDC.

33. Servando Arbolí Y Faraudo, *La Eucarista y la Inmaculada: devoción española* (Sevilla, 1895).

34. See Bartolomé Bennassar, *The Spanish Character* (California, 1979) p. 86.

35. *Spanish Art collection of the Conde de las Almenas* (New York, 1927).

36. Robert Harding, 'The Mobilization of Confraternities Against the Reformation in France', *Sixteenth-Century Journal*, XI (1980) 100–1; and J. Duhr, 'Confréries', *Dictionnaire de Spiritualité ascetique et mystique*, vol. II, col. 1474.

37. AMZ, leg. 916, *Ordenanzas de la cofradía del Santíssimo Nombre de Jesu, lugar de Muelas*. On a similar rural confraternity in the diocese of

Cuenca, see S. Nalle, 'Religion and Reform in a Spanish Diocese', p. 258.

38. 'Confréres', in DDC, col. 144; and Marc Venard, 'L'Eglise d'Avignon au XVIᵉ siècle' (Thesis, Lille, 1980), vol. III, pp. 1217–54.

39. A. N. Galpern, *The Religions of the People in Sixteenth-Century Champagne* (Cambridge, Mass, 1976) pp. 105–6, 188. The Santíssimo Sacramento appears to have been one of the most popular of the new groups.

40. Statistics are based on my compilation of sixteenth-century confraternities listed in Appendix I of my PhD dissertation, available through Ann Arbor microfilms and the eighteenth-century survey in AHN, Consejos Suprimidos, *leg.* 7098, No. 29.

41. William Christian has calculated that images of the Virgin Mary in New Castile dropped from 65% of all images in 1580, to 55% in 1780; the saints fell from 27% to 14% between the same dates, while images of Christ increased in proportion to the total from 8% in 1580 to 31% in 1780. See Table 6.2, pp. 182–3, in *Local Religion*.

42. Marcel Bataillon, *Erasmus et l'Espagne* (Paris, 1937).

43. Erasmus, 'The Religious Pilgrimage', *Familiar Colloquies*, (London, 1519 reprinted 1900).

44. L. Reau, *Iconographie de l'art chrétien* (Paris, 1955–59) vol. II, p. 123; and Anthony Blunt, *Artistic Theory in Italy, 1450–1600* (Oxford, 1956) pp. 103–36.

45. Marina Warner, *Alone of All her Sex* (New York, 1976) p. 328.

46. Louis Chatellier, 'A l'origine d'une société Catholique, le rôle des Congregations Mariales aux XVIᵉ–XVIIIᵉ siècles', *Histoire, economie et société* (2/84).

47. J. C. Broussole, *Etudes sur la Sainte Vierge*, 2 vols (Paris, 1908) vol. II, p. 324. The other sorrows of the Virgin are: the Prophecy of Simeon, the Flight into Egypt, the Crucifixion, and the Ascension.

48. Emile Mâle, *L'Art religieux à la fin du moyen âge en France* (Paris, 1931) pp. 291–2.

49. On the use and meaning of tears in Spanish Catholicism, see William Christian Jr. 'Provoked Religious Weeping in Early Modern Spain', in J. Davis (ed.), *Religious Organization and Religious Experience* (London, 1982) pp. 97–114.

50. J. Meseguer Fernández, 'Las Cofradías de la Vera Cruz', *Archivo Ibero-americano*, VIII, 109–110 (Madrid, 1968) p. 203.

51. Gabriel Llompart, 'Desfile iconográfico de penitentes españoles (siglos XVI al XX)', *Revista de Dialectología y tradiciones populares*, XXV (Madrid, 1969) p. 43. José Bermejo Carballo, *Glorias religiosas de Sevilla o noticia descriptiva de todas las cofradías de penitencia, sangre y luz fundadas en este ciudad* (Sevilla, 1882) p. 349.

52. Archivo Municipal de Valladolid, *Caja* 13, no. 4, 25 March 1482; and AHPZ, Protocolos, no. 2999bis.

53. AHPZ, *Libro de Actas* (1) and (2), and Archivo de la Vera Cruz, *Caja* 2, no. 2, testament of 1513.

54. The statutes claim to have been copied from a set of 1506, AHN, Codices, no. 1187B. Revised ordinances of 1580 are published in Luis

Calvo Lozano, *Historia* pp. 235–41.
55. AHPZ, Protocolos, no. 7, *fols* 164–167. AMZ, *Libro* 66, *Ordenanzas de la Cofradía de la (Vera) Cruz.*
56. Gabriel Llompart, 'Desfile iconográfico de penitentes españoles', pp. 38–9.
57. Ariès, *Le Homme devant la mort* (Paris, 1977) p. 187.
58. John Henderson. 'The Flagellant Movement and Flagellant Confraternities in Central Italy, 1260–1400', in *Religious Motivation: Papers read at the Sixteenth Summer Meeting and the Seventeenth Winter Meeting of the Ecclesiastical History Society*, edited by Derek Baker (Oxford, 1978) p. 159.
59. Robert Harding. 'The Mobilization of Confraternities Against the Reformation in France', p. 94. And P. Rouillard, 'Quelques symboles pénitentiels', in *Symbolisme et Théologie* (Rome, 1974) pp. 215–28.
60. According to Jean Deschamps, the identical penitential robes were another method of forging solidarity among members, conferring a group identity, *Les Confréries au moyen age*, pp. 71–4.
61. AMZ, *Libro* 66, introduction to ordinances.
62. Pedro Carasa Soto mentions that the Vera Cruz were an eminently rural group in the province of Burgos, with only two of them in the city, both of which were in the suburbs: 'La asistencia social y las cofradías en Burgos desde la crisis del Antiguo Régimen', *Investigaciones Históricas*, III (1982) p. 202.
63. M. Bordes, 'Contribution à l'étude des confréries de penitents à Nice au XVIIᵉ–XVIIIᵉ siécles', *Annales du Midi: Revue archeologique, historique, philologique; Revue de la France Meridionale*, xix, 139 (July–December 1978), says that the Holy Cross in Nice was made up of commoners: p. 382; and Teófanes Egido, 'Religiosidad popular y asistencia social en Valladolid: Las Cofradías Marianas del s. XVI', *Estudios Marianos*, xLv (Salamanca, 1980), mentions that in Valladolid, the least selective confraternities in terms of membership were the penitentials, composed of workers and farmers, without purity of blood statutes, p. 203.
64. Archivo de la Vera Cruz de Zamora. *Caja* 2, *doc.* 5, *fol.* 2.
65. Archivo Parroquial de San Torcuato, *Libro* 33, *fol.* 217. Tomé Pinheiro da Veiga, *Fastiginia*, parts of which are reproduced in Gabriel Llompart, 'Desfile iconográphico de penitentes españoles', pp. 37–9.
66. Archivo de la Vera Cruz de Zamora, *Caja* 2, doc. 38, 1614.
67. Robert Harding, 'The Mobilization of Confraternities', p. 103; and Natalie Zemon Davis, 'From Popular Religion to Religious Cultures', in Steven Ozment (ed.), *Reformation Europe: A Guide to Research* (St Louis; Center for Reformation Research, 1982) p. 327.
68. Fernández-Prieto, *Nobleza de Zamora*, p. 558.
69. For a list of the Vera Cruz of the province, see appendix II, in my PhD dissertation.
70. Llompart, 'Desfile iconográphico de penitentes españoles', p. 44. Marc Venard explores the expansion of penitentials in Avignon after 1560 in 'L'Eglise d'Avignon au XVIᵉ siècle', vol. IV, pp. 1449–56.
71. Gabriel Llompart, 'Desfile iconográphico de penitentes españōles', p. 38.

72. Real Academia de la Historia, Codice de Jesuitas, vol.. 105, no. 88. *Letters from the King to the Bishop of Zamora*, Madrid: 19 March 1575 and 29 March 1575.

73. AMZ, uncatalogued, *Ordenanzas de la Cofradía de la Vera Cruz de la Deçeplina*, Pueblo de Matilla, on or before 1628.

74. José Franciso de Isla, 'Fray Gerundio de Campazas', *Clásicos Castellanos* (Madrid, 1758) vol. 148, pp. 81–2; other suggestions of the erotic character of flagellation are made by Bartolomé Bennassar in *The Spanish Character*, p. 39.

75. AHPZ, Protocolos, no. 721, *fol*. 156.

76. *Ordenanzas de la Cofradía de la Vera Cruz de Villalpando*, of 1588, p. 239.

77. As William Christian Jr. has described so vividly in *Local Religion in Sixteenth-Century Spain* through the rich documentation of responses to a royal questionnaire between 1575 and 1580.

78. Gabriel Le Bras, 'Les confréries chrétiennes. Problèmes et propositions', *Revue historique de droit français et étranger* (Paris, 1940–1) pp. 325–6. Sara T. Nalle concludes her work on Cuenca with the theme of centralization of devotions after Trent in, '*Religion and Reform in a Spanish Diocese*', pp. 271–2.

79. John Bossy, 'The Counter-Reformation and the People of Catholic Europe', *Past and Present*, 47 (May 1970) pp. 51–70.

80. Ibid., pp. 57–8.

81. John Bossy, *Christianity in the West, 1400–1700* (Oxford, 1985) p. 134. A. D. Wright cautiously upholds this argument in *The Counter Reformation*, p. 54.

82. For an examination of this in England, see Mervyn James, 'Ritual, Drama and Social Body in the Late Medieval English Town', *Past and Present*, 98 (February 1983) pp. 3–29.

83. AHPZ, Municipal. *Libro de Actas* (2) 15 May 1514, 27 May 1514, 29 May 1514, and 21 May 1515; (4) 9 May 1531, 2 June 1531, 5 June 1531; (6) 19 and 23 May 1544, and 9 June 1544; (8) 12 May 1550, 24 April 1551, and 2 May 1551; (10) 6 May 1582, 23 May 1586, 22 May 1587 and 13 June 1588; (13) 21 June 1593; and (14) 3 April 1598.

84. Bossy, 'The Counter Reformation', pp. 62–3, and 67–8; and his introduction to Delumeau's work, *Catholicism from Luther to Voltaire*, p. iv. B. Bennassar characterized Spanish piety after the mid-sixteenth century to have been 'a religion deserted by its spirit', marked by stagnation in speculative thought, empty rituals, and growing use of purity of blood requirements in religious orders. He notes that confraternities and cults to local shrines remained numerous, but argues that they revealed a bigoted, magical approach to religion, no longer fostered by enlightened faith or a faith of works; *The Spanish Character*, pp. 80–9. Sara T. Nalle's dissertation tracing the successes of Tridentine reforms in 'Christianizing' the diocese of Cuenca concludes with the allusive comment that perhaps beneath the formal appearances of orthodoxy stood a more resilient and presumably more vigorous and meaningful faith of the Middle Ages ('Religion and Reform in a Spanish Diocese' pp. 283–4). For Marc Venard's parallel interpretation of the

French situation, see 'L'eglise d'Avignon au XVIe siècle', pp. 1791–99 and 1923–57.

85. Gabriel Le Bras offers ideas on how historians can measure fervor of religion in *Etudes de sociologie religieuse*, vol. II (Paris, 1955) pp. 587–614.

86. Thomas J. Steele, S.J. 'The Spanish Passion Play in New Mexico and Colorado', *New Mexico Historical Review*, 53, 3 (July 1978) pp. 239–60; Marta Weigle, *Brothers of Light, Brothers of Blood* (Albuquerque, 1976).

87. Campomanes, *Apéndice a la educación popular*, vol. II (Madrid, 1775) p. CLXXXV.

88. F. Bustelo García del Real, 'La población española en la segunda mitad del siglo XVIII', *Moneda y Crédito*, 123 (December 1972), chart of population statistics, p. 82; using the *Censo Español executado de orden del Rey communicada por el Excelentísimo Señor Conde de Floridablanca, Primer Secretario de Estado y del Despacho, en el Año de 1787* (Madrid, s.d.). The date of this census is the closest one available to the date of the one taken by the confraternities in 1771; it does not include people institutionalized in hospitals and asylums.

89. AHN, Consejos Suprimidos, *leg*, 7098, no. 29.

90. Ibid. On Burgos, see Pedro Carasa Soto's study, 'La asistencia social y las cofradías en Burgos desde la crisio del Antiguo Régimen'.

91. AMZ, Libro 66, *Ordenanzas*.

92. *The Decrees of the Council of Trent*, Session VI, ch. X; and Llompart, 'Desfile iconográphico de penitentes españole', pp. 48–9.

93. The sacramentals differ from the sacraments in that they do not produce grace *ex opere operato*, by virtue of the rite employed. Theologians are in disagreement today as to whether the sacramentals may confer grace *ex opere operantis*, through the action of the one who uses them. Among the laity in the sixteenth century, however, there appeared to have been little doubt that the rites were efficacious bearers of grace.

94. Darwell Stone, *A History of the Doctrine of the Holy Eucharist* (London, 1909) vol. I, pp. 42–53.

95. Dom Gregory Dix, *The Shape of the Liturgy* (Glasgow, reprint of the second edition, 1954) p. 161; his emphases.

96. O. B. Hardison, Jr., *Christian Rite and Christian drama in the Middle Ages* (Baltimore, Md; Johns Hopkins Press, 1965) p. 82. Medieval theology, particularly that expressed by Augustine, as M.D. Chenu describes, was committed to vivifying sacred history for the present. The sacraments represented the deeds of Christ. Elements in royal ceremonial, ideas of political authority, and much in the plastic arts represented sacred history in symbolic form as well. According to Chenu, 'Augustine ... supplied medieval men with materials and methods for a symbolism capable of laying hold upon time – Christian time: events, bound up with past and present and future as so many stages of the Old Testament, the New Testament, and the final kingdom, not only prepared for the future but prefigured it in the present.' See Marie Dominique Chenu, 'The Symbolist Mentality', in *Nature, Man and Society in the Twelfth Century* (Chicago, 1979) p. 127.

On the early church fathers, see also Jean Daneilou, S.J., *The Bible and the Liturgy* (Notre Dame, Indiana, 1964) pp. 136–7.

97. *Summa Theologica.* Part III, Q. 83.

98. Francis Clark, *Eucharistic Sacrifice and the Reformation*, 2nd edn (Oxford, 1967) chapter 4, 'Practical abuses and superstitious observances connected with the altar in the pre-Reformation period', pp. 56–72. Belief in the redemptive character of the mass appears to have been stronger in Spain than in other parts of Europe, according to Bartolomé Bennassar. Even lowly peasants in Castile saved for the services of masses after their deaths – not just one or two, but for hundreds. Wealthier persons arranged for a thousand and more masses on their own behalf, a quantity apparently unheard of in England and France, where five or six masses might do; *The Spanish Character*, pp. 71–72.

99. Clark, *Eucharistic Sacrifice*, p. 100. Peter Martyr Vermigli shared Luther's view, see Joseph C. McLelland, *The Visible Words of God. An Exposition of the Sacramental Theology of Peter Martyr Vermigli A.D. 1500–1562* (Edinburgh and London, 1957) pp. 230–57.

100. Clark, *Eucharistic Sacrifice*, pp. 101–12.

101. Reformers united in opposition on this point in the articles of Marburg in 1529. Bernard Cottret considers Calvin's re-interpretation of Communion to have amounted to a new epistemology of signs and symbols. 'Pour une semiotique de la Réforme, *Le Consensus Tigurinus* (1549) et *La Brève resolution*... (1555) de Calvin', *Annales, E.S.C.*, no. 2, March–April 1984, pp. 265–85.

102. Felicity Heal's recent study of hospitality in England shows that prior to the Reformation, three Biblical texts had been used to encourage care of travellers: Matthew 25:35 and 36; Romans 12:13; and Hebrews 13:2. She argues that after the Reformation, 'Protestant divines were not wholly at ease in discussing the seven corporal works of mercy' because of their association with a theology of works, and they rarely cited the Matthew passage. She suggests that they turned instead to the Hebrew texts and to classical ethical codes and natural law because they offered alternative reminders of obligations to aid the poor. She concludes that it was probably cultural tradition and social expectation that sustained the belief in hospitality formally sanctioned by Scripture and secular ethics. 'The Idea of Hospitality in Early Modern England', *Past and Present*, 102 (February 1984) pp. 72–3. J. S. McGee, in *The Godly Man in Stuart England* (New Haven, Conn., 1976), suggests that a more radical change in welfare practices occurred after the Reformation in England, arguing that Puritans concentrated on spiritual charity to the nuclear family and less on material charity to the poor. On the decline of confraternities and chantries with the Reformation in England, see Susan Brigdan, 'Religion and Social Obligation in early Sixteenth-Century London', *Past and Present*, 103 (March 1984) pp. 101–04.

103. John Calvin, *Commentary on a Harmony of the Evangelists, Matthew* ..., translated from the Latin and collated with the French text, Torrance edition (Edinburgh, 1972) vol. III, p. 116 (Matt. 25:35).

104. *Libro de la Vida*, chapters 9:6 and 4:7.
105. Wm. J. Callahan, Introduction to *Church and Society in Catholic Europe of the Eighteenth Century* (Cambridge, 1979) p. 8. Edited by Callahan and David Higgs.
106. Mary Douglas explores these attitudes in *Natural Symbols. Explorations in Cosmology* (New York, 1982) pp. 1–36, and 156–7.

Sources and Bibliography

I ARCHIVAL GUIDES AND SOURCES

A. Zamora

Both the public and private archives of the city of Zamora have been catalogued in the guide by Antonio Matilla Tascón, *Guia-inventario de los archivos de Zamora y su provincia* (Madrid, 1964). Documentation in the Archivo Histórico Provincial de Zamora has been catalogued in a more detailed manner by María del Carmen Pescador del Hoyo, *Documentos históricos del Archivo Municipal de Zamora* (Zamora, 1948).

1. Archivo Histórico Provincial de Zamora (AHPZ)
Sections:
Protocolos, nos. 1–740, years 1508–1599
Hacienda, Orden 1889, nos. 14, 15, 18
Diputación Provincial, Beneficencia, Legajos, 1, 2, 4, 8, 9, 10, 14, 15, 17–19, 26, 29, 32, 35–9, 43, 47, 48, 53–6, 60–5, 69–72, 77, 79, 85–7, 91 (8) (14–26), 165, 166, 188, 191, 192, 194.

2. Archivo de la Mitra de Zamora (AMZ)
Archivo de los Ciento (newly catalogued) Legajos: 69, 74–80, 332, 971, 1341
Archivos parroquiales: Archivo parroquial de Santa María; San Julián, Santa Lucía, San Leonardo, Santo Tomás, San Simón, la Magdalena. Archivo parroquial de San Cipriano, San Claudio, San Isidoro, San Ildefonso, Cathedral.

3. Archivos parroquiales
Archivo de San Lázaro (with the parish of Espíritu Santo)
Archivo de San Vicente (with San Andrés, San Salvador, Santa Eulalia, Santiago del Burgo)
Archivo de San Torcuato (with San Antolín and San Esteban)
Archivo de San Juan de la Puerta Nueva (with San Bartolomé, Santa María la Nueva)
Archivo de San Frontis (with San Sepulcro).

4. *Archivo de la Catedral de Zamora (ACZ)*
Legajos: 17, 18, 19, 36 (14) (15) (18), 139a, 199, 225.

5. *Archivo Particular de don Enrique Fernández-Prieto*

6. *Archivo de la Cofradía de la Santa Vera Cruz*

B. National archives

The Archivo Histórico Nacional in Madrid has enormous collections yielding information on confraternities throughout the peninsula, as yet primarily uncatalogued. The principal general guide to provinces and cities in Luís Sánchez Belda, *Guía del Archivo Histórico Nacional* (Madrid, 1958). See *Clero Secular y Regular: Inventario de procedencias* (1924) for guidance through the richest source material on confraternities connected with the Church.

The national archives of the Archivo General de Simancas have been useful for information on the economy and demography of Zamora. Sections of Camara de Castilla, Expedientes de Hacienda, Real Patronato Eclesiástico, Consejo Real, Contaduría Mayor de Cuentas, Dirección General de Tesoro and the Patronato Real all provided useful material, and their catalogues can be found at the archives.

II WORKS ON THE CITY AND PROVINCE OF ZAMORA

Alvarez Martínez, Ursicino, *Historia General Civil y eclesiástica de la provincia de Zamora* (Zamora, 1889).

Alvarez Vázquez, José Antonio, *Los diezmos en Zamora* (1500–1840) (Zamora, 1984).

Boizas, M., *La Virgen de la Concha y su Cofradía* (Zamora, 1943).

Bueno Dominguez, María Luisa, *El Monasterio de Santa María de Moreruela (1143–1300)* (Zamora, 1975).

Castro, Americo and F. de Onis y Sánchez, *Fueros Leoneses de Zamora, Salamanca, Ledesma y Alba de Tormes* (Madrid, 1916).

Díaz Medina, A., 'La población zamorana en el siglo XVI', *Studia Zamorensia*, 1 (1980).

Fernández Duro, Cesário, *Colección Bibliográfico-biográfico de noticias referentes a la provincia de Zamora* (Madrid, 1891).

————, *Memorias históricas de la ciudad de Zamora, su provincia y obispado* (Madrid, 1882–83) 4 vols.

Fernández-Prieto, E., *La Nobleza de Zamora* (Madrid, 1953).

Fuente Mangas, J., *Aspecto del paisaje urbano en Zamora. Sectores secundario y terciario* (Salamanca, 1972).

Fundación del Hospital, Seminario, Cappillas y Memorias, que dijo El Señor Dr. D. Diego del Val, Chantre y Canónigo que fue de la Sancta Iglessia de Zamora (Zamora, Delegación Provincial del Ministerio de Cultura, 1978).

García Diego, F., *Apuntes para la historia de Zamora. Catálogo de sus Obispos* (1808: handwritten book in the AMZ).

Gómez-Moreno, Manuel, *Catálogo Monumental de la Provincia de Zamora* (Leon, 1980).

Guía sinóptica estadística de las parroquias de la diócesis de Zamora y la vicaría de Alba y Aliste de Santiago de Compostela (Zamora, 1868).

Guilarte, Alfonso M., *El Obispo Acuña, historia de un comunero* (Valladolid, 1979).

Marquina, Javier R., 'Crecidas extraordinarios del rio Duero', *Revista de Obras Públicas* (Madrid, 1949) pp. 202–13.

Pescador del Hoyo, María del Carmen 'Los gremios de Artesanos en Zamora', *Revista de Archivos, Bibliotecas y Museos* (Madrid: LXXV, 1–2, January 1968–December 1972, pp. 183–200; LXXVI, 1, January–June 1973, pp. 13–60; LXXVIII, 1, January–June 1974, pp. 67–101; LXXVII, 2, July–December 1974, pp. 449–520; LXXVIII, 1, January–June 1975, pp. 111–88; LXXVIII, 2, July–December 1975, pp. 605–91).

Piñuela, Antonio? (cited as A.P.X.), *Rebuscos para formar la Historia de Zamora como Antigua Numancia* (1858, handwritten book in the AMZ).

Puig y Larraz, Gabriel, *La descripción física y geológica de la provincia de Zamora* (Madrid, 1883).

Ramos de Castro, Guadalupe, *El Arte Románico en la Provincia de Zamora* (Zamora: Diputación Provincial de Zamora, 1977).

Represa, A., 'Génesis y evolución urbana de la Zamora medieval', *Hispania*, 122 (1972) pp. 525–45.

Rueda Fernández, José Carlos, 'La Ciudad de Zamora en los siglos XVI y XVII: Estudio Demográfico', *Studia Zamorensia*, II (1981) pp. 117–34.

————, 'Introducción al estudio de la economia Zamorana a mediados del siglo XVI: Su estructura socio-profesional en 1561', *Studia Histórica*, II, 3 (1984) pp. 113–150.

Zatarain Fernández, M., *Apuntes y Noticias curiosas para formalizar la historia eclesiástica de Zamora y su diócesis* (Zamora, 1898).

III TREATISES ON POOR RELIEF IN SPAIN

Anglico, Alexandro, trans. by Pero Gonzáles, *Tractado muy útil de las obras de misericordia* (Toledo: Casa Lázaro Salvago, 1530).

Anonymous, *Reducción de mendigos a hostales o asilos* (Madrid: 1550, in the Biblioteca del Real Monasterio del Escorial).

Anonymous, *Que los hospitales generales es buen medio para el remedio de los pobres de la república en común se encarga del sustento dellos* (Biblioteca del Real Monasterio del Escorial, 1555).

Caja de Leruela, M., *Discursos sobre las causas y reparos de la necesidad común* (Madrid, 1627).

Giginta, Miguel de, *Tratado de remedio de pobres* (Coimbra, 1579).

————, *Exhortación a la compasión de los pobres* (Barcelona, 1583).

————, *Tratado intitulado Cadena de Oro* (Perpiñan, 1584).

————, *Atalaya e Caridad* (Zaragoza, 1587).

González de Cellorigo, Martín, *Memorial de la política necessaria, y útil restauración a la República de España, y estados de ella, y del desempeño universal de estos reynos* (Valladolid, 1600).

Guzmán, Pedro de, *Bienes del honesto trabajo y daños de la ociosidad* (Madrid, 1614).

Lanuza, Martín Batista de, *Tratado sobre el modo de distribuir y repartir la limosna con discreción, mérito y utilidad* (1606).

Magdalena de San Jerónimo, *Razón y forma de la galera y Casa Real, que el Rey nuestro Señor manda hazer en estos Reynos, para castigar de las mujeres vagantes, ladrones, alcahuetas y otras semejantes* (Valladolid, 1608).

Mariana, Juan, *De Roge et Regis institutione* (Toledo, 1559).

Márquez, P. Juan, *El Governador Christiano* (Salamanca, 1612).

Medina, Juan de (Fray Juan de Robles, O.S.B.), *De la orden que en algunos pueblos de España se ha puesto en la limosna* (Salamanca: Juan de Junta, 20 March 1545); reprinted in Madrid, Instituto de Estudios Políticos, 1965).

Pérez de Herrera, Cristóbal, *Discursos para el amparo de los legítimos pobres y reducción de los fingidos: y de la fundación y principio de los Albergues destos Reynos, y amparo de la milicia de ellos* (Madrid: Luís Sánchez, 1598; reprinted in *Clásicos Castellanos*, Madrid, 1975) vol. 199.

——————, *Discurso de la reclusión y castigo de las mugeres vagamundas y delinquentes destos Reynos* (no date).

——————, *Respuestas del Doctor Christóbal Pérez de Herrera, Protome- 'dico de las Galeras de España ... a las objecciones y dudas que se le han opuesto al discurso que escribió a su Majestad de la redución y amparo de los pobres* (no date, copy in the Biblioteca Nacional de Madrid).

Sandoval, Bernardino de, *Tratado de cuán piadosa obra sea proveer a los necesidades corporales y espirituales que padecen los presos pobres, ... por el maestrescuela de Toledo* (sixteenth century).

Soto, Domingo de, *Deliberación en la causa de los pobres* (Salamanca: Juan de Junta, 30 January 1545; reprinted in Madrid, Instituto de Estudios Políticos, 1965).

Toro, Gabriel de, *Thesoro de misericordia divina y humana sobre el cuidado que tuvieron los antiguos gentiles, hebreos, y cristianos, de los necesitados* (Salamanca: Juan de Junta, 1548).

Trujillo, Tomás de, *Tratado de la limosna* (Estella, 1563).

Villavicencio, Lorenzo de, *De oeconomia sacra circa pauperum curam* (Antwerp: Christopher Plantin, 1564).

Vives, Juan Luis, *De subventione pauperum* (Bruges, 1526); translated into Spanish by Juan de Gonzalo Nieto é Ivarra as *Tratado del Socorro de los pobres* (Valencia, 1781); and into English by Alice Tobriner, as *A Sixteenth Century Urban Report*, (Chicago, 1971).

IV SECONDARY SOURCES ON POOR RELIEF IN SPAIN

A pobreza e a Assitência a os pobres na península ibérica durante a idad média, Actas das las Jornadas Luso-Espanholas de Historia Medieval (Lisbon, 25–30 September, 1972) 2 vols.

Alvarea Santaló, León Carlos, 'La casa de expósitos de Sevilla en el siglo XVII', *Cuadernos de la Historia de la Medicina Española*, 7 (1977) 491–532.

Alvarez Sierra, J., *Los hospitales de Madrid* (Madrid, 1952).

Arco, Ricardo del, 'Una notable institución social: el padre de Huérfanos', *Estudios de Historia Social de España* (Madrid, 1955) III, 189–222.

Auidobro Serna, L., *Estadística de las Arcas de Misericordia de la Diócesis de Burgos* (Burgos, 1956).

Aznar y Embid, Severino, *Los seguros sociales por Severino Aznar* (Madrid: Instituto de estudios politicos, 1947).

Bádenes Gasset, Ramón, *Legislación de beneficencia particular* (Barcelona, 1962).

Balbín y Unquera, Antonio, *Reseña histórico y teoría de la Beneficencia* (Madrid, 1862).

Bataillon, Marcel, 'Les idées de XVIe siècle español sur les pauvres, sur l'aumône, sur l'assistance', *Annuaire du Collège de France* (1949) 204–14.

Batlle, Carmen, 'La asistencia a los pobres en la Cataluña medieval', *Historia*, VIII, 82, 42–8.

Bennassar, Bartolomé, *Recherches sur les grandes épidémies dans le nord de l'Espagne à la fin du XVIe siècle, problèmes de documentation et de méthode* (Paris, 1969).

————, *Valladolid au siècle d'or* (Paris, 1967).

Callahan, Wm. J., 'Confinement and Poor Relief in Eighteenth-Century Spain', *Hispanic American Historical Review*, LI (1971) 1–24.

————, 'Corporate Charity in Spain: The *Hermandad del Refugio* of Madrid, 1618–1814', *Histoire Social*, 9, (1976) 159–86.

————, 'Pobreza y caridad en Madrid', *Historia 16*, 16, (May 1977) 48–52.

Carmona García, Juan, *El sistema de la hospitalidad pública en la Sevilla del Antiguo Régimen* (Sevilla, Diputación Provincial de Sevilla, 1979).

Casado, Demetrio, *La Pobreza en la estructura social de España* (Madrid, 1976).

Constituciones del Real Colegio de Niños huérfanos de la Provincia de La Mancha (Madrid, Real, 1787).

Corts Grau, J., 'La doctrina social de Luis Vives', *Estudios de Historia Social de España*, II (Madrid, 1952) 65–89.

Criado Cervera, Desiderio, *Estudio de algunas instituciones de protección de menores en la historia de Valencia*, (Valencia, 1949).

Deuringer, Karl, *Probleme der Caritas in der Schule von Salamanca* (Freiburg, 1959).

Egido, Teófanes, 'Aportación al estudio de la demografía española: los niños expósitos de Valladolid (siglos XVI–XVIII)', *Jornadas de Metodología aplicada a las ciencias históricas*, III.

Falero, Juan, *Madrid: Sus instituciones de enseñanza, de beneficencia y de administración: sus centros científicos y artísticos, su organización municipal* (Madrid, 1881).

Farré, Luis, 'Ricos y pobres en la Edad Media', *Revista de Occidente*, 17 (March 1977) 32–9.

Fernández Fernández, M., *La beneficencia pública y los hospicios* (Madrid, 1923).

Friedman, Ellen, 'Trinitarian Hospitals in Algiers: an early example of Health Care for Prisoners of War', *The Catholic Historical Review*, LXVI, (1980) 551–64.

Friedmann, Ellen, *Spanish Captives in North Africa in the Early Modern Age* (Madison, 1983).

Galdiano y Croy, Leonardo, *Breve tratado de los hospitales y casas de recogimiento desta Corte* (Madrid, 1677).

Galicia Pinto, María Isabel, *La Real Casa Hospicio de Zamora. Asistencia social a marginados* (1798–1850) (Zamora, 1985).

García, Santiago, *Breve instrucción sobre el modo de conservar los niños expósitos* (Madrid, 1794).

González Muñoz, M. del Carmen, 'Epidemia y enfermedades en Talavera de la Reina (ss XVI y XVII)', *Hispania*, 126, (January–April, 1974) 149–68.

Granjel, Luis S., 'Vida y obra del Dr. Cristóbal Pérez de Herrera', *Estudios de la Historica de la Medicina Española*, 1, 1 (Salamanca, 1959).

Hermandad de el Real Hospicio de pobres de el Ave María, *Forma, como se pueden recoger los pobres, y desterrar los vagamundos* (Madrid, 1712).

Hernández Iglesias, Fermín, *La beneficencia en España* (Madrid, 1876).

Herrera Puga, P., *Sociedad y delincuencia en el Siglo de Oro* (Granada, 1971).

Imamuddin, M., 'Māristān (Hospitals) in Medieval Spain', *Islamic Studies*, 17 (1978) 45–55.

Jiménez Salas, María, *Historia de la Asistencia Social en España en la edad moderna* (Madrid, 1958).

López Alonso, C., 'Conflictividad social y pobreza en la Edad Media', *Hispania*, 140 (1978) 475–567.

Maravall, José Antonio, 'De la misericordia a la justicia social en la economia del trabajo: la obra de fray Juan de Robles', *Moneda y Crédito*, 148 (March 1979) 57–88.

————, *Estado moderno y mentalidad social* (Madrid, 1972).

Marcos, Martín, A., 'La asistencia social en España: el sistema hospitalario de Medina del Campo en el siglo XVI', *Cuadernos de Investigación Histórica*, II (1978) 341–62.

Martz, Linda, *Poverty and Welfare in Hapsburg Spain. The Example of Toledo* (Cambridge, 1983).

Ministerio de la Gobernación, *Apuntes para el Estudio y la Organización en España de las Instituciones de Beneficencia y de Previsión* (Madrid, 1909).

Muñiz Fernández, Carmen, 'Hospitales españoles. Información para su Historia', *Fuentes legales de la medicina española (siglos XIII–XIX)*, edited by Rafael Muñoz Garrido (Salamanca, 1969) pp. 109–74.

Murcia, Pedro Joaquín de, *Discurso político sobre la importancia y necesidad de los hospicios, casas de expósitos y hospitales* (Madrid, 1798).

Nenclares, E. M. de, *Legislación española de Beneficencia desde Isabel I la Católica hasta el año 1769, recopilada y anotada* (Madrid, 1869).

Pérez Estévez, María Rosa, *El problema de los vagos en la España del siglo XVIII* (Madrid, 1976).

Perry, Mary Elizabeth, '"Lost Women" in Early Modern Seville: The Politics of Prostitution', *Feminist Studies*, IV, 1 (February 1978) 195–214.

Ribeiro, Vítor, 'Historia de Beneficencia Publica em Portugal', *O Instituto*, XLVIII–LIV (1901–07).

Rico Avello, C., 'Evolución histórico de la asistencia hospitalaria en España', *Revista de la Universidad de Madrid*, vol. 3 (1940).

Rumeu de Armas, Antonio, *Historia de la Previsión Social en España* (Madrid, 1944).

Sarrailh, Jean, 'Note sur la réforme de la bienfaisance en Espagne à la fin du XVIIIe siècle', *Eventail de l'histoire vivante...Hommage à Lucien Febvre*, vol. 2 (Paris, 1953) pp. 371–80.

Sempere y Guarinos, Juan, *Biblioteca Español. Económico-política* (Madrid, 1801).

————, *Memoria sobre el exercicio ... de la caridad en el repartimiento de la limosna. Colección de las Memorias premiades por la Sociedad Económica de Madrid* (1784).

Soubeyroux, J., 'Sur un project original d'organization de la bienfaisance en Espagne au XVI', *Bulletin Hispanique*, 74 (1–2) (Bordeaux, 1972) 118–24.

————, *Pauperisme et rapports sociaux à Madrid au XVIIIe siècle* (Lille-Paris, 1978).

————, 'Pauperismo y relaciones sociales en el Madrid del siglo XVIII', *Estudios de Historia Social*, 12–13 (1980) 7–227.

————, 'El encuentro del pobre y la sociedad: asistencia y represión en el Madrid del siglo XVIII', *Estudios de Historia Social*, 20–1 (1982) 7–225.

V CONFRATERNITIES IN SPAIN

Abbad, F., 'La Confrérie condamnée ou une spontanéité festive confisquée', *Mélanges de la Casa de Velázquez*, XIII (1977) 361–84.

Arco, Roicardo del (ed.), *Antigua Gremios de Huesca, (ordinaciones documentos, transcripción y estudio preliminar)*, VI (Saragoza, 1911).

Carasa Soto, Pedro, 'La asistencia social y las cofradías en Burgos desde la crisis del Antiguo Régimen', *Investigaciones Históricas*, III (1982) 179–229.

Cervera, Miguel de, *Compendio histórico de la fundación, instituto y piadosos exercicios de la Real Arch-cofradía de Nuestra Señora de Caridad* (Madrid, 1768).

Correia, Fernando da Silva, *Origens e formação das Misericórdias portuguêsas; estudios sôbre a história da Assistência* (Lisbon, 1944).

Egido, Teófanes, 'La cofradía de San José y los niños expósitos de Valladolid', *Estudios Josefinos*, 53 (Valladolid, 1973) 77–100.

————, 'Religiosidad popular y asistencia social en Valladolid: Las Cofradías Marianas del s. XVI', *Estudios Marianos*, XLV (Salamanca, 1980) 197–217.

Escagués Javierre, Isidro, 'Datos sobre algunas cofradías y hermandades medievales', *Revista de Trabajo*, 10 (October 1945) 877–9.

Falcón Pérez, María Isabel, 'La Cofradía de cuchilleros zaragozanos en el siglo XV. Las Ordenanças de 1423', *Homenage a Don José María Lacarra de Miguel en su Jubilación del Profesorado*, IV (Zaragoza, 1977) pp. 59–77.

————, 'Las cofradías artesanales aragonesas en la edad media', *Jornados sobre el estado actual de los estudios sobre Aragon*, II (Saragoza,

1979) 644–9.

Fouguet Marsal, José, *Cofradías-Gremios, especialment fluviales de la ribera del Ebro en Tortosa* (Madrid, J. Pueyo, 1923).

Freire, Braamcamp, 'Compromisso de Confraria em 1346', *Archivo Historico Portuguez*, I (1903) 349–55.

Gerbet, Maria-Claude, 'Les confréries religieuse à Caceres de 1467 à 1523', *Mélanges de la Casa de Velázquez*, VII (1971) 75–113.

Gómez Ortiz, Juan María, 'Los gremios y la vida gremial', *Historia y Vida*, 90 (September 1975) 74–87.

Granjel, Luis, 'Prehistoria de los Colegios Médicos. Las Cofradías de San Cosme, San Damián, y San Lucas', *Tribuna Médica*, V, 205 (Madrid, 22 March 1968).

Klein, Julius, 'Medieval Spanish Gilds', *Facts and Factors in Economic History, Articles by former students of E. F. Gay* (Cambridge, Mass., 1932) pp. 164–88.

Layna Serrano, F., 'La histórica cofradía de "La Caballada" en Atienza', *Hispania*, II (1942) 483–556.

Llompart, Gabriel, 'Desfile iconográfico de penitentes españoles (siglos xvi al XX)', *Revista de Dialectología y tradiciones populares*, XXV (Madrid, 1969) 31–51.

Longás Pedro, 'Estatutos de la Cofradía de Santa Cristina, en Tudela (Navarra) a fines del siglo XII', *Revista Internacional de Sociología*, I (January–March 1943) 209–17.

Lozoya, Juan de Contreras, *Historia de las corporaciones de Menestrales en Segovia* (Segovia, 1921).

——————, *Los Gremios españoles* (Madrid, 1944).

Meseguer Fernández, J., 'Las Cofradías de la Vera Cruz. Documentos y notas para su historia', *Archivo Ibero-Americano*, xxviii (1968) 109–10, 199–213.

Montoto de Sedas, Santiago, *Cofradías Sevillanas* (Sevilla, 1976).

Nalle, Sara Tilghman, 'Religion and Reform in a Spanish Diocese: Cuenca 1545–1650 (PhD dissertation, Johns Hopkins University, 1983).

Nuevas ordenanzas que la muy ilustres y antigua Congregación de Pobres vergonzantes de esta ciudad de Salamanca (Salamanca 1872).

Oliveira, Eduardo, *Elementos para a Historia do Municipio de Lisboa* (Lisbon, 1882–85).

Ortega Sagrista, Rafael, 'Historia de las cofradías de la Pasión de Semana Santa', *Boletín del Instituto de Estudios Giennenses*, II:10 (1956) 9–71.

Pérez Pujol, E., *Historia de las instituciones sociales de la España goda* (Valencia, 1896) vol. IV.

Rumeu de Armas, Antonio, *Historia de la previsión social en España* (Madrid, 1944).

Sánchez Herrero, José, 'Cofradías, hospitales y beneficencia en algunas diócesis del Valle del Duero, siglos XIV y XV', *Hispania*, cxxvi (January–April 1974) 5–51.

Sancho Seral, Martín Luis, *El gremio zaragozano del siglo XVI* (Zaragoza, 1925).

Sanfeliú, Lorenzo, *La Cofradía de San Martín de hijosdalgos navegantes y mareantes de Laredo* (Madrid, 1944).

Tramoyers Blasco, Luis, *Instituciones gremiales; su origen y organización en Valencia* (Valencia, 1889).

Uña y Sarthou, Juan, *Las asociaciones obreras en España* (Madrid, 1900).

Very, F.G., *The Spanish Corpus Christi Procession: A Literary and Folkloric Study* (Valencia, 1962).

Villanueva, J., *Viage literario a las iglesias de España* (Madrid, 1850).

VI   GENERAL   WORKS   ON   CONFRATERNITIES   AND GUILDS IN EUROPE

Armagier, L., 'Sur la confrérie du Saint-Esprit au Moyen Age', *Cahiers de Fanjeaux* (1976) 305–19.

Angelozzi, Giancarlo, *Le confraternite laicali. Un'esperienze cristiana tra medioevo e età moderne* (Brescia, 1978).

Beauretour, Michaud de, *Notice Historique de la Venérable Archiconfrérie de la Miséricorde* (Maliveno-Mignon, 1881).

Berlière, U., 'Confraternités monastiques au moyen âge', *Revue liturgique et monastique*, II (1925–26) 9–33.

Billioud, J., *De la confrérie à la corporation. Les classes industrielles en Provence aux XIVᵉ, XVᵉ et XVIᵉ siècle* (Marseille, 1929).

Boileau, Abbé, *Histoire des flagellants* (Amsterdam, 1732).

Bordes, Maurice, 'Contribution à l'étude des confréries de pénitents à Nice aux XVIIᵉ-XVIIIᵉ siècles', *Annales du Midi: Revue archeologique, historique, et philologique; Revue de la France Meridionale*, XIX, 139 (July–December 1978) 377–88.

Bovier-Ajam, Maurice, *Recherches sur la genèse et la date d'apparition des corporations medievales en France* (Paris, 1978).

Brentano, Lujo, *Essay on the history and development of Gilds* (London, 1870).

Caremska, Hanna, *Brastwa W Sredniowieczn ym Krakowie: Studium Form Spolecznych Zycia religijnego* (Wrocklaw, 1977).

Celestino, Olinda, and Meyers, Albert, *Las cofradías en el Perú: Región central* (Frankfurt, Main, 1981)

Chenu, M.-D., '"Fraternitas", Evangile et condition socio-culturelle', *Revue d'histoire de la spiritualité*, 49 (1973) 385–400.

Coornaert, E., *Les Corporations en France avant 1789* (Paris, 1941).

————, 'Les ghildes médiévales (V–XIVᵉ siècles)', *Revue Historique*, CXCIX (1948) 22–55, 208–43.

Deschamps, Jean, *Les confréries au Moyen Age* (Bordeaux, 1958).

Ducoudray, Marie-Bernard, *Etude historique sur le rosaire, confrérie du rosaire, rosaire perpétual, rosaire vivant, dans le diocèse d'Angers* (Angers, 1887).

Duhr, Joseph, 'Confréries', in *Dictionnaire de Spiritualité ascétique et mystique* (Paris, 1953).

————, 'La confrérie dans l'histoire de l'Eglise', *Revue d'Histoire ecclésiastique*, XXXV (July 1939) 37–478.

Duparc, Pierre, 'Confréries du Saint-Esprit et communautés d'habitants au moyen-âge', *Revue historique de droit français et étranger*, 4th series, 36

(1958) 349–367, 555, 585.

Durand H., 'Confrérie', *Dictionnaire de Droit Canonique*, vol. 4, pp. 127–76.

Fougères, M., 'Entr'aide et piété: Les associations urbaines au moyen âge', *Mélanges d'historie sociale*, V (1944) 100–06.

Gross, Charles, *The Guild Merchant. A Contribution to British Municipal History* (Oxford, 1890).

Harding, Robert, 'The Mobilization of Confraternities Against the Reformation in France', *Sixteenth Century Journal*, xi, 2 (1980) 85–107.

Henderson, John, 'The Flagellant Movement and Flagellant Confraternities in Central Italy, 1260–1400', in Derek Baker (ed.), *Religious Motivation: Papers read at the Sixteenth Summer Meeting and the Seventeenth Winter Meeting of the Ecclesiastical History Society* (Oxford, 1978).

Hoffman, Philip T., *Church and Community in the Diocese of Lyon, 1500–1789* (New Haven, 1984).

Jones, W. R., 'English Religious Brotherhoods and Medieval Lay Piety', *The Historian*, xxxvi, 4 (August 1974) 646–59.

Larmour, Ronda, 'Merchant guild of sixteenth-century France: the grocerers of Paris', *Economic History Review*, 2nd series, 20 (1967) 467–81.

Le Bras, Gabriel, 'Les confréries chrétiennes. Problèmes et propositions', *Revue historique de droit français et étranger* (Paris, 1940–1) 310–63.

——————, *Etudes de sociologie religieuse* (Paris, 1955).

——————, *Introduction à l'histoire de la pratique religieuse en France* (Paris, 1942–5).

Levasseur, Emile, *Histoire des classes ouvrières en France* (Paris, 1859).

Martin Saint-León, Etienne, *Histoire des corporations de métiers* (Paris, 1922).

Maunier, R., 'Les confréries et le pouvoir francais en Algérie', *Revue de l'histoire des religion* (1936) 256–74.

Meersseman, Giles-Gérard, O.P., 'Etudes sur les anciennes confréries dominicaines', *Archivum Fratrum Praedicatorum*, 22 (1951) 275–93.

——————, 'La loi purement pénale d'après les statuts des confréries médiévales', *Mélanges Joseph de Ghellinck* (Gembloux, 1951) pp. 975–1002.

——————, *Ordo fraternitatis: confraternite e pietà dei laici nel Medioevo* (Rome, Herder, 1977).

——————, 'Pénitents ruraux communitaires en Italie au XIIᵉ siècle', *Revue d'histoire ecclésiastique*, xlix (1954) 343–90.

Mommsen, Theodor, *De Collegiis et Sodaliciis Romanorum* (Kiliae, 1843).

Monti, G. M., *Le confraternitá medievali dell'alta e media Italia* (Venice, 1927).

——————, *Il movimento dei disciplinati nel settimo centenario dal suo inizio (Perugia 1260). Convegno Internazionale, Perugia 25–28 settembre 1960* (Spoleto, 1962).

Pappenheim, Max, *Die altdänischen Schutzgilden* (Breslau, 1885).

Pullan, Brian, *Rich and Poor in Renaissance Venice. The Social Institutions of a Catholic State, to 1620* (Cambridge, Mass., 1971).

Schmitt, J. C., 'Apostolat mendiant et société, Une confrérie dominicaine à la veille de la réforme', *Annales E.S.C.*, 6 (1971) 83–104.

Smith, Joshua Toulmin (ed)., *English gilds. The original ordinances of more than 100 early English gilds from original mss. of the 14th and 15th centuries* (London, 1870).

Spicciani, Amleto, 'The "Poveri Vergognosi" in Fifteenth-Century Florence', in Thomas Riis (ed.), *Aspects of Poverty in Early Modern Europe* (Firenze, 1981).

Thrupp Silvia L., 'The Gilds', *The Cambridge Economic History of Europe* (Cambridge, 1963) vol. III, pp. 230–80.

——————, 'Medieval Guilds reconsidered', *Journal of Economic History*, II (1942) 164–73.

——————, *The Merchant Class of Medieval London, (1300–1500)* (Chicago, 1948).

Truant, Cynthia M., 'Solidarity and Symbolism among Journeymen Artisans: The Case of Compagnonnage', *Comparative Studies in Society and History*, XXI, 2 (April 1979) pp. 214–26.

Vryonis, Speros, 'Byzantine *Ahmokpatia* and the guilds in the eleventh century', *Dumbarton Oaks Papers*, 17 (1963) 289–314.

Waltzing, J. P., *Etude historique sur les corporations Professionelles chez les Romains depuis les origines jusqu'à la chute de l'Empire de l'Occident* (Louvain, 1895–1900).

Weissman, Ronald, *Ritual Brotherhood in Renaissance Florence* (New York, 1982).

Westlake, Herbert Francis, *The Parish Gilds of Medieval England* (London, 1919).

Wilda, W. E., *Das Gildenwesen im Mittelalter*, (Aalen, 1831, repr. 1964).

Zaremska, Hanna, *Bractwa w średniowiecznym Krakowie: Studium form spotecznych życia religijnego* (Wroclaw, 1977).

Zymslony, Monika, *Die Bruderschaften in Lübeck bis zur Reformation* (Kiel, 1977).

VII   POOR RELIEF IN EUROPE

Bataillon, Marcel, 'J. L. Vives, réformateur de la bienfaisance', *Bibliothèque d'Humanisme et de Renaissance*, 14 (1952) 141–58.

Boissieu, Henri de, 'L'aumône-générale de 1534 à 1562', *Revue d'histoire de Lyon*, 8 (1909).

Bonenfant, Paul, 'Les origines et le caractère de la réforme de la bienfaisance publique aux Pays-Bas sous le règne de Charles-Quint', *Revue belge de philologie et d'histoire*, V–VI (1926–27).

——————, 'La création à Bruxelles de la Suprême Charité', *Annales de la Société Belge d'Histoire des Hôpitaux*, III (1965) 149–68.

——————, 'Le problème du pauperisme en Belgique à la fin de l'ancien régime', *Memoires de l'Academie Royale de Belgique*, XXXV (Brussels, 1934).

——————, 'Hôpitaux et bienfaisance publique dans les anciens Pays-Bas des origines à la fin du XVIIIe siècle', *Annales de la Société belge d'histoire des hôpitaux*, III (1965).

Bosl, Karl, *Armut Christi Ideal der Mönche und Ketzer, Ideologie der aufsteigenden Gesellschaftsschichten*, vom II, biszum 13, Jahrhundert (Munich, 1981).

————, *Beiträge zur wirtschaftsund sozialgeschichte des Mittelalters*, 'Armut, Arbeit, Emanzipation' (Bohlau verlag koln wein, 1976).

Bouyer, L., *La Pauvreté* (Paris, 1964).

Caille, Jacqueline, *Hôpitaux et charité publique à Narbonne au Moyen Age: de la fin du XIe a la fin du XVe siècle* (Toulouse, 1978).

Candille, M., 'Pour un précis d'histoire des institutions charitable-quelques données des XII–XIVe siècles', *Société francaise d'histoire des hôpitaux*, xxx (1974) 79–88.

Chill, Emmanuel, 'Religion and Mendicity in Seventeenth-Century France', *International Review of Social History*, vii (1962) 400–25.

Chrisman, Mirian,'Urban Poor in the Sixteenth Century: The Case of Strasbourg', *Studies in Medieval Culture*, xiii (1978) 59–67.

Clay, R. M., *The Hospitals of Medieval England* (London, 1909).

Courtenay, William J.,'Token Coinage and the Administration of Poor Relief during the late Middle Ages', *Journal of Interdisciplinary History*, iii (1972–73) 275–95.

Couvreur, G.,'Les pauvres ont-ils des droits? Recherches sur le vol en cas d'extrême nécessité dupuis la Concordia de Gratien (1140) jusqu'à Guillaume d'Auxerre (1231)', *Analecta gregoriana*, iii (Rome, 1961).

————, 'Pauvreté et droits des pauvres à la fin du XII^{e}s.', *La pauvrété. Des sociétés de penurie a la société d'abondance-Recherches et débats du Centre Cath. d'Intellectuels* (Paris, 1964).

Davis, Natalie, 'Poor Relief, Humanism, and Heresy', *Society and Culture in Early Modern France* (Stanford, 1975).

Fairchilds, Cissie C., *Poverty and Charity in Aix-en-Provence, 1640–1789* (Baltimore, 1976).

Farquhar, Helen, 'Royal Charities', *British Numismatic Journal*, xvii (1923–24) 132–64.

Fischer, Thomas, *Städtische Armut und Armenfürsorge im 15. und 16. Jahrhundert* (Gottingen, 1979).

Forrest Alan, *The French Revolution and the Poor* (Oxford, 1981).

Fosseyeux, M., 'Les premiers budgets municipaux d'assistance. La taxe des pauvres au XVIe siècle', *Revue d'Histoire de l'Eglise de France* (1934) 407–32.

Foucault, Michel, *Histoire de la Folie à l'âge Classique* (Paris, 1972).

Geremek, Bronislaw, 'Il pauperismo nell'età preindustriale (secoli XIV–XVIII)', in *Storia d'Italia*, edited by R. Romano and C. Vivanti (Turin 1973) vol. V, pp. 669–98.

————, *Truands et misérables dans l'Europe moderne (1350–1600)* (Paris, Gallimard, 1980).

Gonnet, Paul, *L'adoption lyonnais des orphelins légitimes* (Paris, 1935).

Gonthier, N., 'Les Hôpitaux et les pauvres à la fin du Moyen Age: l'exemple de Lyon', *Le Moyen Age: Revue d'Histoire et de Philologie*, lxxxiv, 2 (1979) 279–308.

Grimm, H. J., 'Luther's Contributions to sixteenth century Organization of Poor Relief', *Archiv für Reformationgeschichte*, lxi (1970) 222–34.

Gutton, J. P., *La Société et les pauvres: L'Exemple de la généralité de*

Lyon, 1534–1789 (Paris, 1971).

——, *La Société et les pauvres en Europe, XVIᵉ–XVIIIᵉ siècles* (Paris, 1974).

Hands, A. R., *Charities and Social Aid in Greece and Rome* (Ithaca, N.Y., 1968).

Harvey, Richard, 'English Poverty and God's Providence, 1675–1725', *The Historian*, XLI, 3 (May 1979).

Herlan, Ronald W., 'Poor Relief in London during the English Revolution', *The Journal of British Studies* (Spring 1979) 30–51.

Jones, William R., 'Pious Endowments in Medieval Christianity and Islam', *Diogenes*, 109 (Spring 1980).

Jordan, W. K., *Philanthropy in England 1480–1660* (London, 1959).

Kingdon, Robert, 'Social Welfare in Calvin's Geneva', *American Historical Review*, 76:1 (February 1971) 50–70.

Lallemand, León, *Histoire de la Charité*, 4 vols (Paris, 1910).

Lindberg, Carter, '"There Should Be No Beggars Among Christians:" Karlstadt, Luther, and the Origins of Protestant Poor Relief', *Church History*, XLVI (1977) 313–34.

Lis, Catharina and Soly, Hugo, *Poverty and Capitalism in Pre-industrial Europe* (Sussex, 1979).

Little, Lester K., *Religious Poverty and the Profit Economy in Medieval Europe* (Ithaca, N.Y., 1978).

McKee, Elsie Anne, *John Calvin on the Diaconate and Liturgical Almsgiving* (Geneva, 1984).

Mollat, M., 'La notion de la pauvrété au Moyen Age', *Revue d'Histoire de l'Eglise de France*, LII (1966) 14–19.

——, *Etudes sur l'Histoire de la pauvrété* (Paris, 1974).

Monnier, Alexandre, *Histoire de l'assistance publique dans le temps anciens et modernes* (Paris, 1866).

Mundy, J. H., 'Charity and Social Work in Toulouse, 1100–1250', *Traditio*, XXII (1966) 203–87.

Nolf, J., *La réforme de la bienfaisance à Ypres au XVIᵉ siècle* (Ghent, 1915).

Norberg, Kathryn, *Rich and Poor in Grenoble 1600–1814*. (Berkeley, 1985).

Olson, Jeannine E., *The Bourse francaise: deacons and social welfare in Calvin's Geneva* (Stanford University PhD dissertation, 1980).

Pugh, Wilma J., 'Social Welfare and the Edict of Nantes: Lyon and Nîmes', *French Historical Review* (Spring 1974) 349–76.

——, 'Catholics, Protestants and Testamentary Charity in Seventeenth-Century Lyon and Nîmes', *French Historical Studies*, XI, 4 (Fall 1980) 479–504.

Pullan, Brian, *Rich and Poor in Renaissance Venice: The Social Institutions of a Catholic State* (Cambridge, Mass., 1971).

——, 'The Old Catholicism, The New Catholicism, and the Poor', *Timore e Carità l Poveri nell'Italia Moderna* (Cremona, 1982).

Romano, Dennis, 'Charity and Community in Early Renaissance Venice', *Journal of Urban History* (November 1984) 63–81.

Russell-Wood, A. J. R., *Fidalgos and Philanthropists: The Santa Casa da Misericordia of Bahia, 1550–1755* (Berkeley, 1968).

Salter, F. R. (ed.), *Some Early Tracts on Poor Relief* (London, 1926).

Shoshan, Boaz, 'Grain riots and the "moral economy": Cairo, 1350–1517', *Journal of Interdisciplinary History*, X, 3 (Winter 1980) 459–78.

Slack, Paul A., 'Vagrants and Vagrancy in England, 1598–1664', *Economic History Review*, 2nd ser., xxvii, (1974) 360–79.

Steinbicker, Carl E., *Poor Relief in the Sixteenth Century* (Washington D.C., 1937).

Tierney, Brian, *Medieval Poor Law: A Sketch of Canonical Theory and its Application in England* (Berkeley, 1959).

—————, 'Catholics and the Poor in Early Modern Europe', *Transactions of the Royal Historical Society*, 5th ser., xxvi (1976) 15–34.

Ullmann, Walter, 'Public Welfare and Social Legislation in the Early Medieval Councils', *Councils and Assemblies: Papers Read at the Eighth Summer Meeting and the Ninth Winter Meeting of the Ecclesiastical History Society (Studies in Church History*, no. 7) edited by G. L. Cumming and Derek Baker (New York, 1971).

Webb, Sidney and Beatrice, *English Local Government: English Poor Law History* (London, 1927).

VIII   POPULAR RELIGION

One of the most useful official sources on religious customs in Spain has been the synodal constitutions, which include a variety of proscriptions relating to belief and practice. Secondary works on popular religion have been increasing tremendously over the past decade and promise to multiply as historians pursue interest in the third estate and local cultures. Some of the most interesting in terms of both methodology and information for the study of confraternities have been:

John Bossy, 'The Counter-Reformation and the People of Catholic Europe', *Past and Present*, 47 (May 1970) 51–70.

Brown, Peter, *The Cult of the Saints: its rise and function in Latin Christianity* (Chicago, 1981).

Burke, Peter, *Popular Culture in Early Modern Europe* (New York, 1978).

Chaunu, Pierre, *Le temps des deux réformes de l'Eglise* (Paris, 1975).

Chenu, Marie Dominique, *Nature, man and society in the twelfth century* (Chicago, 1968)

Davis, Natalie, 'Some tasks and themes in the Study of Popular Religion', in *The Pursuit of Holiness in Late Medieval and Renaissance Religion. Papers from the University of Michigan Conference* (Leiden, 1974).

——, *Society and Culture in Early Modern France* (Stanford, 1975).

Delaruelle, E., *La pieté populaire au Moyen Age* (Turin, 1975).

Delumeau, Jean, *Catholicism between Luther and Voltaire* (Original French text published in 1971; English edition, London, 1977).

Febvre, Lucien, *Au coeur religieux du XVIe siècle* (Paris, 1957).

Freeman, Susan Tax, 'Religious Aspects of the Social Organization of a Castilian Village', *American Anthropologist*, 70 (1968) 38–49.

Galpern, A. N., *The Religions of the People in Sixteenth-Century Champagne* (Harvard, 1976).

Gennep, Arnold van, *Manuel de Folklore Français contemporain* (Paris,

1946–).

Giordano, Oronzio, *Religiosità popolare nell'alto medioevo* (Bari, 1979).

Grundmann, Herbert, *Religiöse bewegungen im mittelalter; untersuchungen über die geschichtlichen zusammenhäge zwischen der ketzerei* (Berlin, 1935).

Manselli, R., *La religion populaire au moyen âge* (Montreal-Paris, 1975).

Scarisbrick, J., *The Reformation and the English People* (Oxford, 1984).

Thomas, Keith, *Religion and the Decline of Magic* (London, 1971).

Toussaert, Jacques, *Le Sentiment religieux en Flandre à la fin du Moyen Age* (Paris, 1963).

Vauchez, André, *La sainteté en Occident aux derniers siècles du moyen âge* (Rome, 1981).

Violante, Cinzio, *Studi sulla cristianità medioevale* (Milan, 1972).

Index